CLEY

LIVING WITH MEMORIES

Look at the river Glaven today, gently flowing, narrow and meandering along its course, and it is difficult to imagine it as it once was - wide and tidal as far as Glandford and powering as many as sixteen water mills along its course, from its source, just south of Baconsthorpe Castle, through sixteen parishes to the sea.

If that is difficult to believe, then stand in front of Cley church and look across the valley towards the church at Wiveton. You would once have witnessed a much different scene - a view across one of the busiest ports in the whole of England, with wharves both sides of the harbour and ships, up to 130 tons in size, discharging their cargoes of fish, spices, oriental cloths and coal, to be either stored in the many warehouses which then existed in Cley (some remaining today) or loaded onto carts and wagons for transport inland. Along the bustling quays, which stretched either side of the estuary to gain frontage to the channel, would be other carts waiting to empty their burdens of barley, oats and malt for export to such places as Norway, Greece, Marseilles, Carthaginia and the Hanseatic ports. The Customs Officer would be conspicuous, as would the King's Buyer and the foreign merchants, mixing with local fishermen, dockers, coal carriers, and street urchins eager to earn, or steal, the odd coin.

During the reign of King John Ralph de Hauville held land in Cley in return for keeping the King's hawks. At the time of Domesday (1086) Cley was part of King Edward's Royal Manor of Holt and as late as 1790 "all the grocery etc. sent to this town (Holt) by sea is shipped...to Blakeney or Cley, the nearest sea ports."

By the thirteenth century Blakeney Haven (Blakeney, Cley and Wiveton) was one of the greatest ports in the country, being fourth in a list of ten directed to provide ships with bridges and hurdles to go to Sluys for the passage of Edward I and his retinue. The earliest reference to Cley (and Blakeney) port is a judgement of the local Port Court in 1285, which accepted that both communities belonged to the Lords of the Manors who held the right to claim wrecks at sea from Kettle Hill in Morston to Carvel Mill in Kelling.

The development of the Haven grew out of its strategic importance in providing the only safe anchorage between King's Lynn and Great Yarmouth. With the easy access between Cley and Blakeney it was inevitable that the prosperity of one depended to a large extent on the other and, because of this interweaving interest, the reader is invited to read the companion booklet in this series, "Have you Heard about Blakeney?", in order to appreciate the history of the two ports.

1

Let us start our story at the church, a fully descriptive booklet of which is available there. Standing on the site of a much earlier building, the present church dates from about 1250, the tower remaining from that time. A vast rebuilding programme was started in the fourteenth century and was to continue, with interruptions, until well into the fifteenth. The size of the church reflects the wealth of the village (then a 'town') at that time, with money coming from the many wealthy merchants, native and foreign, whose prosperity was founded on international trade; so much so that Blomefield could report the existence of a chapel in the church "formerly belonging to the German merchants".

PIRATES

The early days of seafaring history in Cley, as in Blakeney, were not peaceful ones. By 1317 the Haven was reported as being "in the grip of organised gangs of pirates" and, on the 17th April 1404, a Royal Licence was issued granting permission for armed ships to go to sea, at their own expense, to both protect the coast and attack enemy craft. It was not unknown for ships to be actually attacked and robbed while in the Haven itself and evidence that local men were not above acts of piracy on the high seas is illustrated by the action, in 1405, when some boarded, and captured, the 'Maryenknight' out of Danzig, which was found to be carrying the nine year old Prince James, youngest son of Robert III of Scotland, who was on his way to France under the patronage of the Earl of Orkney and other noblemen and knights. Nicholas Steyard of Cley was one of those credited and rewarded for capturing the young prince.

Despite this unsettling background trade and commerce continued to flourish and by 1544 Cley and Wiveton could each boast more, and bigger, ships than Blakeney, while in 1565 the population of Cley was 450 against 360 for Blakeney.

Other important statistics of the time included crediting Cley with 35 mariners against Blakeney's 30; 25 fishermen against Blakeney's 18; nine ships trading with Scotland (against four); and "fourteen ships of burden" against the neighbour's eight. Another return, dated 1570, showed Cley possessing 65 mariners and thirteen ships against Blakeney's 52 and eleven, with Wiveton having 43 mariners and eight ships.

The main reason for this temporary superiority was the apparent willingness of the authorities at Cley and Wiveton to provide proper quays and facilities for the bigger ships which were then coming into use.

There is also evidence to suggest the presence of boat building businesses at Wiveton and these must have contributed to the importance of the area.

As with many other communities, especially seafaring ones, local Guilds provided a most valuable service, operating in many

Cley and Blakeney, 1586. The comparative size of the Salthouse channel is noticeable. (Courtesy Mrs F. Long).

respects as do our modern friendly societies by looking after those in need. Cley had four Guilds - dedicated to St George, St Katherine, St Margaret and the Guild of Our Lady. They all benefited from bequests, such as those made by John Symondes, an apparently wealthy merchant and ship owner. In addition to bequests to the Guilds he left money to the Friars at Blakeney, Walsingham, Burnham and Norwich, plus money to several local churches, including those at Holt and Salthouse. His wife was to inherit three ships, the *'Leonard'*, the *'Agnes'* and "the great ship *'James'* whan she comys home owte of Iseland." A fourth ship, the *'Margaret'*, was bequeathed to two friends so that they could "stand by my wife and help her order her ships". Son Raufe was to have the *'Trynite'* on reaching the age of 20, when he would also inherit his father's lands in Cley, Salthouse, Holt, Edgefield, Hunworth, "Lerynette", "Glawmfurth" and Saxlingham. He was also generous in bequests to friends and relations and the importance of salt at that time is underlined by the specific bequest of "£40 and 40 wey of salt" to his three daughters (one 'wey' was equivalent to 40 bushels.)

Salt was a most important commodity for the local fishermen and merchants and, while nearby Salthouse may have provided enough for local domestic needs, imports were certainly needed to sustain commercial trade. The Ordnance Survey sheet for 1834 shows "saltpans" in

3

Cley (immediately past the last house on the left hand side as you leave Cley for Salthouse) and in 1794 Defoe is recorded as describing "large salt works in Cley which produce very good salt...which is sold all over the country and sometimes to Holland and the Baltick."

At this time the 'centre' of the village was round the church - a fact confirmed by the number of old wells found in this area - and some idea of the size of the community can be gained from the damage caused by a disastrous fire, which broke out on the 1st September 1612 in the premises of one Thomas Coe. It spread rapidly and by the time it was under control 117 properties had been destroyed, together with most of their contents and all to the value of £4550. Thankfully, as far as is known, there were no casualties. At least two buildings pre-dating the fire survive, their original uses as possible warehouse and store, they now form part of extended and modernized residential properties.

SOCIAL STANDARDS

Times must have been hard for the poor of the parish, for while the wealthy were largely immune from prevailing conditions, the Questmen were always vigilant and seeking to find wrongdoers to present to the Church authorities for punishment. As we have seen in other booklets in this series, the imposition of social standards on parishioners was often strict and open to public gaze. The Archidiaconal Records for Cley tell us, for instance, that in 1567 one Stephen Becham

Cley Church and Village, c.1930 (P. Brooks collection)

was admonished for "having two wives living" - a fault not to be found in George Dunham who "contrarie to the lawes of the land doth not cohabite with his wyffe." Joan Gobrets was accused of being a "common brawle" and ordered to acknowledge her faults in church "on bended knee." John Briggs was ordered to purge himself "by four neighbours" for not attending church and when he did not appear he was excommunicated, only to be subsequently absolved when he paid 2d into the Poor Box.

In 1601 Alice Shorten not only abused the Minister "with most shameful and reproachful words but blasphemed his doctrine saying he doth no good in the towne but what he heard on the week-daie doth upon the sondaie babble it in the church."

Absence from church, playing games and either engaging in work, or allowing employees to do it, on a Sunday were common causes for reporting, but Richard Okelbie was somewhat different. He threw stones into the churchyard "and with the same did hit a woman named widow Wittleson." In those days of long sermons one can, however, sympathise with Thomas Wright for usually "sleeping during divine service."

As we have seen in the booklet on Salthouse, the marshes have always played a vital role in the life of these coastal villages and their development. Prior to the seventeenth century those at Cley were no more than tidal saltings, such as we see today at Morston, although the higher ground of the 'Eye' to the east of the Beach Road, once 70 acres in extent, has always provided valuable grazing land.

There had been some embanking and draining of the marshes in 1522 by Sir John Heydon, this altering the flow of water in Cley Channel. It was an exercise to be repeated in 1630 when John Van Hasedunck once more began enclosing the Salthouse marshes, while seven years later Sir Henry Calthorpe and his son Philip embarked on a similar scheme for the Blakeney marshes. Their plans included putting a dam across the river Glaven, thereby effectively cutting off seaborne traffic along the two arms of the Glaven coming south toward Wiveton Bridge, one serving the wharves below Cley church and the other the wharves at Wiveton, and clearly shown on the Cloudesley Shovell Presentation Map reproduced in the Blakeney book.

Local merchants, lodging house keepers, coal carriers, ship owners and ship builders all complained and petitioned Charles I who ordered an Admiralty Court to hear their grievances. This it did on 31st January 1638 and again on 22nd October the same year, but without taking any positive action. The Port Court of Cley, which could be compared with our modern Port and Haven Commissioners, sitting on 11th December, found against the Calthorpes and following another petition to the King, the bank was demolished.

Thomas Coe, foreman of the Jury, testified that the Ports of Cley and Wiveton possessed 20 "good shipps, some of 140 and one of 160

The beach, about 1910 (P. Brooks Collection)

tons belonging to the same towne, six being built at Wiveton near unto the main channel beside many others belonging to Cleye." There would appear to be no evidence of ship building at Cley - apart from Howard Brett's and Kenneth Newton's later businesses - although Peter Catling has suggested that this could have been done at the mouth of the Holtfleet Creek which ran at the rear of properties (Post Office side) in Holt Road.

A lodging house keeper, Mary Ringall, stated that since the erection of the bank coal was costing her 17s 6d per chaldron (twenty five and a half hundredweight) as against 12s 8d previously and she had become impoverished because whereas she "was wont to make 7 or 8 bedds on one night" she was now reduced to "but one in one night for strangers." In those days eight overnight visitors must have represented a fairly flourishing trade, all of whom would have come from the seafaring community.

Others testified that the "poore porters" had also lost money and that trade had diminished, both in the number of ships using the port (from 30 in 1637 to 14 in 1638) and the volume of cargo handled.

DAMAGE DONE

Although the Calthorpes demolished their bank the damage had been done, for the river course, denied the scouring action of the tide, had already begun to silt up, and continued to do so to the extent that Wiveton ceased to trade as a port. The valley, however, remained tidal until 1824 when the present bank and coast road were built and Cley's decline and ruin as a port became assured. It also had serious effects on Blakeney harbour. The bank was breached in the floods of 1897 and in 1953 when, for a few hours, Wiveton valley became a rough sea again.

In June 1821 Commissioners met to implement the Inclosure Award "for dividing and allotting the said Commons, Salt Marshes, Commonable Lands and Waste Ground...and for embanking and draining the said Common Salt Marshes."

6

Having made their allotments the Commissioners also went on to make several interesting provisions. The Fair, for instance, was to be "for ever afterwards" held on its traditional site on Lee's Marsh, although local residents can recall it being held at the Fairstead and combined with a horse fair on the village green - also known as the Fairstead on an 1839 map. Special Commissioners were appointed "for the purpose of improving and rendering more productive" the marshes and "for preventing the same being overflowed by the Waters of the Sea."

They were under special instructions not to do anything which might injure or damage any house, "especially Glandford Mill." At that time the mill could not work at certain tides because the sea water held back the flow of fresh water needed to turn the water-wheels. The main trouble was at Spring Tide when the mill was out of commission for about 28 hours. If the Commissioners did anything to increase this time then they had to compensate the mill owner at the rate of two shillings "for each and every hour of such extra time lost."

No one could remove stock or equipment from the marshes in order to avoid paying taxes, and there were restrictions on cutting new dykes or destroying any new work, the penalty being transportation for seven years. Any master or ship-owner of any craft causing damage "spoil or mischief" had to pay compensation, this not exceeding £10 "plus 40/- to the informer."

The George, with the Institute on the left, c1926 (P. Brooks collection)

Prior to the construction of the present coast road the only vehicular route to Blakeney was via Wiveton Bridge, although there was a wooden bridge, known as Eson's Bridge, because Patrick Eson, the local collector of Customs, had raised the necessary subscription of £60-£70 in 1739 to enable it to be built. It was later (October 1789) to be damaged when a gale blew a new ship, the *'Abbicorne'*, from its moorings into it. Further damage was done by the digging of a channel to release the ship, but another public subscription quickly raised the 50 guineas needed for repairs and it then lasted as a valuable pedestrian shortcut to Blakeney for many years.

In 1649 Simon Britiffe, Lord of the Manor of Cley and living in Cley Old Hall, had built another bank, this time from opposite what is now Cley Old Hall due north to the Eye, turning along the southern side of Cley Channel to high ground and then back again to meet what is now the main coast road. As he was merely enclosing his own property in order to improve the grazing value and was not interfering with either the flow in any channel or depriving anyone of their livelihood he met no opposition.

This area, known to ornithologists the world over as Cley Marsh, has changed little over the years. The exception is an old right of way, known as the 'Long Drift', which followed the line of an ancient causeway giving access to the 'Eye', which has been closed in exchange for land given by the Cozens Hardy family to form the present Beach Road. The northern portion of Britiffe's enclosure was breached in 1897 and finally went in the flood on 1921, not to be replaced. The 435 acres of the marsh, which for generations had ranked as one of the best wildfowling areas in the kingdom, were bought by the Norfolk Naturalists Trust in 1926 and became the first nature reserve in the county, with the official designation as the Cley Bird Sanctuary under the Wild Birds (Cley Sanctuary) Order 1966, coming into force on the 30th May 1966. The Information Centre can supply full information on the sanctuary and is open every day, except Mondays, (Bank Holidays excepted) April to October between 10.00 am and 5.00 pm.

An indication of the amount of land lost to the sea can be gained by the knowledge that some of today's residents can recall their grandfathers tilling soil and cutting grass on a seven acre field on the seaward side of the present bank, which itself has receded at least half a mile during the last hundred or so years.

VILLAGE MOVED

The effect of the embankments, plus the damage caused by the fire, led to the concentration of trade on the wharves, warehouses and granaries in the area of the present mill; in effect the village moved north. Ships were still going out in February and March to the Icelandic fishing grounds, returning during July and August, while others, like the 100 ton *'Ambrose'* with its 40 man crew, were carrying grain, wool, fish, peas and malt to such destinations as Spain, Marseilles and Crete and returning laden with salt, spices, oriental cloths and other luxury items.

The bulk of the trade, however, was increasingly with the Low Countries, mainly through Rotterdam. As the harbour continued to silt up this international trade declined and coastal trade increased. Cley, like Blakeney, was a major outlet for the farm produce of North Norfolk with cargoes of barley, malt, fish, wheat, beer, peas and beeswax going to London and the north-east ports, with holds full of coal, wine, groceries, linen, cordage, glassware, wood, cloth, luxury food items, pepper, nutmeg, green ginger, treacle, raisins, currants, sugar and French wine coming back.

One interesting export was oysters, the Norfolk Chronicle reporting in July 1836 "Many hundred tons of oysters have been caught off Cley, where there are very extensive beds, during the last season and sold to Kent dealers at less than sixpence a bushel." A map, published a year earlier, showed the beds to be just east of Blakeney Pit.

The success of Cley as a grain exporting port led to great resentment in Norwich and, in 1631, the City Fathers complained to the Privy Council that while they had to borrow some £300 in order to distribute corn to the poor to relieve their misery, this commodity was being exported from Cley and Wells. They requested that the licences permitting this be revoked. Their plea must have gone unanswered for exports continued and reminders of these days can still be seen in the village - in its architecture, layout and individual buildings where glimpses of craftsmanship, unusual decorations (animal bones, for example) and symbolisms still survive today. Look for the little terracotta angel high in the wall of one of the new properties on the former garage site in High Street. She survives from an old maltings once on this piece of land; her two companions are in safe keeping in the church.

As late as 1871 the Highway Rate Book contained details of five malthouses, a warehouse, three granaries, a salthouse and a counting house, the latter, together with one malthouse and three granaries, belonging to Turner and Sons who also had interests in Blakeney trade. As the size of ships increased they found it increasingly difficult to negotiate the silting channel and the number visiting Cley rapidly diminished, two of the last to tie up at the quay by the mill being the 'New Walter and Anne' and the 'Angerona'.

Local inhabitants have recalled horses and wagons lining High Street as they waited to discharge their loads to ships tied up at the quay. It is more likely, however, that these were lighters being used to ferry cargoes the three miles out to Blakeney Pit where they were loaded into ocean going craft. These were poled all the way out and back by four man crews; fourteen hours for the round trip. The usual cargo was 45 tons of grain out and 45 tons of coal back, although until well into the late 1800s Cley carried on a "fair trade" in oil cake and the quay was a busy place. Reports of the time speak of a bone manure factory in the

High Street with "huge quantities of bones" being unloaded at the quay. This trade could well have supplied the many bones to be seen in the walls and decorative stonework of Whalebone House, formerly the village Post Office. One of the last foreign going ships was the *'Homer'* which, in the late 1800s, under Captain Pinchen, set sail to the Baltic, Marseilles and the Dardanelles.

The decline of Cley as a port was confirmed in 1865 when it was transferred to the jurisdiction of Wells, that port suffering the same fate in 1881 when, in turn, King's Lynn became the superior port. The final straw was the coming of the railway to Holt in 1884 when merchants realised they could transport their goods faster and cheaper, and trading ships all but vanished from the local scene.

That other well known seafaring activity, smuggling, was also well practised in the area, despite the presence of coastguard officers in stations along the coast and a Customs House in the village. As early as 1676 official action had been taken to try and curb it by specifying the limits of ports and quays where cargoes could be unloaded. The Port of Blakeney, Cley and Wiveton extended from Morston sluice in the west to Cromer church in the east and for Cley there were two "approved" quays - Captain Simon Britif's measuring 138 feet by 36 feet and Burton's Wharf measuring 67 feet by 36 feet.

Despite this, smuggling continued through the years, not dying out as an organised activity until the late 1800s along this stretch of coast. In 1812 the Sheringham revenue cutter captured a smugglers' boat laden with 600 casks of Geneva just off Salthouse, the cargo being impounded and brought to "the King's Warehouse" in Cley. The year 1833 saw a pitched battle between smugglers and revenue men on the marshes, the latter under the command of Lieutenant George Howes from the Weybourne Preventative Station. In 1935 a reporter from the Norfolk Chronicle interviewed Mr Howard Brett, local carpenter and boatbuilder, then 84, who recalled seeing a "quantity of cases" in a pit hole on Cley allotments. Many village properties still possess convenient 'hidey-holes' where, no doubt, contraband goods were safely hidden in years gone by; one is in the roof of Commerce House near the corner of High Street as it curves towards Blakeney.

White's Directory of 1845 describes Cley as a "small town and port" (the Town Hall in High Street is dated 1596) with a Customs House and a "narrow and shallow" harbour. The previous year's statistics had shown that there were 115 registered vessels within the limits of the port, plus a further 380 fishing boats, these being chiefly from Cromer, Sheringham and the Runtons - a clear indication that while trade had declined the Haven was still offering shelter, particularly during the winter months, for local boats. It is known that the Great Boats from Sheringham sought haven here when not out at sea.

Opposite-Top: The village, c1913. The reverse of the postcard refers to Cley as a 'gentry resort' with local boys 'so countryfied!' Bottom: Cley Institute in 1912 (P.Brooks).

A village scene early in the century (Courtesy Mrs M. Catling).

The year 1844 had seen 38,000 quarters (9500 tons) of corn and "above 10,000" sacks of flour exported from Cley, while imports included more than 20,000 chaldrons (25,500 tons) of coal, buildings close to the mill acting as temporary stores pending its removal inland.

Reference is made to a "former" small Saturday market (it was still being held in 1836) and to a Pleasure Fair held on the last Friday and Saturday in July. A Lancastrian School had been established in 1834 and provided education for 70 boys and 40 girls "who pay 2d each per week". Local residents included a Comptroller of Customs, two "tide waiters", a shipbuilder (John Richardson), a cooper, four grocers and drapers, 6 master mariners, a surgeon, 3 shoemakers, a tinsmith, 3 bakers, 2 blacksmiths, 3 butchers, 7 joiners and 4 tailors. Pubs included the Fishmongers Arms, George and Dragon, King's Head and the Three Swallows, plus up to 6 beerhouses. A sailing packet left for London and Hull "once a fortnight."

The 28th October 1845 saw the visit to Cley of Commissioner Joseph Hume to inquire into the state and future of the ports of Cley and Blakeney. The passage through to Salthouse Broad was by now closed although "within the memory of witnesses there was a passage to admit boats from Cley harbour to the Broad." Hume could find no authority for the enclosing of the tidal land north of the village nor for land on each side of the channel, thereby depriving it of the benefit of tidal waters from some 1021 acres.

He estimated that this work had deprived the channel of some two million tons of scouring water at each ordinary tide and had contributed to the fact that only vessels drawing six feet of water could use the quay, instead of nine feet as late at 1824. And, importantly, the channel had narrowed so much that even these boats could not swing.

Commissioner Hume recorded that in 1824 Cley enjoyed "considerable trade" and had several general merchants; "now there is little trade and only one merchant remains. All property in the town, except land, has decreased in value 50 per cent; and many properties formerly in demand cannot now be let or sold on any terms. The population, which in 1831 was 828, has since that period remained stationary."

He left no doubt as to his feelings regarding the 1824 enclosures, saying they afforded "striking proof of the mischief resulting from these inconsiderate proceedings." He put the blame for the ruin of Cley harbour squarely on the shoulders of the promoters of the Bill, which had resulted in these conditions, and drew official attention to the evils arising from a state of affairs in which a public harbour had been almost destroyed by the actions of a private company who "profited largely therefrom".

Cley "Underhill", about 1913 (P. Brooks collection)

Above: The Old George corner before 1907. "Lawrence Randall, licensee", on the right; in the centre "Cheap modern household furniture"; on the left a baker's shop. (Courtesy Mrs M. Catling). Below: From a postcard known as "The Stangroom Wedding Card", published by E.A. Stangroom, Cley (P. Brooks collection).

Above: An early shooting party, c.1880. Below: The Queen Victoria Inn, c.1890, popularly known as "The Hole in the Wall" (Courtesy of Mrs M. Catling).

In 1846 the Post Office Directory was listing the chief trades as the exporting and importing of coal, timber, oil cake and malt, and civilisation had arrived in the form of a straw hat maker. The post box closed at 3.15pm, but letters could be posted up to 3.30pm on payment of an extra penny and up to 3.45pm by paying two pence extra. The previously listed pubs had been joined by the 'Angel' and the population of 995 included nine master mariners.

By 1875 the Customs House had "removed to Wells" and the diminished population of 764 included eleven master mariners and three ship owners. The Stangroom family, James (tailor and draper), Stephen (grocer and draper) and Frederick (grocer, draper, chemist and druggist) had set up their respective shops. Local people have recalled the latter gentleman with affection. His shop was where the present grocery shop is in High Street, and in addition to his other interests he was agent for the Imperial Fire and Reliance Mutual Life Insurance companies. Also he was always willing to pull a tooth or two and carried a pair of tweezers ever ready for immediate use. His favourite 'pulling' spot was by the railings which used to front the house next to the former garage in High Street, and one can so easily conjure up a mental picture of Fred pulling for all his worth while his 'patient' clung desperately to the railings for support. He sold opium and laudenam, the opium being an ingredient of

The village about 1904. Compare with picture on page 10. (P. Brooks collection).

At the post office, early 20th century (P. Brooks collection)

Godfrey's Cordial, a mixture of opium, treacle and an infusion of Sassafras, which a British Medical Association report of 1867 described as "the usual comfort administered to a squalling baby when its mother was too busy to feed it." This report stated that Lincolnshire and Norfolk, between them, consumed more than half the opium imported into the country, "there not being a labourer's house without its penny stick or pill of opium and not a child that did not have it in some form." Fred's shop was taken over by Ernest Stangroom who continued in business to 1941, when it was let to Rusts Ltd. James's shop on the Holt Road, passed to daughter Hannah, then to Leslie and finally Alec, who retired in 1972. The adjoining building, now the Post Office, was formerly a chapel, then was used by the Salvation Army and during the First World War saw service as a troop billet.

As we have seen for Weybourne and Salthouse, there was an abortive attempt to bring a railway line to Blakeney Quay and out to the Pit. In 1883 White's Directory could report "The Eastern and Midlands Railway (formerly Lynn and Fakenham) now in course of construction is planned to pass through this parish and a station is proposed to be built near the centre of the village"; in fact just behind the High Street, near the George Hotel. By now the School Board, established in 1874 "now use what was formerly the British School established in 1860 in Elizabethan style at a cost of £6090"; there was an attendance of 140 children.

The village's growing importance as a holiday centre was foretold in Kelly's Directory of 1896 for in addition to Barclays Bank "attending on Tuesdays 1-3 pm" there was now a Coffee Room, two lots of apartments, a newspaper reporter, a painter and bird preserver (Harry Nash Pashley) and a Temperance Hotel (Mrs Elizabeth Nicholls, manageress).

The same Directory could also report that "this town is lighted by oil by the Parish Council" and this was in operation certainly by 1887, for an Account of Income and Expenditure under the Lighting Act showed income to be £15 16s 0d with £4 4s 10d coming from the Jubilee Fund. The scheme cost an average of £1 12s 1d per month over the six month period October to March. Paving of the streets had begun as far back as 1738 when Thomas Rogers was responsible for raising money by subscription to pay for the work.

FASCINATING BUILDINGS

The village is full of fascinating buildings, not least those which formerly carried the names 'Umtata', 'Umgeni', 'Umvolosi' and 'Umona'. The names are of Zulu origin and come from territories, townships and rivers in South Africa from Zimbabwe down to Cape Province. They were also names of ships and originated with the Rennie Line which operated a joint service to Natal with ships belonging to Bullard King and Company, the fleet being acquired in 1919 by the Union Castle Line. The names found their way to Cley where a Captain Lewis, who had sailed in the fleet, bought and built properties in the village. The cottages - three on the coast road and one in High Street have, in recent years, changed ownership and it is sad to record that the new owners have either changed the property names or simply done away with the old names. Thus the village has lost a bit more of its historic past.

The Customs House was built in 1680, had a new front built on in 1729, and was in use until May 1853 when the Comptroller was moved to King's Lynn. The quay was, at one time, just at the bottom of the garden for, when excavations were made to install a septic tank some years ago, the remains of substantial mooring posts were found about four feet down.

The property on the corner of Town Yard and Holt Road known as 'The Barn' was built during the early 1700s and was originally known as 'The Town House', providing accommodation for eight male and eight female vagabonds. It subsequently became a cattle shed and was bought and converted in 1970 into the pleasant home it is today. Parts of Cley Old Hall date back to the fifteenth century and it was one of the village's big houses until Cley Hall was built for the Cozens Hardy family. Among many fascinating features within Old Hall are part of a sixteenth century oak screen, an identical design of the sitting room mantelpiece to that of the pulpit in the Church and a handrail comprising a figure tiller from a French collier wrecked in 1913.

Like most villages of its size Cley has had its share of public houses; perhaps even more than most because of its maritime connections. Today only the present George (originally George and Dragon and built in the 1800s on the site of a previous pub) and the Three Swallows survive. At one time or another the village could claim eight. The two most recent to close have been the King's Head in the High Street, a

Top: The village, 1904. Bottom: 1905. Fred Stangroom's 'pulling' spot by the railings on the right.

Morgans house which closed in 1973 and to which, traditionally, drowned bodies were taken to be coffined, and the Fishmongers' Arms, now a private house called 'Sunbeams', formerly a Greene King House which closed in the mid 1950s. The latter was sold in 1802 for £232 and again in 1843 for £400, a plan of the time showing a 'brewhouse' at the back, plus two stables and a cellar, all fronting on to 'Common Street', now High Street. It had its own bowling green just over the road, a plaque on the wall of one of the new houses built on the site recording its existence from 1807 to 1957. It could well have been the site for the "match of bowls" played between three gentlemen of Cley and three from Holt, the wager being fifty guineas a side; the team from Holt won by five games to two.

The 'Victoria' beerhouse, immediately west of the old arch in High Street, was known affectionately as 'The Hole in the Wall' and a favourite haunt of wildfowlers and collectors of eggs and bird specimens around the late 1800s and early 1900s. It opened in 1829 and the clubroom was a regular meeting point for many local organisations, residents recalling needlework classes being held there under the auspices of the County Council until about 1910.

The 'Chequers' stood immediately south of the Customs House, closing its doors around 1850. The old 'Mariners Arms', probably built c1700, closed in about 1865 and was later to become Starr's shop, formerly known as Commerce House, but now renamed "Starr House" in memory of its former occupants. There are records of the 'Angel' public house although the site is unknown. Old records also refer to the existence of several beerhouses and there have been at least two breweries in the village, one at the Mariner's Arms and a second one operating in premises behind the old Institute, this closing about 1890. It is known that there was a maltings on the site at this time, with the Institute at the front. The maltings were demolished just after 1900 and the present houses built.

Argument still surrounds the origin of the old arch in High Street and, although doubt surrounds the theory that it came from an old chapel on Cley Eye, the 1835 map accompanying the second report of the Tidal Harbours Commissioners shows ruins described as 'Cley Chapel'.

The antiquity of the village is highlighted by the discovery in 1976 of a medieval wall painting in a house in High Street. Similar to one discovered in France and dating back to 1430, it was thought to have associations with Roman Catholicism and date from the time of the Civil War when it would have been considered dangerous to have such a painting on open view. The layout of the village is, in at least one respect, reminiscent of that of Great Yarmouth for we see a series of Lokes or Lanes coming down from the higher ground to the busy commercial and port areas. Town Yard, Taylor's Loke, Post Office Lane, Short Stone Lane, Beck Lane and Stangroom's Lane all provide this means of communication although Howes Yard, formerly known as Ratcliffe Highway (or Rattle Alley Highway by some) between the former garage site, now redeveloped, and the Harnser Restaurant, now a dead end, once gave access to the Fairstead and was the acknowledged "red light" area of this bustling port.

As we have seen at Salthouse, the threat of floods has always been a very real one. The Parish Church registers contain many graphic entries. On 25th November 1665 a tide destroyed wheat on the marshes and some of the banks "and tossed a ship out of the sea over the beach into Salthouse Channel, which was brought to Cley to be repaired." There is an interesting footnote which tells us that at that time "there was a channel between the beach and the 'Eye' (once 70 acres in extent - look at it today!) leading to Salthouse which is now filled up by the beach."

The flood of 7th February 1742 tore through all the banks, destroyed some 40 acres of wheat on the marshes, flooded many houses to a depth of four feet and drowned a horse belonging to one named Morgan "who lived under the hill." Total damage was put at £815 and following this the banks were rebuilt and strengthened sufficiently well to withstand another 'rage' on 28th February 1749, when the sea overflowed the East Bank but did not breach it.

Further serious "inundations" occurred in 1767, 1779, 1789, 1791, 1808, 1810, 1829, 1879 and 1921 and there was, of course, the flood of 31st January 1953 when, as in 1921, some houses had seven feet of water in them with mud and filth everywhere. Some idea of the nightmare events of that time are recalled by the late Miss Freda Starr in her eminently readable book "A Village Shop" and which is also a very personal and entertaining account of her life in the village to which she moved in 1906. Copies are available locally.

Local people have long kept weather records, Harry Pashley remembering the wreck of the steamboat 'Leven' in November 1893, when little auks were killed by being blown against the wire rigging; a steamboat blown ashore in December 1899 and the "worst storm I have known" on 16th June 1910 when the school bell turret was blown down.

CLEY REMEMBERED

And so we come to Cley as remembered by its inhabitants. Miss Starr's book really is a 'must' if you wish to capture the everyday feel of the village. In this space I can do no more than highlight some of the more interesting local events and characters.

Childhood memories recall the bowling of hoops along High Street; stringing skipping ropes across the same street and jumping over them; a game of marbles with holes in the unmade road as the 'target'; early trips on Sunday School outings and to Norwich Theatre and other exotic places in Hilary Heseltine's canvas covered lorry with the hard wooden benches emphasising every jolt and jar; and cinema shows at the Town Hall, a granary prior to conversion in 1896. For the young men of the village there were billiards and snooker at the Institute, formerly the Cley Parish Church Rooms, built about 1905 when the adjoining maltings were rebuilt. The Institute, whose original steps remain, was also the venue for well attended boxing matches - the ring anchor marks are still there - and Cley seems to have had a long association with this sport, for in August 1815 the Norfolk Chronicle was reporting:

> "Last week a well attended battle was fought at Cley between John Bell and the noted Mathew Randall, well known for his skill in gymnastic exercises. Betting was 2 and 3 to 1 in favour of Randall. After 20 minutes hard fighting Bell won. The known bottom of Bell and the tried science of Randall drew a considerable concourse of people among whom were noticed many distinguished characters of the neighbourhood. A handsome subscription was made for the conqueror who was taken from the ground in a gentleman's carriage."

That there were characters in the area cannot be denied, as we have seen for Salthouse and Weybourne. In addition to 'Jimma' and his two "wives", Annie Rooney and 'Thank You Ma'am', Cley also had John Bone from Wiveton. He sold home grown vegetables from - depending on your point of view - either an original and attractive, or a grossly dilapidated, wooden cart, green with age with odd bits of wood nailed on in a higgledy piggledy manner to replace those which had either fallen off or decayed with old age. Despite losing a leg in the first World War

Work on ditching and embanking was a constant process (P. Brooks collection).

The mill and marshes (P. Brooks collection).

he is remembered as a cheerful, happy man and was much mourned when he died.

Tramps came and went to and from Beckham (Palace) Workhouse and the annual visits by German dancing bears, cheapjacks with their assorted pottery and organ grinders were always welcome. And, of course, there was Harry Pashley, born in Holt in 1843, with his shop window full of stuffed birds - and sometimes live ones in the back yard, the tame white cranes being particularly remembered. They were always an attraction to the village youngsters and his reputation as a taxidermist extended well beyond the county boundaries.

Before settling in his final cottage he had run his business from the Manor House, the Customs House and the Gables. He died on 30th January 1925 at the age of 82. It was largely through his work that Cley became a mecca for bird collectors, this small area of Norfolk coastline providing more rare migrants than any other comparable area in the whole country.

The village can also claim two distinguished sons. John Greeve was an assistant to Sir Cloudesley Shovell, when he burnt the enemy's ships in the port of Tripoli on 14th January 1676, for which action he was made captain of the *'Orange Tree'*. He died on 14th April 1686 and an inscription recording his valour can be seen on his table-tomb in the parish church. Captain Grenville Collins is also remembered as the first to make a survey of the English coastline in 1693.

Fred Massingham was at work in his forge on the corner of Holt Road, reputedly built in 1607 to make cannons for the English fleet, those standing mutely outside being reminders of these early days. The building was restored in 1968 and is well worth a visit, not just for its delicatessen foods, but for the many reminders of days past - the unique beam drill, original double-clambered bellows embellished with a cow's horn, anvil, tyre moulds, cannon ball, forges and horseshaft.

There was also, during the sixteenth and seventeenth centuries, a fairly remote smithy down Blacksmith's Road across the marsh oppo-

23

site the council houses on the Holt Road, and much of the trade for this business could well have come from the ships.

Cley was, like many of its contemporaries, a self-contained community with two butchers and two bakers, both offering a 'home-baking' service whereby anyone could take their own pies, cakes and puddings to be cooked, all at a halfpenny each. The Rating Book for 1823 listed twelve shops in the village, the same number existing in 1926, plus five granaries, maltings and warehouses.

There were bathing huts on the beach - "too many" according to some, but cheap at a shilling a day; boat trips to Blakeney Point; a Regatta (until about 1930); cinema shows, dances and concert parties at the Town Hall. For many life would appear to have been rather idyllic, until you recall that in March 1907 there were 31 inhabitants receiving assistance from the old Erpingham Union, this ranging from one to five shillings a week, plus free milk in some cases. In October 1910 a bereaved wife was awarded 15s 8d to pay for her husband's coffin and £2 3s 6d to pay the funeral expenses. And it was not unknown for a knock on the door to herald the arrival of a child begging for tealeaves or any other item of food or drink that could be spared.

The mill, a current Grade II listed building, built during the early 1800s, was in use until about 1920 after which it became, in turn, a family home, self catering accommodation, a rumoured home for Princess Margaret (in 1982) and then to its present use as a guesthouse, a public meeting being called to discuss this latest development, and at which there were no objections. Increased motorised traffic brought demand for more petrol and this was met by two suppliers, in addition to the former Cley Garage, the new pumps were at the Smithy opposite the Manor House and on the western side of High Street close to the very sharp bend to Blakeney. Both have now gone and Blakeney offers the nearest filling up point.

WAR YEARS

War came suddenly to Cley, with recruiting meetings on the Saltpans, Peter Catling recalling a "blowsy female" singing in a loud contralto voice "We don't want to lose you but we think you ought to go". There were trenches on the 'Eye' and the beach, and troops billeted in houses, barns and granaries. There was an aerodrome at Swans Lodge, tents and huts appeared on nearby heaths and commons and there were hand-grenade practices on the marshes, which also saw use as a bombing range. The marshes were closed to everyone except military personnel, only the officers being allowed to shoot there. As Harry Pashley once recalled, "A few were good shots but the majority couldn't hit a hayrick!"

A wide eyed Charlie Francis watched troops practising bayonet charges against sacks of straw slung across the road at the Fairstead. There was a canteen in the King's Head clubroom and the Gables became both a billet and the venue for the 1919 Peace Celebrations. With Blakeney Point being used by Zeppelin pilots as a landmark these craft were a fairly common sight and sound as they crossed and recrossed the coast on their bombing missions. Despite all this activity the only real scare was on 23rd September 1916, when a bomb was dropped on the marsh opposite Anterton Hill, although a raid on the airfield at Swans Lodge on 7th January the same year was both clearly seen and heard in the village.

In November 1914 the wreck of the coal ship *'Vera'*, a collier from South Shields, with a full cargo of best steam coal, provided something of a godsend, the coal being sold at 2s 6d a ton on a "come and get it yourself" basis. The three man crew was saved by the local rocket company and the ship's boilers can still be seen at very low tides. A much more tragic wreck was that of the *'Hjordis'*, a Norwegian ship en route from Hull to Calais with 435 tons of coal. She came aground in February 1916 and of the eleven man crew only one survived, despite the efforts of the rocket brigade. He was taken to the King's Head where host and hostess Baines saw to his creature comforts and many parishioners came to see him in the course of the day.

This view of Cley beach in 1920 illustrates the change in the configuration of the beach. (P. Brooks collection).

The years between the wars saw the village becoming increasingly attractive to holidaymakers, especially those with ornithological interests. The basis was laid for the present day situation where some 20-25% of properties serve as holiday retreats occupied at selective weekends and short periods during the summer season.

World War II was marked by the arrival of troops and evacuees, the mining of the beach and the blowing up of every bridge leading to it - all of them being hurriedly rebuilt so that a Royal Artillery battery of six inch guns could be stationed there. A camp, housing some 160 men, was built on the 'Eye' and this subsequently became a Prisoner of War Camp, with Italian prisoners - but not the Germans - being allowed out at night to attend dances at the light anti-aircraft camp at Stiffkey!

Towards the end of the war the camp became a transit site for displaced refugees from Eastern Europe and was finally pulled down in 1948, the land being bought by the Norfolk Naturalists Trust. Then, on 15th August 1955, the Eastern Daily Press could report:

Cley High Street, with the old arch, about 1920 (P. Brooks collection).

"A large building on the seafront at Cley which formerly housed a battery observation post and the Coastguard Station was blown up yesterday by the 250th Field Squadron RE (TA) and two pillboxes on the beach at Salthouse were also demolished. The building which stood about 40 feet high was erected at the beginning of the last war as an observation post for two 6 inch guns. The Coastguard Station was transferred from a building about 50 yards to the east and accommodated in an extension on the seaward side below the main observation gallery. The premises continued to be used by coast guards and when the main part was no longer required for military purposes it was taken over by the Norfolk Naturalists Trust as an observatory."

The present observation building was formerly the camp generator house and when the building on the beach was demolished this was taken over by the coastguard service as a permanent lookout with two full-time men on duty. From 1967 it became a rough weather lookout and in 1983 was sold to the Norfolk Naturalists Trust who now use the top part as an observatory over their sanctuary. The old Cley Voluntary Rocket Life Saving Apparatus Company has been superseded by the present day HM Coastguard Auxiliary Service, an Initial Response Team of five members trained in marsh search and rescue techniques and providing assistance through the use of flares, life jackets and first aid to those in distress. Although members, through the years, have helped to save many lives they have had their disappointments, as in the case of the French ship *'St Joseph Dunkerque'*, a two-masted schooner driven ashore in November 1880 when the marshes were covered in snow. Although the local men tried hard they could not make the French crew understand how to work the breeches-buoy and only one of the five survived.

During the war, despite the presence of thousands of military personnel in the area, the village suffered no air raid, the nearest approach by an enemy aircraft being a Heinkell III which came down at Blakeney Creek on 9th June 1940.

On 30th October 1941 the Montreal registered ship *'SS Hall'* got into difficulties off Cley and the Sheringham lifeboat was summoned. Most of the crew, as well as the military personnel manning the ship's anti-aircraft guns, were taken off and the action was to win the RNLI's Bronze Medal for the Coxswain James Dumble for his "determination and seamanship". His son James recalls that the ship's propeller caught in the barrage about a mile off shore. This took the form of a wire encased in rubber tubing filled with kapok like material, attached to floats with strips of wire suspended just below the surface so that they would foul the propellers of enemy E-boats. The *'Eaglescliff's'* propellers had done just that and she was drifting in-shore when the lifeboat arrived. The wire was subsequently removed and the ship went on its way.

The year 1947 saw another coal-ship, the *'Billsdale'*, come ashore, this one being stranded on the west beach from November to well beyond Christmas, it not being released until a channel was dug around it.

Post war years saw the village developing more and more as a holiday centre and this has led, increasingly, for the village centre, to resemble a 'ghost' community during the winter months. An ageing community - about half the population is over 60 years of age - and a lack of industry mean that young people, inevitably look to other places for their livelihood and home. Not a good omen for the future.

Despite these trends the village's optimism is reflected in its £27,000 Village Hall opened in 1980, its continuing popularity as a centre for ornithological research and study, and the real attempts being made by both local and national bodies to balance the needs of visitors against the effects they have on the very environment they come to enjoy. Conservation Area status for the main part of the village, together with the surrounding Area of Outstanding Natural Beauty and Site of Special Scientific Interest, plus close monitoring by North Norfolk District Council of all forms of development should ensure that Cley retains its unique character. Future development would appear to be restricted to infilling and at the time of preparing this new edition it is understood that a Conservation Area Statement is in preparation by the local Council, with publication targeted for the summer of 1998. Concern over future flooding has been partially allayed by the construction of a new protective bank behind High Street. Total satisfaction, however, will not be achieved until an integrated coastal defence policy has been agreed, and implemented, for this vulnerable stretch of coastline. One suggestion has been the construction of a new earth bank extending eastwards to Kelling, with material coming from the Norfolk Wildlife Trust Reserve. This would allow new reed beds to be created in an attempt to encourage bitterns to breed here.The Reserve has seen new scrapes (shallow ponds) provided, new hides constructed, the Visitor Centre refurbished and boardwalks introduced - all designed to cater for, and manage, the increasing number of visitors who come every year to study the wildlife of the north Norfolk marshes. If walking in a wild environment has an appeal then follow the coastal bank eastwards to Salthouse, or westward to the loneliness of Blakeney Point. But check tides and weather conditions before you go, and remember that Arkwright's Cafe on Cley Beach car park is open at weekends during the winter months and daily between April and October for a cup that cheers and food to refresh.

ROMAPHOBIA

ABOUT THE AUTHOR

Dr Aidan McGarry is principal lecturer in politics at the University of Brighton.

ROMAPHOBIA

THE LAST ACCEPTABLE FORM OF RACISM

Aidan McGarry

ZED

Zed Books

LONDON

Romaphobia: The last acceptable form of racism was first published in 2017
by Zed Books Ltd, The Foundry, 17 Oval Way, London SE11 5RR, UK.

www.zedbooks.net

Typeset in Book Antiqua by seagulls.net
Index by Ed Emery
Cover design by Clare Turner
Cover photo: Villeneuve d'Ascq, 2013 © Philippe Huguen/AFP/Getty

ISBN 978-1-78360-400-5 hb
ISBN 978-1-78360-399-2 pb
ISBN 978-1-78360-401-2 pdf
ISBN 978-1-78360-402-9 epub
ISBN 978-1-78360-403-6 mobi

Printed and bound by CPI Group (UK) Ltd, Croydon, CR0 4YY

CONTENTS

ACKNOWLEDGEMENTS

It was only possible to write this book due to a research grant from the University of Brighton in 2013. I was awarded a 'Rising Star' research grant, which allowed me to conduct research in the Czech Republic, Slovakia, Hungary and Macedonia in 2014 and 2015. It also afforded me the opportunity to hire the wonderful Dr Nick McGlynn, whose literature review of territoriality in urban geography, sociology, law and political science helped outline the key debates and focus the investigation.

I am fortunate to have friends and colleagues who read early versions of the chapters and offered invaluable critiques. I want to thank Timofey Agarin, Nicholas DeGenova, Lucie Fremlova, Nana Håkansson, Ciaran McKenna, Annabel Tremlett, Huub Van Baar, Tommaso Vitale and Can Yildiz for taking the time to share their knowledge and insights, which I gratefully took on board. Of course, any shortcomings are mine alone. Early versions of different chapters were presented at conferences and symposia at City University of New York; Uppsala University; Queen's University, Belfast; Sciences Po, Paris; Al-Quds University, Jerusalem; and Comenius University, Bratislava. I am particularly grateful for the comments received from the University of Brighton Social

Movement Network when I presented at the monthly seminar in October 2015.

I also want to thank the participants at a 'Romaphobia' symposium that I organized at the University of Brighton in November 2015. Some of the debates at this symposium have found their way into this book either directly or indirectly.

My field research was greatly aided by certain individuals who helped me gain access to interviewees or resources that would have ordinarily remained out of reach. I particularly want to thank Benjamin Abtan, Mustafa Asanowski, Lili Mitrová and Violeta Vajda, each of whom was especially generous with their time and expertise. The interviews in Macedonia would not have been possible without the signposting and contacts provided by Eben Friedman, Julija Sardelic and Dejan Stepanovic. The research in Lunik IX was helped through the contacts provided by Lenka Kissová. I also want to thank the people I interviewed who shared their stories, insights, knowledge and time.

My gratitude also to Kim Walker and her team at Zed Books for editing the book and giving me the space I needed to complete it.

My special thanks go to Rowan McConnell for his unwavering support.

CHAPTER 1

ROMAPHOBIA: MARGINALIZATION AND STIGMATIZATION IN EUROPE

Today, Roma are one of the most marginalized groups in Europe, with anti-Roma attitudes on the rise. In many societies it is perfectly acceptable to denigrate Roma by invoking so-called traits and characteristics that all Roma supposedly possess. These qualities are invariably negative: Roma, as a group, are accused of criminality, deviancy, and living parasitic lifestyles. Romaphobia is the hatred or fear of those individuals perceived as being Roma, Gypsy or Traveller; it involves the negative ascription of group identity and can result in marginalization, persecution and violence. Romaphobia is a manifestation of racism: it is cut from the same cloth. Romaphobia is no different in form and content to Islamophobia or anti-Semitism, both of which are on the rise in Europe, but its causes can be particularized. There is something *specific* about Romaphobia, even if its racist core is familiar. I intend to explore the specifics. Instead of detailing manifestations of Romaphobia, this book uncovers the causes of racism towards Roma communities and points to constructive ways to combat Romaphobia.

While defining Roma is challenging due to the prevalence of multiple societal and political-legal representations (McGarry 2014), I follow the Council of Europe's (2012) definition: 'Roma' includes 'Roma, Sinti, Kale, and related groups in Europe, including Travellers and the Eastern groups (Dom and Lom) and covers the wide diversity of the groups concerned including persons who identify themselves as Gypsies'. Roma number between 10 million and 12 million people and are present in every state in Europe. Let me start with a simple but illuminating fact: legally sanctioned forms of discrimination against Roma have receded but anti-Roma prejudice persists – indeed, Roma are more segregated and unequal than ever before. This requires investigation. The extensive list of negative stereotypes of Roma, Gypsies and Travellers is instructive and depressing: Roma are regarded as a menace, a scourge and a disease, as secretive, unadaptable and ungovernable. But why? Why are Roma so vilified in every society and in every state in which they reside? Why is it somehow acceptable to discuss Roma in terms we would not apply to other communities? I want to know why this is the case for several reasons. First, like homophobia and Islamophobia, Romaphobia is an irrational fear that serves political ends: it is man-made and thus can be confronted and ultimately changed. In order to do this we need to understand why Romaphobia exists. Second, any attempt to improve the social, economic and political position of Roma must grapple with the root causes of anti-Roma prejudice. Policy interventions in education, employment, housing and health are doomed to failure unless they meet the challenge of Romaphobia head on. Only by understanding the causes of Romaphobia can meaningful solutions be found. Third, the issue of responsibility is oft discussed but a common solution has found little traction. Who is responsible for the integration of Roma communities (if we agree that integration is the goal anyway)? International organizations, national governments and civil society have failed to address the most pressing socio-economic concerns of this group, and the socio-economic position of Roma has actually deteriorated in the last thirty years across Europe. So, whose fault is that? Many Roma have been unable to mobilize politically in a significant manner to articulate their needs and interests because of structural disadvantages, yet failure to improve their condition is met with accusations from the majority that Roma are helpless and hopeless. It is commonly believed that Roma do not want to integrate so should be left alone to inhabit a parallel society. However, I intend to show that Roma have never lived separate from the majority; indeed, their perceived difference has been harnessed by the state and by other actors to foster national unity, with disastrous results for Roma, who in the process have been constructed as the perennial outsider community that does not belong.

Roma have never been so high up the political agenda of national governments and the European Union, with significant media interest in Roma communities (on television and film and in books). However, despite this spike in interest, there is no clear understanding of *why* Roma are so vilified and so excluded in every state in which they reside. *Romaphobia* diverts attention from the current academic and policy trends of documenting the regrettable situation of Roma across Europe and argues that it is crucial to understand the causes of Romaphobia and not just its consequences. It challenges some of the dominant trends in academic literature on Roma and seeks to explain *who* Roma are. Many academics who work on Roma start by asking why Roma are the poorest, most vilified minority group in Europe, but somehow we lose our way as we evidence instances of anti-Roma prejudice and draw attention to the discrimination and persecution of Roma communities and individuals across Europe. Of course, it is imperative that we spotlight violence against Roma, the destruction of housing by authorities, the targeting and expulsion of Roma communities, ethnic profiling by the police, school segregation of Romani children, coercive sterilization of Roma women, intimidation, hate speech by elected representatives from across the political spectrum, and accusations of child abduction. However, we lack any clear comprehension of where this prejudice comes from or how it is sustained. *Romaphobia* therefore seeks to uncover distinct processes of exclusion and persecution by exploring the relationship between identity, territory and belonging.

I use 'Romaphobia' in preference to other similar terms such as anti-Tsiganism or anti-Gypsyism partly because 'Gypsy' and 'Tsigan' are considered offensive and many prefer the endonym 'Roma'. Romaphobia does have a number of drawbacks because it does not refer to those who do not consider themselves 'Roma' or who are not identified by others as such. Anti-Tsiganism/anti-Ziganism and anti-Gypsyism help capture the negative attitudes and legacies of stigmatization regarding those whom others consider to be 'Gypsies', 'Tsigan' or 'Zigans'. I prefer the term Romaphobia because it captures the fear that motivates negative attitudes towards Roma communities. While there are certain benefits of fear, such as foresight and caution, it can also lead to factionalism. In *History*, Thucydides argues that fear is necessary and beneficial, acting as an important incentive to the formation of states, that it can be found everywhere, and that therefore fear is fundamental to the human condition. The collective fear of Roma communities is created and maintained by physical and symbolic segregation between Roma and non-Roma, and it is sustained by suspicion and distrust. Over time, conjecture replaces fact, with the majority regarding Roma as secretive, untrustworthy, and distinct from the rest of society. As Roma are seen as being different, they do not belong to mainstream society and, importantly, they do not have the same investment in the collective community, such as the nation. Even as Roma communities seek to integrate and assimilate, through the adoption of religion or language, their presence is seen as hostile and threatening, inducing fear of the 'other'. But fear alone is not enough to explain anti-Roma prejudice and attitudes; this is why it is important to focus on diverse causes of Romaphobia. I argue that Roma communities have been used by nation-builders and state-builders to furnish material power and to generate ideas of solidarity, belonging and identity that have served to exclude Roma from mainstream society. The main questions guiding the book are as follows: why is Romaphobia so prevalent in European societies and how is it manifest? What impact does Romaphobia have on understandings of Roma identity, territoriality and belonging? How can Roma communities address negative associations of group identity and participate in the economic, cultural and political life of mainstream societies?

I am aware that I run the risk of painting Roma as a hopeless community beset by stigma and persecution, a picture that disregards the wonderfully mundane and ordinary lives of many Roma. Not all Roma experience their lives as targets of oppression. Our eyes may search for the sensationalistic or dramatic images of Roma persecution but this reveals more about us than anything else. We must be careful not to mask the joy and hope in the lives of Roma individuals by reducing Roma people to oppressed caricatures drudging through their lives on the margins of society. Furthermore, Romaphobia can inspire positive reactions, such as the celebration of Roma history and identity. Indeed, recent years have seen a reawakening of Roma pride – a direct challenge to narratives of stigma and persecution – as well as ownership over these narratives and discourses through the emergence of the European Roma Institute to promote Romani culture, arts and heritage.

The book is guided by the conviction that we cannot hope to understand the causes of Romaphobia by focusing on purported characteristics of Roma. In order to understand where Romaphobia comes from it is necessary to widen our analytical lens to capture the relationships and processes that have created Romaphobia historically and fuel it today. For this reason, I look beyond ethnicity and race as causes of marginalization and examine how they have been used to create difference, fear and hatred. One of the arguments of the book is that Romaphobia is a legacy of nation-building and state-building exercises in Europe. The key to understanding why Roma are marginalized across Europe lies in our conception of territory and space as well as in processes of identity construction and maintenance. This 'identity work' includes European state nationalism as well as articulations of Roma identity and, importantly, the negative ascription of Roma identity by the majority. One example of the latter is the stereotype of Roma as itinerant 'nomads' who have no home or fixed roots, which serves to justify their exclusion today as Roma are not regarded as 'one of us'. As a nation without a territory, Roma do not fit the model of Westphalian nationalism that equates one nation with one sovereign territory. As a result, Roma are excluded from public life and serve as a foil for the interests of

the political elite; Roma are seen as a problem community that does not 'fit' the projection of the nation. Due to
the heterogeneity of Roma communities across Europe,
which are unique in that they lack any claims to territory, do not share a common religion, do not all speak
the same language (although a common language exists)
and are geographically dispersed, efforts to mobilize
politically have foundered (McGarry 2010). Moreover,
attempts to forge a collective identity are further impeded
by the myriad sub-groups and cultures that are housed
under the endonym 'Roma'. Indeed, it is more accurate
to conceive of Roma as a political project or phenomenon
(Vermeersch 2006) rather than as a bounded cohesive
group, and this has implications for Romaphobia.

Romaphobia has clear links to other major racisms in
Europe's history, notably anti-Semitism and Islamophobia.
It is beyond the scope of the book to outline the similari-
ties and differences between Romaphobia, anti-Semitism
and Islamophobia, but European state nationalism was –
and continues to be – underpinned by principles of racism
as it facilitated the inclusion of some at the expense of
others. This delineation acts as a source of strength for the
nation but requires active policing of symbolic identity
boundaries, inevitably leading to marginalization. Romaphobia, anti-Semitism and Islamophobia are realized
through othering and sustained resistance to integration
efforts by the minority, often by discrimination and persecution. These different forms of racism continue to play a
key role in the history of Europe, as can be seen in rising

fascism and xenophobia across the continent. This book focuses on Romaphobia in Europe because of the significant number of Roma living in Europe, the historical and contemporary persecution that Roma communities in diverse states experience, and the acutely hostile attitudes of societies towards Roma in their midst – but this is not to say that Romaphobia does not exist elsewhere.

The continued pursuit of the European project and the recent institutional commitment to Roma from the European Union (EU) through the elaboration of the EU Framework for National Roma Integration Strategies offer some hope for the future in terms of promoting Roma agency and empowerment, both of which are vital weapons in combating Romaphobia. But even as the EU offers a framework for integration, there is a danger that Roma are increasingly regarded as a 'European problem': that is, a problem to be dealt with by the institutions of the EU, thereby absolving states of their responsibilities vis-à-vis Roma people living on their territory. It is clear that efforts to integrate Roma and attempts to fight manifestations of Romaphobia cannot be addressed through the EU alone; local and national commitment and political will are required too. While the EU offers resources, both symbolic and material, to combat Romaphobia, it also maintains Romaphobia through its commitment to neoliberalism, which creates social inequalities and economic marginalization. The EU is reluctant to interfere in the affairs of member states on the issue of minorities, meaning that the European state retains primary sovereignty over its people.

THE STATE AND THE NATION

The state is a sovereign institution of governance to control a population within a given territory. The state is not a unitary, amorphous actor. It is constituted by myriad institutions (legislatures, police forces, local authorities, etc.) underpinned by norms, rules and laws that attempt to govern relationships within the state. It might appear that the state carries out any number of formal and legal functions (as well as informal and illegal ones), such as collecting taxes, patrolling borders, and suppressing minorities or protest movements, but in reality the state does none of these activities: these are carried out by 'sub-players' of the state, such as tax agencies, which collect tax, and the police, which monitors protestors (Jasper 2015). Thus when I refer to the state throughout this book, I refer to multiple agencies and institutions that may or may not act in a coherent and rational manner.

In early modern Europe, a patchwork of sovereignties including empires, kingdoms and city states traded with one another and went to war intermittently to accrue more power and, by extension, more security. The Westphalian sovereign state that emerged from the seventeenth century onwards has become the one enduring polity of the modern age. The state cultivates a relationship with its subjects, who later became citizens, through a contract to guarantee protection from their fellow subjects, societal progress and eventually rights. Loyalty was given if the state met these conditions, while failure to do so could result in rebellion. To fulfil its duties, the state established taxation and conscription and sought to supress dissent. But the early modern state was relatively ignorant about its subjects, including about their wealth, their landholdings, their crop yields and their identity. The state had to find ways of handling its subjects in order to get the most out of them (particularly their labour, but also their freedom); this resulted in the creation of surnames, the standardization of weights and measures, the standardization of language, population registers, the design of cities and the organization of transportation across the defined territory (Scott 1998: 2). States organize and calibrate in such a way as to make their subjects more legible, which means that they are more understandable and by extension easier to appropriate, manipulate and control, as well as to provide services to.

An illegible society is an obstacle to any intervention by the state; this includes those interventions that are welcomed (such as universal vaccinations) and those that are not (such as income taxes) (Scott 1998). On the one hand, legibility can be seen today in universal school attendance of children to provide an educational baseline standard in numeracy and literacy. On the other, it can result in the extreme abuse of state power: prior to and during World War Two the distribution of Jews across Nazi Germany, its allies and the annexed territories was documented by the state and subsequently used to identify, round up, deport and ultimately kill Jews and Roma. Legibility is one thing; how states use it is something else entirely.

The working, taxpaying, educated citizen is the easiest to monitor, assess and manage. But Roma historically have not been so easy to control for various reasons, one of which is their pursuit of employment and livelihoods that provide more independence from the state, such as self-employed trading. Tilly argues that 'states generally worked to homogenise their populations and break down their segmentation' (1990: 100). But segmentation can never be fully eradicated. If states are concerned with legibility and control, then how have states made Roma more legible? Scott (1998: 220) draws an explicit link between illegibility and Roma ('gypsies') because of their temporary encampments. After 1945, socialist regimes initiated a programme of sedentarization, meaning that citizens, including Roma, could be identified, observed, counted and monitored. As a further step, authorities attempted to homogenize populations through the assimilation of cultural specificity, particularly language, with the result that most Roma in Hungary speak Hungarian rather than Romanes (the language of Roma). The state is not an abstract concept but a self-realized actor that encompasses a broad range of services and responsibilities and relies on diverse agencies to control Roma populations; these agencies include border police, local governments, municipalities, mayors, interior ministries and the police.

One could argue that today the state has abandoned any hope of making Roma legible: the persistent stereotypes of Roma as nomadic, unadaptable and unteachable suggest some truth in this claim. Equally, one could say

that states willingly affirm Roma's illegibility for ulterior
motives, such as fostering nationalism by claiming an
adversarial narrative of 'them and us' that goes something
like this: 'We are civilized, retain common values and
characteristics and share the same history while Roma are
not like us, and do not share our principles and aspira-
tions.' Roma, while not immune to processes of legibility,
are seen as a necessary aberration in the homogenizing
forces of nationalism that aim to foster a common identity
built on a shared understanding of the nation. Successive governments have given up on perfecting legibility
with less pliant Roma individuals and communities and
have instead pursued containment: in designated schools
as well as in camps, villages, ghettos or settlements. For
state agencies, Roma communities are difficult to count
owing to an absence of objective criteria to determine
Roma identity as well as a widespread distrust of data
collection on ethnicity. This results in under-representa-
tion in census figures as well as a lack of identification
documents across Europe, making access to state services
more problematic. Territorial and symbolic containment
allows the state to make Roma more legible through
regulation but also provides an opportunity for Roma
to inhabit non-state spaces. These spaces are within the
territorial confines of the state but can be characterized as
zones of exclusion where populations live essentially off
grid, so to speak, relatively untouched by the tentacles of
the state leviathan. It may be a stretch to call some spaces
'stateless' but such liminal spaces and their inhabitants

are certainly illegible. These spaces are fertile grounds for subversion on the part of the excluded community but can equally breed suspicion and distrust between 'them and us', between Roma and the majority and vice versa.

Bauman (2004: 15) argues that each generation has its people who are 'shipwrecks marooned in the social void: the "collateral casualties" of progress', suggesting that casualties are a *necessary* vestige of societal progress. Those less adaptable will be left behind. And if something is created then something else must be consigned to waste. Waste is produced by society in order to foster progress: 'the bad is the waste of human improvement' (ibid.: 29) and is determined by those who drive the engines of progress. Human detritus includes the 'underclass', asylum seekers, refugees, those who inhabit zones of exclusion such as refugee camps and favelas, and those who risk life and limb crossing borders and treacherous waters illegally in search of a better life. On the one hand, societies dispose of this waste by making it invisible, simultaneously finding it repulsive and compelling. On the other, states make populations legible through design (categorization, bureaucratization and homogenization) in order to pacify and exploit (Scott 1998). Roma communities are exploited through exclusion from the labour market and are often regarded as 'useless' (Fassin 2015a) by states and unusable as labour. However, the story is not so straightforward, for while Roma are frequently seen as useless, they are a crucial component in the forging of a national identity by the state. Nationalism has proven the preferred tactic to

pacify peoples, shoring up affective bonds of solidarity
with one's supposed kin. Like all design it is deliberate
and has a purpose – to produce order from chaos (Bauman
2004: 31) – and so it is therefore reasonable to ask whether

the exclusion of Roma is by design. Marginalization is
then a by-product of state-making and nation-building,
both of which march hand in hand towards a particular
vision of progress. Today, for most states, that progress
is marked by economic and political liberalism, broadly
defined and understood. Roma, embodying the eternal
European 'other', are seen as wild and chaotic. Whether
Roma are objectively unpredictable or not is neither here
nor there; they are constructed as such by the majority. By
emphasizing the power of the majority in the construction
of Roma identity, I do not mean to suggest that Roma lack
cultural or political agency; rather, this points to processes
of identity-building where exogenous forces can brand
Roma communities in particular ways (as outsiders,
untrustworthy, parasitic) for political purposes and illustrates how very difficult it is to counteract this. These
processes mark Roma as superfluous waste, unwanted
in a progressive society, making it virtually impossible to
rebrand oneself as a productive, useful member of society
who can help drive the engines of progress.

IDENTITY AND STIGMA

I will not expend too much effort on the (still) hotly
contested matter of nouns, adjectives, verbs, endonyms

and exonyms to determine who Roma are. This is not because the matter is unimportant; rather, it has generated a wealth of interest and academic and policymaking energy already, with no consensus reached. When co-editing a special issue of the journal *Ethnicities* in 2014 with Annabel Tremlett and Timofey Agarin, we compared this exercise to the futile efforts of Sisyphus as he repeatedly pushed a boulder to the top of a hill only for it to roll down again. Every academic article or book must explain very early on the appropriate nomenclature to refer to Roma. The matter has diverted attention away from the myriad complex puzzles relating to the marginalization of Roma communities in which this book is more interested.

 Are Roma simplified, stripped of heterogeneity and cultural complexity in order to be captured and digested? This simplification, promoted by the majority to make Roma legible, comes with caveats. The image of Roma, re-fractured and imagined from mythic true selves, is owned by non-Roma through narratives, discourses, images and symbols. When an image or representation of Roma is summoned in everyday language it perpetuates racism as it comes loaded with an essentializing view. Like prefacing a statement with 'I'm not a racist but ...', it highlights that those making the statement know how it will be interpreted and attempt to pre-empt the inevitable finger wagging. Calling a racist a racist does not necessarily change anything: either they already know and do not care, or they refuse to believe that they are capable of being racist, which means that any accusation of racism can be swatted away. How many people harbour prejudicial feelings towards Roma but do not consider themselves racist? This is what Van Barr (2014) refers to as 'reasonable anti-Gypsyism'. Another predictable reaction is for the majority to counter-blame Roma for *their* racism against the majority, as they deliberately exclude themselves from society, ignoring the processes that maintain divisions between Roma and the majority. Romaphobia is the last acceptable form of racism. It is acceptable in as much as it is palatable or understandable given the overwhelmingly negative attitudes towards Roma across Europe. Research by the World Bank explored societal attitudes towards different groups in society: Roma communities across Europe generated negative attitudes comparable to paedophiles and drug takers in some states (Lakhani et al. 2014). Romaphobia is present in casual conversations in homes and at work, in media portrayals of the carnivalesque Gypsy, when state authorities accuse Roma of abducting blond-haired, blue-eyed children, in the town planners who place Roma in ghettos, in political elites who target Roma for special treatment and bulldoze their homes, or who deport Roma communities en masse. Here it is the identity of Roma that is targeted as troubling or threatening. The widespread conflation of Roma culture with criminality in countries such as Hungary and Italy is a testament to this.

At a conference on 'anti-Gypsyism' in Uppsala University in Sweden in 2013, the keynote address was delivered by Rom Professor Ian Hancock, who argued that addressing anti-Roma prejudice starts with legal redress. He said that if laws that prohibited discrimination on the basis of nationality or ethnic origin were changed, then we could fight visible manifestations of racism and show, as a society, that racism was unacceptable. But even though the European Court of Human Rights case *D.H. and others v Czech Republic* ruled in 2007 that placing Roma in special segregated schools is a form of discrimination, the practice of segregation continues in the Czech Republic and elsewhere. Even though we can recognize the importance of the law in fighting what might be termed overt forms of racism, it does not really help with covert racism, which is a more malignant strain. Changing laws and legal protection against discrimination is the minimum we should expect. Covert racism is found in subtle prejudicial views and attitudes and is the soil in which overt racism grows. Those wishing to fight Romaphobia will need to pay attention to covert racism, too, which is found in everyday action and language.

Stigma, following Goffman's social psychological approach, is a way to categorize and understand people and their attributes that become normative expectations or stereotypes. Stigma is a 'situation of the individual who is disqualified from full social acceptance' (Goffman 1963: 9). Those who are stigmatized are presented and understood as not being 'normal', or as a deviation from the majority or mainstream. But Goffman (ibid.: 24) argues that the causes and effects of stigma must be confronted directly, which suggests that processes of stigmatization can be challenged through the majority and those who are stigmatized engaging in social interaction. The majority and the stigmatized are part of one another: they require one another to exist. It is this symbiotic relationship that is central to transforming an attribute such as skin colour or tone or an accent into a fully blown stigma. Goffman tries to stretch the conceptual power of stigma too far; stigma should best be understood on a spectrum that covers phobia, prejudice, oppression and dehumanization, and that relates in different ways in different contexts to racism, discrimination, marginality and exclusion. This spectrum allows us to see how stigma is manifest in different ways in different contexts through different agencies.

There are several propositions that might explain why Roma are stigmatized. The first proposition is avoidance: that Roma communities want to be forgotten to avoid the enveloping arms of the state, and thus they create opt-out strategies and in the process they actively resist incorporation into the state polity. The ultimate aim here is to retain control over one's own affairs, believing that survival cannot be left in the hands of others. This strategy is called 'dissimilation' and refers to the cultural distance between societies (Scott 2009: 174); it can be seen in the maintenance of linguistic differences, differences in attire, housing styles, labour practices, and burial and marriage rites. Some Roma communities have developed cultural practices including courts (*kris*), purity rituals (*marime*), early marriage, and kings. Their difference or marginality can be seen as a political stance, even if it is not the product of a collective decision. Significantly, dissimilation can lead to ethnogenesis, where the group is understood by supposedly essential characteristics such as nomadism; this means that a practice with no cultural content can come to be understood as part of an ethnicized identity. Through the pursuit of employment, which was often mobile, flexible and adaptable, nomadism is understood to be a fundamental component of Romani identity in the same way that speaking French is for the French. Furthermore, the flexibility of oral over written histories has several advantages for communities that want to evade state bondage, capture or manipulation (ibid.: 24). Dissimilation implies an act of defiance as it is a direct challenge to the state, one that can be used by the majority political elite to stigmatize Roma as a hostile or threatening community.

The second proposition is exclusion. From the beginning of nation-building exercises (and indeed, before) Roma have been excluded from the articulation of the nation promoted by political entrepreneurs, their difference harnessed in order to build the nation as 'us' (the majority), not 'them' (Roma). Roma, as a heavily constructed and policed identity, become necessary 'others' positioned outside the nation; this is the rule rather than the exception. Roma have been stigmatized and persecuted in every European polity at some point or another since they arrived in Europe in the fourteenth century – with predictable results. As some Roma have eluded state capture in the form of conscription or taxation, they come to be seen as lawless or evasive by key institutions of the state and by the majority society. Their utility, such as it is, is served best by treating Roma as a distinct yet problematic entity inhabiting the state, yet separate from the nation. The unwillingness to coalesce around a collective identity could be seen as strategic. If Roma are a defined ethnic group then they are more visible to authorities, which might see their solidarity as a threat and could make them more susceptible to integration and assimilation. Roma have not risen up through armed opposition in a concerted resistance against nation-building or state-making forces but this does not mean that they are not a threat to the nation. The exclusion of Roma fosters a context of fear, while the relative lack of interaction between Roma and the majority fuels discrimination and negative stereotypes of Roma identity, which in turn reinforces exclusion. It is not surprising that some Roma individuals and communities seek to exclude themselves, for example by not sending their children to school. A willingness to exclude oneself from society should only be understood as a reaction to living in a hostile, racist society and should not be read as an endemic part of Roma identity.

It is misleading to suggest that Roma communities have pursued such strategies after a collective decision. We must also remember that there are those who identify as Roma who seek assimilation and want to be seen and treated like everyone else. But there is no uniform approach pursued or advocated. Some have adapted to the majority society for various reasons and play the 'game of integration', as it were, and some do this successfully (defined according to the rules of the game). Roma are an interesting case because of heterogeneity; Roma do not all speak the same language or practise the same religion, they have divergent levels of wealth and education, and their national affiliations are not all the same. And it is important to recognize that not all Roma are separate from the nation: many Roma identify as Hungarian or Finnish or Bulgarian, and so on. Between the First and Second World Wars, the collapse of three empires (Austro-Hungarian, Ottoman and Russian) had an impact on Roma residing on those territories and led to an increase in Roma political consciousness. New states emerging from the ashes of empires pursued divergent strategies towards Roma, including restrictions on participation in cultural and economic life as well as assimilation and integration. Moreover, newly created constitutions after the collapse of communism across Central and Eastern Europe recognized Roma as national and ethnic minorities, as legally constitutive *of* and belonging *to* the state and nation. Roma communities feel that they belong to the nation in spite of the stigmatization of identity as Roma, or perhaps because of the overt and covert forms of discrimination that Roma endure.

Thobani offers an explanation of stigma whereby the 'exalted subject' of the nation is venerated and exalted above all others as the embodiment of quintessential characteristics and the personification of the nation's values

and ethics (2007: 3). As a result, the outsider provokes
anxiety as well as outright hostility. Writing in the context
of Canadian colonial conquest, she argues that the
national subject is constituted through its exaltation and
points out that binary constructions whereby the self is
constituted in relation to its excluded 'other' have been
critiqued by Edward Said and Frantz Fanon. The exaltation of the national subject at the expense of the outsider
presents the relationship as antagonistic rather than
symbiotic. Crucially, the exaltation is policed through
discursive interventions that prohibit the 'possibilities for
coevality, mutuality and reciprocity' (ibid.: 6). In Central
and Eastern Europe, the patchwork quilt of identities
across borders is stitched together from categorized hierarchies articulated through legal and political recognition.
Being recognized as belonging to an ethnic minority
means being marked as different from the national ideal
and can result in stigmatization and potentially persecution. Thobani argues that outsiders are needed to build
the image of the national subject and that this is achieved
through exaltation as a technique of power that accultur-
ates the national subject and 'facilitates their "belonging"
to the community through the recognition and cultivation
of such shared nationality' (ibid.: 9).

Exaltation is demanded by the nation and confirmed
by the state, which becomes the cumulative expression
of this community of belonging. National subjects hail
each other as possessing the necessary characteristics of
the nation, and, according to Thobani, can override their

internal differences such as gender, class, religion, and so on, in the face of outsiders by expelling those outsiders who lack those necessary characteristics. So, why is one difference overridden in this context while others, such as ethnicity, are not? The characteristics that seem to be exalted are 'Western' and 'modern', two epithets that are not readily attributed to Roma. Frantz Fanon (1968) argues that 'the colonised is elevated above his jungle status in proportion to his adoption of the mother country's cultural standards', which suggests that the exaltation has a corrective. But the power remains in the hands of the colonizer and those who can express the necessary characteristics of the nation.

I want to emphasize that this is not about the exclusion of Roma from any one nation but from all nations in Europe. The historical experience of Roma communities in Romania or Slovakia or Spain has been unique in each case; however, despite different experiences, Romaphobia is prevalent in every state in Europe. Historically, we can point to acts of violence and dehumanizing treatment of Roma, such as being hunted for sport, expelled and deported, murdered, and enslaved – all of these have been supported by nation-building projects. Even where Roma are recognized as a national minority they are denigrated and excluded for being different. The promotion of nationalism is necessary to demand recognition but also reinforces difference and suggests that Roma are separate from the majority community rather than being equal citizens with rights and responsibilities. Public discourse and attitudes today reveal a level of animosity towards Roma which is alarming. I argue that Roma, while stigmatized, enjoy a qualified inclusion within the state which translates to a precarious position as second-class citizens. The internal other's identity is marked through moments of interaction with the exalted national subject, meaning that this identity is created in circumstances not of their own choosing, and they lack the ability to impose or challenge prevalent ascriptions of group identity. Nationhood arises through articulations of common characteristics – ethnicity, language, history, myths and values – but nations are built on exclusion as much as inclusion. This constant disequilibrium requires interaction between the exalted subject and the internal other. Thobani (2007: 20) maintains that the 'nation depends on the preservation of its distinctiveness if it is to maintain its self-identity and its coherence … should this exclusion ever be transcended the nation itself would cease to exist'. The identity of Roma communities is constructed and maintained by the exalted subject; this is particularly acute today with the rise of the far right across Europe, and with populist and nationalistic parties vying to protect the so-called fundamental values and characteristics of the nation.

The stigmatized identity becomes, over time, shackled to the internal 'other' and proves almost impossible to escape. Those who are stigmatized can internalize the image that the exalted subject, the oppressor, has prescribed. Usually a stigmatized identity becomes so rooted in everyday language and practice that it is

self-sustaining: Roma who are stigmatized as impoverished and helpless often cannot get work and may end up
begging on the streets, which means that stereotypes are
confirmed. This Romaphobia 'loop' is fuelled by distrust
and a lack of understanding between the majority and
Roma communities. Any interaction between Roma and
non-Roma is conducted in the context of the exalted
subject who holds all the cards and decides on the rules of
the game. Changing the hearts and minds of the majority
is made more challenging by the presence of Romaphobic statements uttered by political representatives,
the persistence of entrenched negative associations of
Roma or Gypsy identity in everyday discourse, as well
as the inability of Roma communities to effectively break
these stereotypes. Stereotypes, unless challenged, will
endure. There have been groups in the past – such as
women, African Americans and gays and lesbians – who
have protested against the negative ascription of group
identity, to varying degrees of success. Roma too have
mobilized over time in different ways, including trans-
nationally with the creation of the International Romani
Union and Roma Nation Day/International Roma
Day as well as through recent Roma Pride parades and
demands to be included in Holocaust commemorations.
The impetus here is to stake a claim to be recognized as a
political identity that is visible in the national and international context and to affirm and publicly own a positive
group identity. Freire (2004) believes that those who are
oppressed are complicit in their oppression and become

fearful of being free. He argues that freedom from oppression is 'acquired by conquest, not by gift' (ibid.: 47) and must be led by those who are oppressed, which is why it is important to understand Roma participation and agency in challenging Romaphobia (McGarry and Agarin 2014).

One may point out that the causes of Romaphobia are not so relevant: if a community is persecuted then does it really matter why or how? However, whether the position of marginalized communities in society has come about by design or default does matter in recognizing strategies to address stigmatization and persecution. The historical construction of Roma as indolent, untrustworthy thieves who leech off society and cheat and swindle at every opportunity because of inherent cultural traits matters for its cure and its remedy. It may appear that the only redress is for the majority to change their minds about Roma, but the catalyst for change must come from Roma themselves. If Roma individuals try to adapt (Get an education! Get a job! Be a good citizen!), they can only do so by shedding cultural baggage and integrating. How many Romani teachers and nurses, when colleagues learn of their ethnicity, are assured, 'Oh, but you're not like the others,' and are duly welcomed into society? Some Roma recognize the futility of challenging prevalent attitudes, but this can lead to internalizing visions of inferiority or living separate lives from the majority, both of which corroborate that majority's long-held suspicions that Roma don't want to integrate, they don't want to be helped, and they cannot even help themselves. Increasingly, though, Roma

are agitating for change on the local, national and transnational level across political, economic and cultural fields.

Equally, attempts to mobilize public fears of a deviant
other who jeopardizes personal and societal safety are
prevalent. Roma become a security threat in targeted
campaigns, for example in Italy in 2007–08 and in France
in 2010. In both cases, rhetoric from the political elite
goaded a sensationalist media and accentuated extant,
and sometimes dormant, negative feelings towards Roma
in the public. Roma have never been so visible but they do
not control the narrative of public presence and lack the
material resources to mount an effective counter-narrative
campaign. European states have recently lurched to the
right, with right-wing populist parties espousing ideals of
the nation and protection from unwanted immigrants. In
2013, former British Home Secretary David Blunkett said
that Roma migrants from Slovakia were causing problems
in his constituency of Sheffield, and that this could result
in rioting unless Roma changed their 'behaviour and
the culture' (Bowers 2013). All Roma migrants in the UK
have been tarnished, not just as a problem community
but as a threat to order and peace because of perceived
cultural characteristics. Some have argued that as the
state has ceded sovereignty in core areas of power due
to economic globalization, it has attempted to reassert its
domestic sovereignty, and that this has taken the form of
increasingly restrictive public order and penal interventions (Tyler 2013). As Roma communities across Europe
are in the cross hairs of far-right parties and nationalists,

prospects for improving their position remain limited and grim as long as different Roma communities are regarded as threatening groups living in the midst of civilized Europeans, the ultimate exalted subject.

It is thus important to understand and to try to explain not only why Romaphobia emerges and what are its main causes, but also how, and to what extent, it changes under socio-historically different circumstances. I will focus on identity, belonging and territoriality within the context of the nation and the state. This does not mean that I see in modern European history an almost continuous re-emergence of contexts of nationalism that, simultaneously, interact with the conditions under which Romaphobia becomes manifest. We must be careful not to consider Romaphobia as something that is historically a more or less constant phenomenon: its societal presence and how it manifests change over time. Nationalism, of course, played and continues to play a key role in various forms of xenophobia and racism, but, at the same time, nationalism alone cannot explain the changing faces of Romaphobia. I want to shed light on this area but it does not mean that I relegate other issues to the darkness. In the age of empire and in the age of the nation-state, fundamentally diverse mechanisms of inclusion and exclusion (or differential inclusion) were developed. The societal relevance of forms of Romaphobia in the contexts of the Habsburg, Ottoman and Russian empires therefore cannot easily be explained from the point of view of nationalism, even though the latter emerged at some critical point in each of these

imperial histories. Dynasty, class and religion were significant in socially organizing these three empires (though in
different ways), whereas the nation-state would not take
over this role until much later, in the context of the territorialized states and nationalized churches that emerged
from these empires, or, rather, at the moments of their
gradual dissolution. In these older imperial contexts,
in which Romaphobia certainly was a strong phenomenon, diverse forms of exclusion, marginalization and
denial (including murder) of Roma were not supported
by nation-building processes. Today, as state sovereignty
is much more disputed, nationalism continues to play a
key role in the maintenance of and changes in xenophobia
and racism. It is important to remember that it is not just
Romaphobia that is on the rise in Europe; anti-Semitism
and Islamophobia are spreading and are fuelled by a
reconfiguration of the nation, particularly in terms of who
belongs and who does not.

TERRITORIALITY

The relationship between peoples, including nations and
minorities, and claims to territory has produced interstate
wars as well as galvanized irredentist movements such
as subnational struggles in Spain, France and Northern
Ireland. The relationship between Roma and territory can
help explain historical persecution and continuing persecution today. While many minorities hold some claim to
territory or homeland, for Roma this is complicated by

the absence of a kin state. There is no Romanistan and no desire to create one. Indeed, the most vocal support for a sovereign state for Roma has come from far-right parties in Central and Eastern Europe that suggest removing all Roma from Europe and placing them somewhere in Africa. Roma have come to understand themselves as 'a nation without a territory' (Acton and Klímová 2001) and are today a transnational, geographically dispersed group with a presence in every state in Europe.

Most conceptions of territory equate it with a bounded space over which the state has sovereignty. But territoriality requires a reconceptualization of territory as multiple spatial sites, meaning that territory is more than mere geophysical locations. Territoriality is 'a form of behaviour that uses a bounded space, a territory, as the instrument for securing a particular outcome' (Taylor 1994: 151). Territoriality can function at the individual, group, sub-state, state and interstate scale and is always directly related to sovereignty. And it is understood as a strategy for organizing political authority (Sack 1986; Agnew 2005). Significantly, it melds the nation and the state by way of their mutual constitution *through* the same space (Taylor 1994). Sovereignty is constructed in part through borders and nationalities, and so we must unravel the discourse of state sovereignty as the conceptual encasing that enframes and enables the narratives of borders, identity and society (Kuus and Agnew 2008: 97). It requires the spatialization of identities and includes citizenship regimes, such as the EU, and the mobilization of ethnic identities across different political spaces (Sassen 2008). Some Roma have chosen to place themselves out of reach of the state and have sought to occupy de-territorialized zones of refuge where they are physically present on state territory but inhabit a different socio-political and cultural space. The implication of choice is important. Many Roma are neglected by the state and then try to resist any attempt by the state to make them legible, which usually translates into policies of control and punishment.

While political authority is always spatialized, it is not always spatialized through the territorial nation-state. The state remains central to our understanding of sovereignty and territory as well as of institutions such as citizenship. For this reason, this book explores the relationship between Roma and territoriality in three cases: in local territorially concentrated spaces within the state (Chapter 4); in expressions of local and transnational mobilization through Roma Pride (Chapter 5); and in transnational de-bordered spaces through a declaration of belonging to the EU polity by performing EU citizenship (Chapter 6). There are multiple cases that might prove useful, but those selected allow the research to explore the causes of Romaphobia through the lenses of identity, territoriality and belonging.

At stake here is whether Roma belong to the nation-state and whether the promotion of a transnational identity fails to anchor Roma in the national territory. States are what guarantee citizenship, which means that Roma must be formally tied to a specific territorial state in order to enjoy rights and responsibilities. With this in mind, the performance of Roma identity does not have to preclude the performance of a national identity. Roma migrants move beyond the confines of formal territorial boundaries and associated identities, but even if social spaces no longer correspond to the borders of the state, dispersed familial, social and cultural networks formed beyond the state mean that borders have to be negotiated. Rather than being borderless, I argue that some Roma have become 'de-territorialized subjects', particularly in the context of EU migration, which produces new forms of social and political agency and new sources of cultural meaning (Smith 1994: 16). This has the potential to develop our understanding of what it means to belong in diverse socio-spatial settings.

CITIZENSHIP, IDENTITY AND BELONGING

As already discussed, it is difficult for a state to impose its sovereignty and maintain control over a population that is on the move or lacks a clear pattern of organization, so the push for sedentarized populations has gone hand in hand with state-making projects. Some Roma have pursued 'dissimilation' as a strategy to remain more autonomous. The state has responded with the creation of an institution that compels even those communities inhabiting zones of refuge to join the flock: citizenship. By codifying rights and responsibilities, the state has formalized its relationship with individual subjects, but critics of citizenship

point to its uneven application. Marshall's (1992) conception of civil, political and social rights is unproblematically
construed as rights being equal to all under the sovereign
protection of the state, and guaranteed by the state. But
citizenship rights are not accessed equally, a point argued
most vociferously by feminist scholars. Because citizenship is bound up with state pageantry, including rites
and rituals creating affective bonds, such as flag raising,
national anthems and national holidays, as well as political practices such as voting and 'associated expressions
of civicness, the nation is the medium through which
exalted subjects can perform their belonging and recognize that of their compatriots' (Thobani 2007: 79). The
difference of those who cannot access the full catalogue of
citizenship rights is reinforced (Sardelic 2015). Moreover,
the deliberate erasure of the presence of Roma in national
historiographies, as witnessed in the refusal to recognize
sites of trauma for Roma communities before and during
the Holocaust, including the continued existence of a pig
farm on the site of a concentration camp in the Czech
Republic, serves to reinforce the exalted status of the
national subject. Romani language and history are not part
of educational curricula and the contribution of Romani
individuals to majority society is consistently denied and
ignored. Thus, the rites and rituals of citizenship constitute the national subject and recognize her as legitimately
belonging to the nation.

Citizenship is membership of a legally constituted
political community and 'consists of rights, duties,

participation and identity' (Delanty 2000: 4). This is a more active form of citizenship and suggests a community in which individual citizens must participate, if the opportunity to participate were open, which in turn would forge solidarity and protection. Citizenship has never adequately realized its universalist application and the paradox of the unequal distribution of citizenship has created a large body of literature exploring how citizenship can accommodate marginalized communities (Lister 1998), something that is possible only if societies accommodate a plurality of identities. Young (1990: 257) points out that some groups will be excluded or put at a disadvantage 'even if they have formally equal citizenship status', but societies prefer to generalize rather than particularize. Nation-building exercises will asseverate bonds of solidarity based on claims to territory or a common language to consolidate a homogenized population (Gellner 1983). Cultural difference is challenged and exteriorized as the 'other' who does not fit the dominant conceptualization of the nation. For those who are excluded from the nation, affective bonds of belonging to both the nation and the state are tenuous and in flux. The creation of the nation is built on exclusion, and those excluded from the nation are symbolically, if not formally, excluded from citizenship. It is not rights that are being excluded but identity. *Romaphobia* will unpack the relationship between identity and belonging but is not principally concerned with the ability of Roma to access citizenship rights; rather, the book intends to shift the focus to antecedent processes of exclusion that have created the context of unequal citizenship.

Exalted subjects preserve their identity at the expense of the 'other'; this process demonizes Romani identity, resulting in exclusion and discrimination. In response to increasing mobility across borders, states and nations have attempted to reassert a restrictive vision of the nation and who belongs in that vision. This can be seen today across Europe in the rise of populist parties that gain political traction with voters by re-orientating what it means to be French or British or Slovakian or Hungarian. In Western European states, the galvanizing force of nationalism is fuelled by fear of those seeking entry to the state – typically immigrants but also longer established groups such as Muslims and Roma – and attempts to protect the nation from those who might seek to disrupt it. In Central and Eastern European states, which experience lower in-migration and have smaller Muslim populations (apart from in Balkan states such as Bulgaria, Albania and former Yugoslavia), the target is typically Roma. In order to challenge increasing ethno-centrism and subsequent dangers, a more inclusive iteration of citizenship should be established that gives significant attention to identity and belonging. It is not enough to argue that excluded groups ought to be included; there needs to be a change in how solidarity is fostered through collective action, which demands the active participation and voice of the excluded, and not solely on the basis of exclusion.

The construction of Roma identity by the majority in negative terms impacts on the capacity of Roma to enjoy equal citizenship. Potentially, the remedy will be found in the articulation of Roma as a political identity rather than as a specific ethnic group per se. A political identity is unhindered by the reduction and production of an essentialist Romani ethnicity (by the majority) and instead emphasizes Roma political agency. It also requires adaptation to the majority community rather than expecting the majority to bend to the minority (it won't!). There is the possibility that Roma draw on their exclusion and marginality in order to make demands, which can in turn lead to further marginalization. Gamson (1995) shows how queer communities that mobilize on the basis of their oppression ultimately undermine their actions as they reinforce their difference and marginalization. Similarly, by drawing attention to difference in order to mobilize, Roma potentially reinforce notions of 'them and us' already dominant in the majority society, and, by extension, of who belongs and who does not.

BOOK OUTLINE

Chapter 2 outlines the concept of territoriality and how it develops our understanding of belonging. Drawing on insights from political science, law and sociology, this chapter uncovers the relationship between authority, identity and belonging in relation to territory. It argues that the geopolitical conceptualization of territory and the Westphalian sovereign nation-state have meant that communities such as Roma are seen as not belonging to the majority nation, which provides the opportunity for Roma to be stigmatized and subsequently excluded from public life. It examines the relationship between Roma communities and space or place and offers a critique of prevalent notions of cultural nomadism.

Chapter 3 explores Roma identity. It problematizes academic understandings of Roma by unpacking the relationship between ethnicity, identity and community. It asserts that because no objective criteria exist to determine who is Roma (and who is not), such ontological debates that have dominated the discipline of Romani studies do not address the most pertinent issues facing Roma communities today. It examines the meaning of the Roma nation and asks whether it is appropriate to conceive of Roma as a community or an identity and whether such constructions are compatible. The chapter outlines the political expediency of the Roma nationalism movement and explores the impact of Roma nationalism on notions of identity and belonging.

Chapter 4 is the first of three case study chapters. It focuses on two areas (Lunik IX in Košice, Eastern Slovakia, and Šuto Orizari in Skopje, Macedonia) where Roma are territorially concentrated and the impact of this for expressions of identity. Roma communities are socio-spatially segregated, inhabiting spaces on the periphery of societies, which highlights the active containment and control policies of state actors and a realization of state power. It examines whether territorial concentration improves the capacity of Roma to articulate their voice and ensure that their interests are represented. It also explores whether the territorial concentration of Roma has the potential to further marginalize Roma by 'ghettoizing' the community.

Chapter 5 explores the nascent Roma Pride movement which started in 2011 and has styled itself on the Gay Pride movement. Roma Pride certainly has the potential to challenge stigmatization in the long term as it seeks to challenge prevailing understandings of Romani identity in a non-territorial space, often by appropriating urban city centres to declare belonging. Roma Pride is primarily a celebration of Romani culture (which contributes to the reification of Romani identity to inoffensive and often positive stereotypes) rather than a political tool to articulate the demands of Roma across Europe, although there are signs that this is changing already. This chapter looks at different Roma Pride protests but compares two of the largest and most politicized in Central and Eastern Europe, in Prague and Budapest.

Chapter 6 explores one of the most topical issues in relation to Roma: migration. Recently, Roma issues have entered public debate in Western European states; this has led to a dramatic increase in attention to Roma, and a significant stigmatization and stereotyping of Roma communities, invariably centring on the unwanted presence of Roma on the streets of major capitals in Western Europe. This chapter explores migration as a de-territorialized space as part of the European integration project and what it means for national and transnational or post-national conceptions of citizenship and belonging. It analyses the impact on Roma communities living in the EU for inclusion and belonging and highlights how Roma declare their belonging to the EU polity by performing acts of citizenship. It examines the duality of belonging in national and transnational or supranational spaces and what this means for Roma people.

The book seeks to advance understandings of the causes of Romaphobia by drawing attention to issues of identity, belonging and territoriality, and the relationship between these concepts. One of the intentions of this book is to pull the discipline of Romani studies more clearly within the purview of the social sciences by introducing concepts and ideas from sociology, political science, geography, cultural studies and humanities literatures in response to claims that Romani studies occupies an academic position of 'splendid isolation' (Willems 1997). The aim is to advance understandings of the position of Roma communities and to point to ways to address this. The academy has a long and complicated relationship with Roma communities and is complicit in the exoti-cization and essentialization of Roma, even expressing racist language and ideas (for a discussion of this issue, see Van Baar 2011b, Chapter 3; Acton 2016). Acton (2016) highlights the impact of scientific racism on discourse in the Gypsy Lore Society, which he argues was 'profoundly racist' from its formation in 1888 until 1945 because it contributed to the oppression and genocide of those

identifying and identified as Roma or Gypsy. Willems
(1997) argues that early scholars orientalized Roma or
Gypsy communities as a nomadic, non-European, ethnically homogeneous people. The legacy of early studies in
the eighteenth century has been to cement Roma communities as fixed and bounded people with clearly defined
cultural practices and as the perennial outsiders. The
history of Roma has largely been written by non-Roma
scholars. I am part of this legacy too, but the intention of
this book is to be sensitive to my role as an academic in
outlining the causes of Romaphobia by drawing on my
personal experience of coming from a minority and stigmatized community. Roma identity has been imagined
and constructed by non-Roma for the most part (Kóczé
2015); it is therefore imperative for Roma agency to take
control of the narratives and discourses that have largely
remained out of reach, and this extends to the academy.
But participation in research and in policy decisions
requires partnership. After all, Romaphobia is not just an
issue for Roma communities; it is a problem for everyone
who lives in a society that tacitly supports Romaphobic
attitudes and actions.

CHAPTER 2

STRANGERS WITHIN THE GATES: TERRITORIALITY AND BELONGING

One of the most enduring stereotypes of Roma is nomadism and the widespread belief that Roma retain no ties to territory in ways that sedentarized groups do. The most troubling aspect of a lack of territorial identification has been how this has been used to fuel negative perceptions of Roma communities as not really belonging to the majority nation, even when Roma have been residing on European territory since before the creation of nation-states. The absence of a material homeland or a so-called Romanistan has also inflated the importance of citizenship in diverse national territories to ensure that Roma feel at home within different states and nations. Our home is where we feel secure, and many Roma will identify home as the place where they live or their family lives. Sometimes home will be a settlement, a village, a camp or a country, but for others home remains tenuous and out of reach. There is a difference between what we consider our home and where we feel at home, as might be experienced by some Kosovar Roma, displaced in 1999 and subsequently raised in France. Similarly, a makeshift settlement on the outskirts of town may be home for many Roma but they may not feel at home there or have the concomitant associations of safety and security. Where we belong is often not where we have been born and bred but arises from what Savage et al. (2005) call 'elective belonging'; this is where people choose to belong to particular places irrespective of historical roots they may have.

This raises some interesting questions in terms of how some groups come to be identified with the territory they reside in, as well as how territory can come to define some groups, such as diasporas. Place has a 'distinctly moral element, containing as it does, notions of belonging, of one's rightful place in the world, locating individuals and places geographically and historically … Place links the metaphysical sense of belonging with the physical present; the act of orienting spatially and temporally is fundamental to the human condition' (Jacobson 2002: 3). Displacement, whether coercive or voluntary, is prevalent all over the world, meaning that people live outside their attributed homelands in diasporas and have to negotiate complex identities, multiple loyalties and belongings (Appadurai 1991). This is not impossible as we house variegated identities at any one time that are never really fixed, even if they appear to be stable (Jasper and McGarry 2015). Diasporas are suspended between two terrains, 'living without belonging in one, belonging without living in the other' (Mishra 2006: 16), and can be

regarded as a social formation that simultaneously desta-
bilizes nationalism while reinforcing it.

So, are Roma a diaspora? Diasporas are 'ethnic
minority groups of migrant origins residing and acting
in host countries but maintaining strong sentimental and
material links with their countries of origin – their homelands' (Sheffer 1986: 3). But Roma lack a homeland in any
practical or meaningful sense. Even the Indian roots of
Roma have atrophied due to a lack of maintenance and
so now Roma are missing one of the critical components
of a diaspora: dual territoriality. The existence of a place
of origin, such as India in the case of Roma, is not enough
to generate an emotional yearning for the homeland. In
the absence of conclusive historical data we are unable to
determine why Roma left India around 1,000 years ago
and whether this was by choice or by force. The connection with India was made late (in the eighteenth century)
and is still contested, even though the linguistic evidence
to support the argument is very convincing. There are
no strong links with India, if ever there were, but Roma
do share some attributes of a diaspora and these relate
to belonging in the national territory. Connor (1986: 18)
argues that:

> diasporas are viewed best as outsiders, strangers within
> the gates. They may be tolerated, even treated most
> equitably, and individual members of the diaspora may
> achieve highest office. Their stay may be multigener-
> ational, but they remain outsiders in the eyes of the

indigenes, who reserve the inalienable right to assert their primary and exclusive proprietary claim to the homeland, should they desire.

Diasporas have a homeland with which they maintain active links, for example by sending back remittances or by maintaining cultural practices, which serve to reinforce the conviction that diaspora communities do not belong in their new home. At the same time, diasporas have a material and symbolic focus of their multi-positionality that can provide succour if a diaspora feels threatened by the host state.

Roma do not possess a kin state to lobby, argue or fight on their behalf but do maintain practices and cultural traditions that mark them as different from the host nation. This serves to accentuate their difference. Hall (1992: 310) holds that:

> people who have been dispersed from their homelands … belong at one and the same time to several 'homes' (and to no one particular 'home') and such multi-positionality can be used by the majority to affirm their difference within the dominant nation justifying policies of expulsion, exclusion, exile, segregation and persecution.

Safran (1991: 86–7, cited in Mishra 2006) argues that Roma are a 'metadiaspora' in their 'economic rootlessness', pursuing professions that require mobility across national borders and thus possess no consciousness: 'The Gypsies have no myth of return because they have no precise notion of their place of origin, no clear geographical focus, and no history of national sovereignty.' But such assertions do not tell the whole story because many Roma identify as Czech or Romanian or Italian and use their national citizenship to affirm belonging in the national political space. Moreover, since their arrival in Europe in the fourteenth century, Roma groups have oscillated between settlement and mobility at different periods; this has continued up to the present day, with only a limited number still 'itinerant' today. There is an important distinction to be made regarding mobility, as many Roma leave Central and Eastern European states to move westwards with the hope of finding a better life. I do not consider such populations 'itinerant' in the same way that I do not consider young Spanish people living in the UK 'itinerant'. They are migrants searching for economic opportunities, cultural freedom, and a higher standard of living. With the right passport and/or visa, anyone can escape one state and reside in another where conditions may or may not be better. The socio-economic and political position of Roma across Europe is, on the whole, substandard, meaning that a change in territory will not necessarily bring a change in circumstance.

This chapter considers territoriality as it relates to Roma communities. Roma are an exemplary case through which to explore ideas of identity, belonging and territoriality because of their historical and contemporary experiences.

This chapter explores the intersection between spatial and racial marginalization and argues that Romaphobia finds fertile ground to flourish in Europe due to the perception of Roma as rootless nomads who do not have ties to any one nation or state. It begins by outlining the role of the state in its execution of territorial power and how nationalism is tied to territory. While territoriality is widely understood as a strategy, I highlight how space impacts upon our identities; this is a crucial observation in the case of Roma. I then explore the impact of cultural nomadism on the belonging of Roma at different points in history and outline how the state sought to curb the movement of groups such as Roma. I also explore the impact of this for the practice of professions and lifestyles. Then I briefly examine the role of slavery in marginalizing Roma but also its impact in terms of assimilation and integration in Romania, where Roma were the last legal slaves in Europe. The chapter then explores the deportation and punishment of Roma, as expressed through physical exclusion, in terms of how belonging in a given space is highly contextual in the way in which identity and emotional attachments are expressed. Finally, the chapter considers the prevalence of separation and segregation among Roma communities and argues that we cannot look only at territory and space as an explanation of Romaphobia; rather, we need to understand how the negotiation of space by the majority, the state and Roma creates zones of exclusion where Roma are banished and how Romaphobia conspires to ensure that Roma remain a separate community.

STATE TERRITORIALITY

States have become the one enduring polity of the modern age by combining the territorial and community aspects of belonging in order to make political sovereignty and national belonging indistinguishable. From the seventeenth century onwards, nation-states successfully wove people and land together to become a singular whole, particularly in republican states such as France (Jacobson 2002). In early modern Europe, the concept of sovereignty changed as it became associated with territory and so heralded the birth of the inter-state system ushered in by the Treaty of Westphalia (1648). From then, states recognize one another's sovereignty over a territory and people, and borders are marked, protected and recognized. As the nation challenged – and in most cases usurped – religion in people's loyalties, the state added fuel to the fire by embarking on nation-building exercises such as war and land acquisition as well defence of the homeland (the Motherland or Fatherland) with the result that people were willing to die to protect that homeland (*dulce et decorum est pro patria mori*). The connection of a nation-state to a bounded territory became part of a civic political culture that emerged after the revolutions in the USA and France in the late eighteenth century. In the civic polity, territory replaces kinship as the principle of governance and organization, because political power is stronger when rooted in the land as the state is more stable and has borders to insulate and protect the sovereign nation within and to regulate the movement of people from outside. States knew that a homogeneous population was unlikely to be realized and nor was it particularly desirable, especially if the state had expansionist ambitions and needed to annex territories and peoples who were foreign and spoke different languages. But kinship remained powerful, particularly for those groups and communities who were excluded from homogenizing nationalism projects at work across Europe. When a group does not fit within the conceptualization of the nation in terms of language or religion or ethnicity, it is either excluded altogether or its presence is tolerated as long as the group knows its place and does not compromise the integrity of the nation or state.

The justificatory discourse of nationalism promotes a group consciousness and determines a collective 'we' differentiated from 'them'. Nationalism is carved from multiple sources including language, religion and claims to a territory. Before the emergence of states, a mosaic of ethnic identities was supported by linguistic concentrations, literacy, religious norms, agricultural production, urban centres, and the administration of regions, empires and city states (Rokkan and Urwin 1983). As the state strengthened in Europe, mobility decreased as people unified under the banner of a national (or subnational) identity. The closure of borders encouraged the increased interdependence between people within a state, giving rise to a national society (Bartolini 2005). We have seen the gradual conflation of nation and territory to the extent

that they are now mutually reinforcing. Under commu-
nist regimes, Roma did not fit the definition of a nation
because they did not possess a kin state. Stalin elaborated four defining components of nationhood: 'common
language, territory, economic life and psychological
make-up manifested in a common culture' (Guy 1975:
222). Because Roma do not meet all the criteria to become
a nation, they were treated as an ethnic group, which
meant assimilation and the concomitant sedentarization. Okely (1997: 68) highlights the centrality of territory
in the creation of national identity: 'territorial identity
predominates. A common language and "economic life"
follow from a specific territory because it is assumed that
the nation is linguistically and economically self-suffi-
cient in a common space.' Nations are not bounded in
any sense; they are constructed, imagined and contested
(Smith 1986), and the idea of a nation without a state is
not unusual: for example, Kurds and Palestinians lack
a sovereign territory although they claim one. For Sami
communities in northern Norway, Sweden, Finland and
Russia, territory is an important part of cultural identity
but only so far as it sustains the migrating reindeer populations that Sami groups herd.

The interplay between territory, identity and power is
complex. Okely's (1997: 69) assertion that 'without recognition as bearers of a sealed and self-contained nation
or geographically located culture, there is greater rationale for incorporation' raises a number of issues. First, it
is unclear what a self-contained nation looks like – one

that is perhaps contained within a sovereign territory? It would be a stretch to argue that even republican nation-states such as France are self-contained, never mind homogeneous. Secondly, states in the twentieth century have increasingly sought to recognize national and ethnic minorities within the constitution of the state polity, including through the granting of territorially based autonomies such as South Tyrol in Italy and Scotland in the UK. In Eastern Europe there exists a range of mechanisms that recognize and protect nations within the state, as in Bosnia-Herzegovina and Hungary. Roma communities, despite not being territorially concentrated in many parts of Europe, have been accorded rights to guaranteed representation in parliament in Kosovo and Romania, for example, and the sovereignty and territorial integrity of the state is not undermined.

Power is manifest in territories in a variety of ways, including, for example, in the prevention of mobility across national borders without the appropriate documentation such as a state-issued passport and/or visa. We might refer to this as the material power of territoriality. Notably, it is exercised by the state but requires territory in order to be realized. One example of the material power of the state articulated through territory internally is the identification and appropriation of land, for example for the building of an additional runway for airport expansion. Territory also carries a social power. In the UK, when signs in the 1970s and 1980s read 'No Blacks, No Dogs, No Irish', it was significant as it selected groups for special restrictive access to certain spaces. The impact was access for the aforementioned groups but the message was one of belonging and supremacy. The ability to exclude is a sure sign of social power. Of course, such expressions of power are context-specific and guided by dominant attitudes and discourses, and supported by policies and laws.

Territoriality is a component of how societies and institutions organize themselves in space with respect to the social and material world, which implies that the human organization of space is important to all communities. We will see that this is acutely relevant for Roma as the organization of space is in the hands of the state and often excludes Roma from particular spaces. The majority nation polices the material and symbolic boundaries of the nation and ensures that territoriality is expressed in ways that constitute the norms, principles and discourses of the majority. Social life is always territorialized, which means that the experiences, identities and relationships of people (including Roma) are shaped by the constitutive impact of territory on the citizen, the refugee, the homeowner, the tenant, the nomad, the prisoner, the homeless, and so on. There is a danger that territory becomes self-evident and taken for granted as an almost natural phenomenon, but we must understand that the appropriation and inscription of territory by the state and society are deliberate and purposeful: they are a political feat (Delaney 2005: 11). By moving beyond the idea of territoriality as a strategy, I am interested in how territorial arrangements impact on group identities and how they shape a collective consciousness. Significantly, territory has an impact on feelings of belonging and exclusion for some group identities, including those relating to age, gender, disability, sexual orientation and ethnicity – that is, those identities that provide us with a sense of self and collective orientation. Geographer Doreen Massey (1991: 28) argues that we should pay attention to the social diversity that animates our understanding of place: 'Instead of thinking of place as areas with boundaries around, they can be imagined and articulated moments in networks of social relationships and understandings.' The explicit link between identity and space is critical for Roma communities, particularly in terms of how racialization and spatialization intersect as processes.

Edward Soja (1971: 19) was one of the first thinkers to tilt our understanding of territoriality to a socio-political strategy and argued that we should focus on the tendency for humans to organize space 'into spheres of influence or clearly demarcated territories which are made distinctive and considered at least partially exclusive by their occupants or definers'. Murphy (2012: 160) believes that this contribution shows that social spaces 'shape identities, understandings of place and attachments to place'. Robert Sack, in one of the most influential works on human territoriality, determined that 'territoriality in humans is best understood as a spatial strategy to affect, influence or control resources and people, by controlling area; and, as a strategy, territoriality can be turned on and off. In geographical terms it is a form of spatial behaviour'

(1986: 1–2). Human agency is placed front and centre, and thus Sack (ibid.: 19) highlights that territory is fundamentally a human strategy 'to affect, influence and control people, phenomena, and relationships by delimiting and asserting control over a geographic area'. It is no surprise that his approach has been taken up by those seeking to understand human efforts to consolidate power by constructing political-territorial arrangements. The key unit of analysis here is invariably the historically situated state and the execution of power over people through sovereign borders and territorial expansion.

In a 1978 lecture, Foucault pointed out that sovereignty is exercised first on a territory, and second on the subjects who inhabit it. He argued that sovereignty is exercised within the borders of a territory, discipline is exercised on the bodies of individuals, and security is exercised over a whole population (Foucault 2007: 11). While this might seem overly simplistic, it does capture the dynamics at play in the nexus of territory, authority and society. For Foucault, citing Guillaume de La Perrière, the government is concerned not with territory but with the general management of *things*, such as resources, risks, populations and alliances, but government is different from the sovereign; the latter acts only for public benefit, the so-called common good. But what if the sovereign, in order to protect the common good, actually targets, subjugates and ignores, separates and persecutes? One example of governmental bio-power is the expulsion of someone with the plague so as to protect the other bodies in the body politic, recognizing that the contaminant is a threat and must be removed for the greater good of the health of the population. Raffestin (1977, cited in Klauser 2012: 110), meanwhile, is influenced by Foucault and understands human territoriality in strictly relational terms as the ensemble of mediated relationships linking individuals and/or social groups on different social and spatial scales. Raffestin's approach is important in capturing the territorial ideas and practices of everyday life that are not concerned with merely strategic control of a particular space. Indeed, territoriality is not concerned with an essential study of space per se but highlights the social actors, instruments and relations that shape and impact upon territory. While Raffestin and Foucault are useful up to a point, they do not help us to understand the prevalence of identities such as nationalism and how they are deployed by the state to augment political power in order to control the population. Territoriality is regarded as a tool for the government to know and understand a population – and therefore to control and exploit it – rather than as a way of constituting a people, as Massey argues. The former position fails to capture processes of consciousness whereby individuals and groups come to identify themselves. Territories are meaningful because they signify belonging and markers intelligible to groups who understand their positionality in relation to others. The capital cities of Bratislava and Vienna are 50 miles apart but have vastly different architectures, histories, societal attitudes, norms and values because the Austrian-

Slovakian national border delineated divergent economic and political regimes that created an indelible mark on the inhabitants of both cities. Territoriality has a decisive impact on identities.

NOMADISM AND MOBILITY

Historically, Roma have been constructed, and even celebrated, as an anachronism due to their perceived territorial dexterity governed by the necessity or preference for self-employment, performing jobs that required residential mobility such as scrap metal collecting, tin-making, leather-working, tailoring and horse-trading. Paradoxically, today people are more and more mobile, particularly educated professionals working for multinational corporations who have been described as 'digital nomads' and do not experience discrimination because of their perceived lack of commitment to a place (Andreotti et al. 2015). The 'dominant sedentarist society has stigmatized and hindered most of these characteristics' with the result that Roma are 'ever vulnerable to the controls and judgements of societies and nation states within which they survive ... a sedentarist ideology has no place for nomads and those without a culture fixed in the past or present geographical locale' (Okely 1997: 64). While Okely's research has focused on English and Scottish Gypsies where halting site provision and exclusion are the dominant issues facing mobile Gypsies and Travellers in the UK (around one in three are mobile), Roma communities across Europe have faced similar choices. In order to prove their belonging or simply to avoid the continued persecution of state and society, Roma must either assimilate or integrate. While assimilation was the modus operandi under socialist regimes in Central and Eastern European states, European institutions today prefer the language of integration and inclusion, which sound more benign but yield similar consequences. At stake is liberal choice: choose the future or choose the past. In order to integrate, Roma must become good citizens, send their children to school, and settle in one place. But the overwhelming majority of Roma have settled in one place due to forced sedentarization under communism and extensive regulations on mobility in Western states. While Roma communities are leaving Central and Eastern Europe and are generating scaremongering headlines in Western European states, this migration is a search for a better social and economic life and should not be construed as part of Roma communities' inherent (and highly problematic) cultural nomadism.

In the past there were a number of benefits from being mobile, particularly if one wanted to avoid state capture such as registration, taxation and conscription, which, of course, necessitated a more independent existence and consciousness. Luccassen et al. (1998) note that in the late seventeenth century Roma were subject to two forms of labour: as galley slaves in the Mediterranean basin and military conscripts in Prussia-Brandenburg. In response, some Roma and Sinti gathered in a narrow strip of land between the two that became known as the 'outlaw territory' where they hoped to remain beyond the reach of authorities. Even during communism some Roma communities were mobile, which had an impact on living conditions and identity. In 1958, Czechoslovakia outlawed nomadism and it is estimated that around three-quarters of all Roma were located in Slovakia by 1970. Towns in the southern part of Slovakia, close to the Hungarian border, often had two separate Roma sections: one for the sedentary Roma who were usually older, and one for the 'nomadic' Roma, who tended to be younger. There were crucial differences between the two sections in terms of housing, with the nomadic Roma living in 'unclean … unsanitary hovels' while sedentary Roma lived in 'neat little houses, imitating within the material reach of Gypsies local standards of the housing of non-Gypsies' (Lípa 1979: 52). Even those semi-nomadic Roma who did settle continued to own a horse and canvassed or wooden wagons and would travel in the surrounding area or around the country in order to sell products or to perform trades and skills. The pursuit of what was perceived to be an itinerant lifestyle generated animosity from the majority society as well as from the sedentary Roma, who considered them to be 'half wild' and their 'behaviour … abrasive to others' (ibid.: 52). Sedentary Roma were regarded by the majority as taking the right step towards assimilation but they were still not included, hence the existence of specially designated Roma spaces in towns. However, the social isolation of Roma from non-Roma, particularly in larger settlements, meant that the Romani language continued to be spoken. In Hungary, Roma were no longer able to make their profession in the service industry and had to join production lines in state-run factories. Roma experienced compulsory school attendance, equal pay for equal work and conscription, which, according to Bíró (2013), all strengthened the feeling of belonging to the nation.

In Western Europe, large numbers of Roma were mobile, much more so than in Eastern Europe, but the basis of the peripatetic lifestyle was that they were insignificant, if not redundant, to the wider economy (Gheorghe 2013). Rather than being seen as nomads, it is more accurate to conceive of Roma as adaptable in their work and employment, often filling niches in local economies, both urban and rural, and sometimes doing jobs that others did not want. But deeply ingrained notions of nomadism have proliferated and were entrenched by early policy interventions in Western European states in the 1960s and 1970s, with debates focusing on the situation of travelling people and the migration of Roma from Eastern Europe. There was a widespread assumption that all Roma were nomads. Different exonyms have helped to fix ideas of Roma culture as nomadic: *gens de voyage* (France) and *nomadi* (Italy). In this context, it is perhaps unsurprising that governments in Italy and France have recently expelled Roma in large numbers based on the conviction that Roma do not belong and are always on the move anyway. The scant attention that was paid to Roma communities by the

EU, up to and during the 1980s, framed and understood Roma principally as an itinerant community (Liégeois and Gheorghe 1995), reinforcing the idea that they did not belong in or to any one state. In the 1990s, as more international organizations and human rights non-governmental organizations (NGOs) focused on Roma, they sought to simplify their experience and situation in order to make Roma more intelligible. Typically, policymakers at the national and European levels embraced age-old stereotypes of cultural nomadism as well as the promotion of Roma as a single, coherent and bounded internally homogeneous community, which served to further exacerbate marginalization as it reinforces their difference vis-à-vis the majority nation. Early debates laid the foundations for national governments and supranational authorities to argue over where responsibility for Roma integration lies, a dispute that continues today.

The dynamic between nomadism and belonging is played out more clearly in the UK where many Gypsies or Travellers are mobile for large parts of the year; this has an impact on access to services such as housing and education. Groups are identified as outsiders because their social institutions and structures are seen as being different to, and thus incompatible with, the majority (Sibley 1981). Roma communities often reside on the periphery of society and have limited interaction with the majority, which can create social distance and physical boundaries as well as a lack of understanding between the majority and Roma. School is one of the institutions in society that even supposedly outsider groups such as Gypsies and Travellers must negotiate (ibid.). Bhopal (2011) argues that 'the spatial element of the school and the structured environment imposes restrictions on Gypsy and Traveller children's behaviour, which they may not be used to', implying that behavioural norms of Gypsy and Traveller children are different and are subject to close external mediation. The school also provides a context of interaction between Gypsy and Traveller children and teachers, parents and children from the majority society. This interaction has the potential to break down stereotypes and facilitate mutual understanding but it also has the capacity to reinforce prejudices, including the belief that because of a perceived itinerant lifestyle, Gypsy and Traveller children will not be staying long in the school and may not be invested with the necessary time and effort or encouraged to achieve their potential. Bhopal (ibid.: 480) argues that:

> schools work on the basis of sedentary lifestyles and it is the norms of such lifestyles that Gypsies and Travellers must conform to ... the difference between the cultural and physical environments of the school and the site and the attitudes of teachers towards these differences serve to perpetuate cycles of underachievement and marginalization.

The belief that Gypsies and Travellers do not want to send their children to school is incorrect. The main impediment for school attendance is the mobility of some Gypsy and Traveller families making enrolment more difficult, particularly in over-subscribed schools. In 2011–12, I chaired a cross-party Independent Scrutiny Panel for Brighton and Hove City Council in the UK on the creation of a 'Traveller strategy' for the city. As part of the panel, I gathered evidence from different individuals, including local members of parliament, local residents, Traveller liaison officers, council services on education and housing, local media, Gypsy and Traveller advocacy groups and representatives, to hear what they thought about the main issues facing Gypsies and Travellers and how these might be addressed, while balancing the concerns of local residents in regard to the creation of a permanent halting site in the city (which was the final recommendation). On a site visit to Horsdean, a temporary site on the outskirts of the city, in December 2011, I was struck by how quiet the site was even though the caravan bays were full. When I inquired why this was, a woman cleaning her caravan told me it was because all the kids were in school. When I asked whether they liked school, she informed me that her kids loved it because they had friends and received a Christmas card from each of their classmates, something they had never experienced before. This anecdote highlights the overlap between belonging and territoriality for a marginalized community but research is needed to understand how children from Gypsy, Traveller and Roma communities negotiate the education system and what impact this social structure has on identity and belonging.

In recent times, the movement of Roma from Eastern to Western Europe has been seen by many as unpredictable and fast and as signifying a form of disorder that threatens to unpick the highly organized, regulated and exclusionary space of the state. Freedom of movement, the cornerstone of the EU's internal market, is discursively regulated to prevent the dissolution of the nation-states' sovereign political power (Voiculescu 2014: 2). Some groups are deemed capable of performing so-called normal mobility (such as tourists, students or the highly skilled) while others of a lower status (such as those lacking skills and/or education and Roma) are treated by the state as unstable and problematic, requiring bureaucratic energy and administrative attention. Following the discussion of James Scott in Chapter 1, the state will tolerate migration and the flow of people in and out as long as it retains some semblance of control. Sibley (1995) demonstrates that the state criminalized populations who were mobile or had unstable ways of life, such as Roma and Jews. Sedentarized populations could be regulated, monitored and controlled easily whereas, for the aforementioned groups, 'mobility is portrayed as an expression of a lack of attachment and commitment to a place, and consequently as an indicator of potential moral flaws' (Voiculescu 2014: 3). Historian Ilsen About (2014) analyses the convergence of public policy aimed at surveying populations, policing mobility and identifying families and individuals alternatively designated as *Nomads*, *Zigeuner*, *Zingari* or *Gypsies* across Western Europe in the inter-war period. He found that categorizations of different Romani individuals incorporated into the nation by a distinct legal or bureaucratic definition are subsequently excluded from citizenship as a result of that recognition: 'the continuous physical pursuit of "Gypsies" throws up for examination at once the deployment of a central authority, the State capacities of an expanded network, and the supposed control of a given territory' (ibid.: 501). So, the construction of Roma as nomadic has served to reinforce the conviction that Roma do not belong to a nation or state and need to be managed through social, economic and political interventions by a 'nervous sedentarized state' (Clark 2004: 244).

Roma communities across Europe differed widely and 'could include long-term settlement rather than nomadism' (Taylor 2014: 17). As Roma moved from the Balkans into Central and Western Europe in the fifteenth and sixteenth centuries, new strategies were needed to avoid persecution and different Roma communities attempted to make themselves more legible to the new territories they were entering. They needed to make themselves understandable to a new world and new populations in Western Europe, a region that was 'inclined to construct boundaries between places, people and religious groups' (ibid.: 38), where some people belonged in certain places while others did not. Fraser (1995) notes that Roma presented themselves as pilgrims who were penancing for sins of apostasy, which allowed some Roma communities to avoid outright persecution, at least initially. But from the early sixteenth century various states responded with measures including banishment and punishment that persisted until the eighteenth century. A spirit of distrust and hostility towards foreigners characterized the formation of nations and states in Europe from the seventeenth century, with states augmenting their sovereign power over a given territory and people by pitting insiders against outsiders, usually on the basis of religion. In this context, minority groups such as Roma, Muslims, some Christian groups and Jews were seen as a threat. In 1619, Philip III ordered the expulsion of all Roma found wandering in Spain, forbidding their return on pain of death. However, those willing to assimilate could stay providing they abandoned their traditional dress and language; this meant that the choice for Spanish Roma (*Gitanos*) 'was between exile and forced assimilation into a society simultaneously assigning them pariah status while demanding they abandon cultural identity' (Taylor 2014: 60). While the state targeted Roma for harsh and torturous treatment, Roma were in fact welcomed locally as they provided much needed services. The vilification was state-led and would filter down to the masses.

Colonial ideas of race constructed northern Europeans as progressive and rational while savagery and backwardness were traits of 'blacks' and 'non-whites' outside Europe, with 'those living on the margins of society positioned as closer to nature, to chaos and to savagery' (ibid.: 98). Nomadism and itinerancy were increasingly regarded as backwards, and mobile groups were seen as potential deviants who needed to be controlled. During the Enlightenment, the state used its power to improve the lives of its subjects but also to control and regulate their behaviour (ibid.: 103); this did not automatically mean banishment and punishment but could include more 'progressive' policies aimed at reform and assimilation such as those of Maria Theresa and her son Joseph II in the Austro-Hungarian empire, with the expectation that undesirable elements within the nation would gradually and forcibly disappear. But the position of Roma remained marginal with persecution taking different forms, such as discrimination or exclusion. States embarked on a formal process of codifying belonging through citizenship laws that emphasized loyalty and a collective identity, with the net cast wide enough to accommodate diverse ethnic identities while promoting a singular national identity.

THE LAST SLAVES IN EUROPE

Roma were the last legal slaves in Europe, in Wallachia and Moldovia (modern-day southern and eastern Romania as well as Moldova), with emancipation taking place in the middle of the nineteenth century. From the end of the fourteenth century until the middle of the nineteenth century, *robi* (slaves) were tied to land owned by lords and monasteries. As large numbers of Roma settled on Romanian lands in the fourteenth and fifteenth centuries, slavery became a widespread phenomenon, with 'the term "Gypsy" being synonymous with that of "slave"' (Achim 1998: 29). Full emancipation was realized in 1855 in Moldavia and 1856 in Wallachia. Just before emancipation, research carried out by Félix Colson showed that there were approximately 139,255 Roma in Moldavia and 119,910 in Wallachia, corresponding to 9.8 per cent and 5 per cent of the total populations respectively. Immediately after emancipation, the authorities were faced with the problem of tens of thousands of free Roma no longer shackled to their owners and lands. In Wallachia, authorities quickly moved to settle Roma on the land they had previously been on with the consent of both Roma and landowners. In Moldovia, Roma had the freedom to move off the land they worked on as slaves and so dispersed more readily, which had the effect of more assimilation of Roma communities in Moldovia than in Wallachia (Ciorou 2009: 155). Due to territorial mobility, Roma communities also moved to urban centres and spread across the entire region of Moldovia and Wallachia, usually residing on the territory of a landowner, but they did not own or work on the land typically.

In contrast to the way in which Romanian peasant serfs were bound to the land, *țigani robi* (Roma slaves) were tied to owners as their property or chattels. While it was impossible to sell or exchange individual serfs, as they were always part of the land, *țigani robi* could be donated or received as a dowry without any accompanying transfer of land: 'these practices made slaves a collective and hereditary juridical and economic institution concerning the person' (Gheorghe 2013), meaning that the landowner had complete juridical control over the slave. Land ownership was not only the basic condition for social and juridical freedom, it was also the prerequisite for full citizenship, but land ownership was denied to Roma who were never legal members of the political community at this time. *Robia* institutionalized a relationship with territory, citizenship and belonging that was exclusionary; it was only after the abolition of slavery that Roma could live as inhabitants of towns and villages across modern-day Romania and that integration – and eventually, for some, assimilation – into the Romanian nation was possible. The relationship between land and former slaves was one of 'compulsory integration' (ibid.). Significantly, Gheorghe argues that Roma did not lack a relationship to territory as such but rather they did not have a relationship to patrimony, which would have meant that land could be owned and inherited over generations.

This brings up an important clarification regarding territoriality and Roma: 'nowhere have significant numbers of Roma turned into peasants or farmers, so that their roots and livelihood have become based on the land' (Bíró 2013: 11). For Bíró, this is the fundamental reason why the majority 'other' Roma, and, while it is not the sole reason for the persecution of Roma communities, the preservation of this intrinsic detachment from the basis of settled societies is an important and long-standing cultural difference. Almost all societies are settled due to the state's desire for legibility (Scott 1998). Roma fulfilled a niche role through service professions offered to the settled communities on which they depended, and vice versa, such as animal trading (especially horse-dealing), iron-working, metal-working, brick-making and wood production, music, fortune-telling, scrap collecting and rubbish collecting. The purpose of these roles was to make a living and to survive. As such, these professions retained a closed and restricted character that may have contributed to the reproduction of the socially marginalized status experienced by Roma for centuries (Bíró 2013: 12). In order to survive, Roma consistently had to negotiate a world created by non-Roma, which sometimes meant (and still means) adapting to the laws and rules that are created to favour the majority.

Time and time again we see the conviction that Roma are not tied to territories, states and nations and this detachment is used to explain why Roma migrate to other states. Using the case of Romania, Achim (1998: 5) demonstrates that the emancipation of Roma from slavery did not mean the granting of land. For this reason, significant numbers of Roma were not integrated into rural communities, partly because the acquisition of land or the adoption of an agricultural occupation meant the loss of Romani identity, becoming relatively assimilated from an ethnic point of view into the majority population. Even under slavery Roma were not necessarily tied to a particular estate but to a particular owner – 'belonging to a master' (ibid.: 31), meaning a feudal master such as a prince, a monastery or a boyar. It was this belonging to a master that made *robie* (slavery) distinct; the subjugation of Roma was expressed in the absence of legal status, with the *rob* (slave) the property of the master. Achim consistently argues that Roma continued to be nomadic and that this is a distinctive part of their identity or 'way of life' (ibid.: 52), but the *rob* paid a tax to the master by plying various trades such as blacksmithing, bear-training or gold-washing – jobs that required mobility. So the lines between cultural nomadism and performing jobs in order to pay taxes and to survive are blurred even during slavery. For Achim (ibid.: 65), the one theme that unites different Roma groups is their 'obstinate refusal to adapt to the values of European civilization and to give in to assimilation'. This bold claim suggests collective agency and a decision-making process that are patently missing and is not supported by the adaptation of Roma communities throughout European history to, for example, diverse languages, political and economic regimes, religions and cultural traditions. It is the ability, capacity and resourcefulness to survive, and in some cases thrive, in spite of an endless series of pogroms, expulsions, persecutions and deportations that has characterized the existence of Roma in Europe. It is perhaps more surprising that the endurance and adaptability of Roma throughout time have not gained sufficient respect among European societies whose own histories are characterized by adaptation and survival in the face of adversity.

EXILE AND PUNISHMENT

In October 2013, Leonarda Dibrani, a 15-year-old Roma girl, was removed from a school bus in France and along with her family expelled to Kosovo, which is where the authorities believed they had come from. This action generated media attention and inspired widespread sympathy as Leonarda was seen as an innocent victim who had known only France and was, to all extents and purposes, French. Her family's expulsion is part of a long-standing policy of the French government that targets Roma communities, usually those inhabiting camps, for expulsion. In recent years, the number of Eastern European Roma coming to France has increased, with most coming from Romania and Bulgaria. Unable to find work and a place to live, many Roma reside in temporary settlements. The then Interior Minister Manuel Valls (and current Prime Minister) argued that 'there is no solution other than dismantling the Roma camps progressively and sending the Roma back to the border ... the majority should return to their countries ... Our role is not to welcome all the world's misery' (Gopnik 2014: 24). Indeed, the visibility of Roma migrants in public life is regarded as a serious issue requiring their immediate removal: 'the presence of domestic or migrant Roma in public spaces is considered to be a security risk and is sufficient to allow the authorities to take special measures, including eviction, confiscation of property and ethnic profiling through fingerprinting' (Van Baar 2015a: 77). Social order is about spacing, about maintaining appropriate social distance through separation. An extreme manifestation of separation is expulsion, when individuals belonging to a racialized group are identified by the state for special treatment. The expulsion of an individual attests to the power of the state. Expulsion demonstrates the state's preferences concerning desirability and belonging.

Belonging in space is highly contextual and an area in which identity and emotional attachments are negotiated and expressed. In her exploration of Roma belonging in Greece, Theodosiou (2011: 100) explains that Roma or Gypsies in the settlement of Parakalamos reject negative ascriptions of group identity such as nomadism, drugs, crime, poverty and illiteracy and instead promote the idea of having 'roots' in Parakalamos with a distinct local identity: 'what frames their desired representation is not a common identity as Gypsies, but the way such an understanding of themselves intersects with a place of origin'. But even when Roma communities have been long established in a particular territory (town, city, village, locale), the idea that they belong remains in the hands of the majority. Roma must articulate belonging, requesting recognition. So, Roma occupy spaces that are fluid and in flux; their presence in a territory tells us nothing of belonging, so the argument goes, because Roma communities 'reproduce their singularity without recourse to the usual anthropological prompts of attachment to land or territory' (Gay y Blasco 1999: 3). However, Lemon (2000: 4) argues that it is crucial 'to see that Roma too belong to places'. This conviction is a direct challenge to those who argue that belonging refers to a set of properties and possessions that identify people vis-à-vis other people (Fortier 1999) according to a set of criteria, such as language. I argue that belonging is not merely belonging to a given space, or to situated identities, but refers to emotional attachments, discourses and values, not all of which are in the hands of Roma themselves but are delineated by the majority. This is particularly resonant for Roma communities, for whom the constellation of belonging, space and identity is mediated in a highly racialized environment, where the subjective articulations of belonging are frequently denied. Because belonging is regulated by non-Roma, an emphasis is naturally placed on aspects of collective identity that are shared and can be owned by Roma without interference; these aspects include *Romanipen*, which is a feeling of common belonging for all Roma. It should be noted that *Romanipen* is expressed and understood very differently by Roma communities depending on experience and history, and can be harnessed by ethnic entrepreneurs seeking to foster solidarity for 10–12 million people living in diverse states, speaking different languages, and enjoying very different levels of education and wealth.

Van Baar (2015a) shows how the mobility of populations across borders has generated securitized processes and transnational governmentalities, creating intra-EU divides between racialized EU citizens (such as Roma and Muslims) and 'regular' EU citizens and disregarding the fact that Roma and Muslim migrants are invariably EU citizens. We are witnessing an increasing number of pre-emptive measures targeting certain potentially threatening communities including highly mobile criminal

gangs, terrorists and human traffickers. The exclusion of
threatening individuals is justified by the state and enjoys
popularity, but the process of exclusion requires the
active targeting and vilification of certain groups. Public
discourse on Roma migrants across Western Europe
stigmatizes all Roma as thieves, beggars, criminals and
parasites who do not contribute to society and only add to
its woes, bringing untold misery and problems. Van Baar
(2015a) argues that the expulsion of Roma is justified on
two grounds: first, the framing of Roma as a public order
or security threat; and second, the construction of Roma as
excessively mobile or problematizing them as 'nomads'.
This conflation of Roma identity with nomadism unfor-
tunately has coloured policy interventions in a number
of fields, especially migration and EU enlargement, with
Western European governments acutely concerned that
eastward expansion of the EU would mean an influx of
unwanted Roma communities in their midst. But the
EU was merely following the lead of Western European
states such as Italy, which had elaborated laws recognizing nomadism as a fundamental cultural trait of
Roma communities with the result that the noun *nomadi*
has become the politically correct way to refer to Roma
(Sigona 2015: 3). In Italy, most Roma are not mobile and
there are not enough halting sites; as a result, less than half
of all Roma inhabit *nomadi* camps and the public assume
that those living in camps choose to do so, fuelling the
idea that Roma contribute to their marginalization, their
segregation being to some extent self-imposed (ibid.).

FROM SEPARATION TO SEGREGATION

Roma communities across Europe inhabit distinct symbolic and territorial spaces, which are frequently delineated, though not always, by non-Roma actors including society and the state. A potent stereotype of Roma is that they do not belong because they live separate lives to non-Roma and often reside in liminal spaces such as temporary settlements, camps and ghettos. This stereotype sustains the idea that Roma are culpable in their marginality and do not want to belong to mainstream society anyway. In France, research comparing Romaphobia with anti-Semitism and Islamophobia reveals that 82 per cent of the population considers Roma to be a 'separate group' in society, an increase of 16 points since January 2011 (Mayer et al. 2016). There is, in France, a tendency to assume that all minorities are closing ranks and policing the boundaries vis-à-vis the majority; however, the conviction that Roma actively auto segregate is almost unanimous, and this is very different to the image of other national and religious minorities in France. Certainly, across Europe Roma occupy spaces where only Romanes is spoken, where distinct cultural traditions are practised or micro economies maintained, but a Roma-only space is erroneous; even Roma 'ghettos' are rarely homogeneous, with abject and poor non-Roma living side by side with Roma. Roma communities never live completely separate from the majority even when they appear to reside in closed communities in a given space. The territory where

Roma live is racialized, which traps the people residing in that community and limits choices and opportunities, and stigmatizes those people as impoverished and socially excluded. Wilson's (1987) seminal intervention on urban economy and poverty related to inner-city minorities linked poverty to place and highlighted the impact of social isolation for African Americans. Territorial stigmatization (Wacquant 2007) is a process that attaches a precarious population to a marginal space and underpins social exclusion: for example, it impacts on the capacity of individuals to access public goods and services, including their ability to get a job; when a Rom applies for a job over the phone and gives her address as Lunik IX (a well-known Roma settlement) in Košice in Slovakia, she might suddenly find that the post is filled. Here, territorial identification is deployed in order to confirm difference, to reinforce divisions, and to assert majority power. Vincze and Raţ (2013: 6) demonstrate that 'the marginal, polluted and dangerous geographic space becomes a force of social exclusion and ethno-cultural stigmatization, and vice versa'. Separation and segregation in this context are an exercise of power that pushes certain 'problematic communities' to the margins, to spaces others do not want to inhabit, such as the edge of town, to rubbish dumps or rural settlements with poor infrastructure and communication. Suffice to say, only the extremely poor housing conditions become visible, and this overshadows other manifestations of Roma representation. Exclusive visibility of very poor conditions produces fear and the mobilization of bias against Roma because of the abject and marginal spaces they occupy (Vitale 2015).

Two recent examples from East and West Europe epitomize the current pattern of targeting Roma for territorial exclusion. First, in the summer of 2015, the government of the city of Miskolc in north-eastern Hungary amended a decree on social housing that in effect seeks to drive Roma out of the city. The decree foresees the demolition of the most impoverished low-comfort social housing neighbourhoods in the city, which are almost exclusively inhabited by Roma (ERRC 2014). The decree explicitly discriminates against people living in low-comfort social housing and it offers compensation to them to terminate their contracts, but only if they buy a property outside the territory of Miskolc. It also states that the property cannot be sold or mortgaged for at least five years. Roma residing in these areas are being removed from the city and could become homeless. Underpinning such examples of Romaphobia are discourses of exclusion and stigma that have been on the ascendency in Hungary since 2009. Public statements from the police chief on the existence of 'gypsy crime', a common refrain in Hungary, and from the mayor, who spoke of his wish to clear the city of 'antisocial' Roma, prepared the ground for this attempt to expel Roma from the town (ibid.). Secondly, in May 2015 in Italy, the Civil Court of Rome decided at the first instance against the municipality of Rome, ruling for the first time in Europe that 'nomadic camps' (as Roma settlements are referred to in Italy) are a form of segregation and discrimination based on ethnic grounds, breaching both Italian and European law. As argued in the complaint, the Italian court stated that the construction of the 'village' La Barbuta was discriminatory in nature and therefore unlawful by the mere fact that a specific ethnic group, Roma, were being segregated from the local population through the provision of housing by the city council (ERRC 2015). Placing Roma in a single-ethnic territorial unit, physically and symbolically removed from the majority, fosters social isolation and has the potential to engender distrust and animosity between Roma and the majority.

Research by the SPAREX project (Spatialization and Racialization of Social Exclusion) explores the social and cultural formation of 'Gypsy ghettos' in Romania; these are widely understood as ethnically and socially homogeneous spaces inhabited by poor Roma. The research showed that a 'Gypsy ghetto' is 'a territory from the peripheries of localities where the mainstream society outcasts its unwanted "elements" in order to keep them as far as possible from itself' (Vincze and Raţ 2013: 12). The ghetto is constituted and understood 'as an intersectional form of socio-spatial exclusion' that differentiates 'between "insiders" and "outsiders", between those who "deserve" belonging to society and those who do not ... [based on a] shared understanding of who is to be included and who is to be excluded from the mainstream and (highly) valued societal space' (ibid.). This research uses the cultural construction of the ghetto to understand social exclusion as a form of injustice involving material

deprivation, stigmatization, and a denial of social participation. To give one example, Vincze focuses on the Pata
Rât area of Cluj-Napoca and shows how geographically
marginalized urban areas, usually in toxic or polluted
environments (such as landfills or former industrial
zones), are separate from the rest of the community; this
means that inhabitants are seen to deserve to belong to
the landfill where they reside and we see 'the naturaliza-
tion of the association of "particular people" with these
"particular places"' (Vincze 2013: 220). Bauman's (2004)
argument that society excludes unwanted elements as
metaphorical waste is realized in the deliberate relocation of Roma communities to polluted areas such as
rubbish dumps. Vincze (2013) shows how this happens
as a legacy of housing policy in post-socialist Romania, a
country that promoted home ownership and the creation
of cheap substandard housing, and to some extent why
this happens through intersectional injustice produced
at the crossroads of poverty, stigma and non-existence.
While it is certainly tempting to argue that because Roma
are not recognized they do not exist, in analytical terms
this fails to comprehend how Roma are highly visibilized
by the state for instrumental reasons. Roma residing in
ghettos are not merely pushed to one side in the hope
that they will disappear; rather, both Roma identity and
the 'Gypsy ghetto' perform a necessary function across
broader society in terms of communicating ideas about
the exalted subject who contributes to the smooth func-
tioning of society. In short, it confirms who belongs and

who does not. Recognition is always in the hands of others (state and society) and is regulated and bestowed on those who are seen to deserve it.

Roma ghettos occupy a marginal urban space whose inhabitants are restricted from human dignity, material well-being, and social inclusion. As society recognizes ghetto inhabitants as not being deserving of the full range of socio-economic provisions and services, the state justifies its minimal incursions into a marginal space by holding back on refuse collection, paving roads, and providing water and electricity, among other things. Political agency among the inhabitants of ghettos is limited, usually to NGOs, whose role it is to convince the state to include the ghetto in regeneration and redevelopment plans. But the state is not interested in investing precious resources in those it deems 'unproductive' or 'useless' citizens. In the eyes of the state, Roma communities inhabiting ghettos are a burden which is best ignored. Roma are not significant enough – socially, economically or politically – to be included and so they remain on the margins in hazardous and isolated areas. The phenomenon of segregated settlements and ghettos across Europe is created by states and societies motivated by racist ideas of belonging, where space and identity intersect to reproduce hierarchies of belonging and citizenship. Vincze (2013: 239) reveals that this logic creates 'an inferior class of non-humans, who threaten the formation of a desired territory of "our own" inhabited by the desired community (by "us") composed of people who deserve belonging to it'. The best hope for improvement in life conditions is to move elsewhere, but, in doing so, the idea that Roma are nomadic and have no fixed home is perpetuated and only assimilation offers the possibility of avoiding stigma. But Romaphobia will persist even with a change of address or home. For Roma families or individuals with the financial means to reside in a better part of town, their acceptance or inclusion may be withheld until they perform their role as 'good citizens' and do not exhibit any purportedly 'typical' unsavoury Romani traits such as being untidy, dirty, loud or unruly.

Szalai (2014: 21) clarifies the difference between integration and inclusion: integration signifies an act on the part of the majority to create certain conditions that open the gates for entry and participation for Roma individuals and communities, usually through policy interventions in housing or education. Integration is necessary for inclusion. Social inclusion requires members of Roma communities to actually feel at home in wider society and to enjoy equal membership and opportunities to participate (of which they actively avail themselves) in the larger community. Here, Szalai captures the importance of belonging and how this is structured and constrained by broader processes and interventions to ensure inclusion. Significantly, 'the collective nature of exclusion is underscored by its visibility, most easily identified in spatial segregation ... excluded communities live apart from the majority and spatial segregation is as much a product as a self-perpetuating cause of the daily reproduction of their excluded living' (ibid.: 21). The intersectional nature of Roma inclusion and exclusion means that access to employment and low levels of education, coupled with living in isolated rural areas as well as marginalized and hazardous urban spaces, exacerbate spatial and social exclusion. Those residing in ghettos are seen to belong there, deserving the substandard living conditions they enjoy, but the majority also claims that Roma want to live in ghettos and separate settlements due to their unwillingness to integrate. Moreover, in this context, poverty can be racialized, thereby blaming the poor for being poor, and thus explanations of why Roma are poor are seen as a natural result of the cultural traits of an 'inferior' and 'uncivilised' race (Vincze 2014: 74). If the majority attributes any agency to Roma, then they believe Roma to be active and seemingly willing players in their own marginalization.

Romaphobia is sustained and reproduced by processes that exclude Roma from schools, the education system, the labour market and the body politic. When territorial exclusion intersects with ethno-spatial segregation, the ability of Roma to access social, economic and political provisions is highly compromised and the terms of Roma belonging is mediated by the majority which actively seeks to exclude. The notion that Roma are nomadic fuels the idea of rootlessness and a concomitant reluctance to commit to a given space, usually a state. This does not automatically produce Romaphobia because agency is needed to turn Roma into objects of fear and hatred. The marginalization and oppression of Roma are absolutely tied up with the intersection between identity and space. Roma are seen as deserving victims and become defined by their weaknesses and their victimization rather than by their contribution to society.

CHAPTER 3

ROMA IDENTITIES: HOW ROMAPHOBIA DISTORTS ROMA IDENTITY

The apparent risk of this attempt at 'authenticity' is that in the end it turns into playacting where 'Roma identity' is constructed by means of imitating stereotypical aspects of an ethnic culture. Representations of Roma culture are often simply responses to other people's expectations of the performance of otherness.

NICOLAE GHEORGHE 2013

The meeting of feminism and Romani politics has already transformed internal discourses within the Roma movements.

ANGÉLA KÓCZÉ 2009

The public voice of Roma has been ignored and sometimes actively silenced. To be sure, it is difficult to amplify this voice and there exists a serious lack of clarity of what that voice should sound like and what it should say. This chapter explores how Romaphobia fixes Roma

identity in negative ways and discusses the implications. There are, however, alternative voices that have the
capacity to change public perceptions but these voices
are struggling themselves to be heard and understood,
and Romaphobia can endanger or distort their projection.
In the above quote, Nicolae Gheorghe captures some
dilemmas at the heart of Roma identity construction:
between self-ascription and external recognition and
between authenticity and fabrication. Roma identity is
no more or less contested than other collective identities,
but Romaphobia means that the voice of Roma is stifled
and non-Roma are able to shape public understandings
of Roma identity. The debate concerning Roma identity
is significant today, as much as it has ever been, because
of claims from Roma (especially the younger generation
and those who are more educated) and because of Roma
taking more ownership over how their identity is understood but also expressed in the public sphere. Roma
identity is produced and reproduced by a diverse range of
actors, including Roma, academics, policymakers, media,
international organizations, state agencies and the nation.
We are left with a confusing blend of mediated meanings
and expressive ascriptions that reify 'the Roma' as a
community or people and also spotlight their difference
as a distinct 'other'. For example, in Sweden, reification
means that all recent Roma migrants from Central and
Eastern Europe are seen as beggars and seeking benefits,
which collapses individual agency into popular tropes
readily digested by the public. In the above quote, Angéla

Kóczé draws our attention to the importance of intersectionality for shedding light on multiple marginalizations and the lived experiences of Roma who are also women (as well as those with other marginalized identities such as LGBTIQ, disabled, class, youth, etc.), which helps us to understand that Roma identity is not fixed, not stable, not 'this' and not 'that', but is instead fluid, complex and contested. It is intersectionality that reveals insights about Roma identity and Romaphobia: what is 'inside' and 'outside' Roma identity is not clear, and why should it be anyway?

It is perhaps more accurate to refer to Roma *identities* given the problematic assumption of a cohesive bounded identity and the interplay between hetero ascription by exogenous actors and the self-ascription by Roma individuals and groups. Roma identities capture the competing articulations of group identity and remind us of the role of different actors in building up an understanding of Roma communities. The work of Mayall (2004) demonstrates that asking the question 'Who are Roma?' misses the point: being Roma or Gypsy has meant different things to different people in different spaces at different times, and this extends to Roma people too. Roma determine who they are and who they are not while non-Roma create and sustain stereotypes and racialized meanings, so Roma identities are the product of this dialectic. I am careful not to overemphasize the capacity of non-Roma to ascribe meaning to Roma identity as it could suggest that 'Roma' is a category of people that outsiders create;

this would negate the significant identity work that goes on within the community. For example, the recent push for the creation of a European Roma Institute for Arts and Culture (ERI) seeks to strengthen the self-esteem of Roma and decrease the prejudice of the majority towards Roma through the promotion of Romani arts, culture, history and media. Although a recent development, the desire to establish the ERI is an attempt for Roma to take more ownership over the public and politicized identity of Roma with the hope of fostering the self-confidence of Roma across Europe. At a symposium on Romaphobia at the University of Brighton in November 2015, one proponent of ERI, Iulius Rostas, argued: 'I see ERI as a space for cultural autonomy of Roma, a public space to find issues important for identity for reacting to issues or shaping discourses.' The goal of the ERI is to challenge the narrative of Roma as a 'problem community' because without counter-narratives young Roma may internalize those messages too. Roma activist Anna Mirga argues: 'It stigmatizes a whole community and ethnicizes a problem that is rooted in social inequality, in discrimination, in unjust societies' (Clark 2015). It suggests that race and ethnicity and identity are the causes of the problem rather than class or inequality. We have also seen an increase in demands for Roma to participate at events (artistic, political, policy, academic), informed by the principle 'Nothing About Us, Without Us', and, in 2015, the European Roma Rights Centre published its journal *Roma Rights* with the same title and included contributions almost exclusively from Roma. This followed the success of Roma-led summer schools organized in Lyon (2013) and Budapest (2015). The issue of Roma identity is being politicized within the community and among activists, advocates and academics. While interventions such as these point to the empowerment of Roma and a growing self-confidence, the pervasiveness of Romaphobia necessitates a battle over Roma identities that is being waged on many fronts simultaneously.

This chapter will pay attention to how Roma public and collective identities are produced and the potential impact of this in terms of manifestations of Romaphobia. Identities are useful to create a sense of 'us and them' that shores up our sense of belonging to different groups and is expedient when building a political voice and making demands related to a minority position, which is where the persecuted and oppressed are likely to be situated. Roma inhabit societies where being Roma is already contextualized according to negative stereotypes. Much more research is required to show how different kinds of identity are activated, displayed and processed in situated interactions in which context plays a key role in the mediation of identity.

It is important to remember that being Roma is not necessarily the most pertinent identity for an individual in a given time and space and that we possess multiple and competing hybrid identities (Tremlett 2009). In spite of the attention given to the construction of Roma identity by elites (McGarry 2014; Sardu and Kovats 2015), we must be attentive to people who may identify as Roma but experience their identity in ways that are mundane and humdrum (Tremlett et al. 2014), the latter being much more difficult to harness for instrumental reasons but are significant nonetheless for those who experience them. Research has demonstrated that Roma possess identities that are characterized much more by hybridity and diversity as by congruence (Tremlett 2009; 2014).

Racism is an expression or activation of group power (Essed 1991: 36). Romaphobia places an emphasis on how non-Roma construct Roma as a particular identity group, distinct from the majority. There is a strong argument that Roma have become 'the marginal group extraordinaire, the quintessential strangers' (Barany 2001: 62–3). During the recent economic crisis in the Czech Republic, Roma were considered as co-culpable allegedly because of high unemployment, reliance on social welfare, and criminal activity. Roma were seen as 'maladjusted citizens' whose values, behaviour and economic position marked them as different from 'normal society' (Hušek and Tvrdá 2015: 51). Of course, Roma may contribute to this distancing from the majority in order to preserve or protect cultural differences and resist assimilation; this is evidenced by the professions practised by Roma groups over the centuries which have required mobility, such as horse-trading and scrap-collecting. Thus, in some contexts, Roma have found it more favourable to deny their identity and adopt another, in order to disappear in the dominant culture, so we also see the adoption of religions and languages by Roma communities as a strategy for survival. This distancing indirectly helps to create Romaphobic practices and legitimate structural racism in institutions as well as societal attitudes and behaviour. Essed (1991: 36) argues that we should not distinguish between institutional and individual racism as it places the individual outside the institutional, thereby severing rules, regulations and procedures from the people who make and enact them. Romaphobia is a system of structural inequalities and prejudicial attitudes and signifies a historical process created and recreated through practices. When a Rom is discriminated against on the basis of her ethnic identity we can say that this practice only makes sense in terms of its consistency with a Romaphobic system. Everyday Romaphobia in the media, in the workplace or in the classroom sustains this system as it reproduces the power of the dominant group (the majority) over the oppressed; and it means that Romaphobia benefits the majority as it confirms their position as the dominant group. The purpose of Roma-phobia is to sustain power.

Autochthony is built on a sense of where ethnic identities belong and tends to create closure and exclusion for some ethnic identities. Ethnicity evokes the existence of a more or less clearly defined ethnic group with its own substance and a specific name in history, and similar notions of autochthony can create a 'them-and-us' opposition (Geschiere and Nyamnjoh 2000). Some scholars have argued that Roma ethnic identity exists only through the active promotion of Romani elite (Stewart 1997: 28), but this hardly differs from other identities, such as nationalism, which are harnessed by the political elite and willed into existence. Nation-building is an open-ended process that emphasizes autochthony and necessitates boundary-making and closure expressed in terms of belonging and exclusion. The European nation-state has promoted protectionism and boundaries between different identities (usually linguistic and/or ethnic) where issues of space, place and belonging are key. This is not to say that autochthonous groups will always feel threatened by minority groups residing in the same territory or that division is inherent in all nation-states, but political elites can activate feelings of fear that can be used to target certain groups, such as Muslims, Jews, LGBTIQ and Roma, when the political opportunity arises. The nation, acting out of collective fear, allows the state to intervene to defend the nation. Across Europe, far-right populist discourses are built on exclusionary autochthony that articulate ideas of keeping the nation pure and cleansing it of unwanted elements (Mudde 2005; Korkut et al. 2013). The persistent conflation of Roma people as dirty or stinking is a reminder to those within the nation of the contaminating potential of Roma as a group and the desirability of expunging Roma from the polity altogether. Those who belong are welcomed and those who do not are feared.

FEAR AND LOATHING

Roma identity is constructed by non-Roma through the lens of fear, which commands an irresistible self-perpetuating quality because the 'enemy within' narrative fences the majority into a position of power that is maintained through stereotypes and scapegoating. It is Roma identity, rather than the Roma people, which is the concern here. To be more specific, I am concerned with the public collective identity of Roma rather than subjective everyday identity or identifications. I am interested in how this is harnessed by the majority and ascribed onto Roma people, with the result that Roma people become understood through dominant, usually negative, ascriptions of group identity, which they have little control over once such ascriptions are in the public sphere. Suffice to say, there are Roma identities that are not seen by the public and it is likely that any attempt to affirm these identities in the public sphere would face stiff resistance from the majority. Roma identity, like all identity, is malleable and has been created by non-Roma in the past to promote a strongly racialized image of criminals. The fear is societal and does not suggest an immediate threat to one's person – or, indeed, a fear of victimization – but reveals an anxiety over societal change, a disruption to the status quo, a tilting of power and control, a shift in values and norms, and an irreversible change for the worse (Bourke 2005). Societal fear is a reaction to social change and is always the product of the will of political entrepreneurs.

There are good reasons to create uncertainty over the identity of a threat or the probability of a risk that has implications for social affiliation (ibid.: 191). Converting social anxieties into fear is a political function: we frequently see Roma communities, particularly poor Roma and/or Roma migrants, being scapegoated by established political elites and the media as a means to influence voter preferences, to foster a sense of threat from unwanted and unknown 'others'. In turn, this legitimates control over subordinate groups. Roma may be named by politicians and media but a lack of interaction between Roma and mainstream society fuels rhetoric that Roma are secretive and untrustworthy, do not belong 'here' and constitute a very real threat. One of the most popular responses to fear is scapegoating or externalizing fears onto others (ibid.: 293). Scapegoating instils fear into the majority and in doing so conveniently presents the political elite with the justification and authority to act in defence of a cowed public.

When Roma, acting individually or in concert, denounce racism or draw attention to Romaphobia they are attempting to challenge the dominant representations of group identity created by non-Roma (McGarry 2014). If the language of racism is one of power and oppression then the narrative cannot ever be changed until systemic racism is overhauled. When Roma feel that they do not belong in the society where they live, where they go to school, where they work, then this is oppressive. It is certainly harmful to millions of Roma across Europe because they are treated unequally. Opportunities for justice and self-respect are often out of their hands. Of course, there are those in the majority who will decry Romaphobia and speak out on behalf of those Roma who are oppressed; this suggests that racism against Roma can be challenged. While we are naturally drawn to the alarming manifestations of Romaphobia such as anti-Roma marches in the Czech Republic or the deportation of Roma communities en masse from France, it is the inaction of the majority who merely accept the status quo of Romaphobia and allow it to go unchecked in either small or significant ways that sustains anti-Roma prejudice. It is the tacit acceptance of Romaphobia that allows it to thrive, which is why it needs to be acknowledged, named, denounced and eradicated at every turn.

We need to make a distinction between identity and groups. There is a tendency to conflate the two but Brubaker (2004) highlights how ethnic identity exists outside of a group. Romaphobia is a complex of ethnic discrimination and prejudicial attitudes that target groups and individuals based on assumptions of inferiority. Prejudice is 'an antipathy based on faulty and inflexible generalizations' (Allport 1954: 9), or what we might term stereotypes. These generalizations are harmful because they reduce all Roma to negative attributes and characteristics simply because they are Roma. Instead of 'that Rom is a criminal', we hear 'all Roma are criminals'. The jump from the individual to the collective is achieved through the negative ascription of group identity, and once you identify with other members of a group, you have the potential to be stereotyped or tarnished with the dominant negative associations levelled at that group. The in-group is not concerned with promoting the heterogeneity of the out-group but only with maintaining its position of power. Stereotypes are the ultimate expression of out-group power, an expression created by diminishing individuality and reducing a group identity to unflattering homogeneous characteristics; in the case of Roma this is criminality, untrustworthiness, secrecy, deception and dirt. Yet, one of the important issues in how Roma have historically been stereotyped is the ambiguity involved in stereotyping, meaning that it is important to look not only at the negative side of the spectrum of stereotypes; Roma have been romanticized and exoticized, and this has served to project a particular homogeneous and positive image of Roma as excellent musicians, for instance. All groups are potential targets of stereotypes but those that occupy a non-dominant position are more at risk of experiencing a negative ascription based on in-group norms, traditions and values, and for this reason I explore the impact of the negative ascription of group identity. Importantly, a group in a non-dominant position will find it harder to challenge negative generalizations because it is unable to change cultural scripts that reinforce difference and ascribe *value* to some groups and not to others. Identity, then, is a means to reduce all members of a group to the same characteristics and values.

We might assume that Romaphobia is so ingrained in European society, tolerated and acceptable even, that it is impossible to break. However, identity is the key to Romaphobia as it creates and sustains it, so it is to identity that I turn in order to understand how to challenge Romaphobia. In the 1990s, appeals to a cosmopolitan imaginary where the rights of all are respected and a vision of society unencumbered by national identity were attractive and had potential, but, in reality, this failed to get to grips with the power of identity in creating difference and oppression. For the past fifty years, Roma agency has reflected trends towards demanding rights or asserting difference or maintaining that integration is key.

Let us consider how questions of identity, otherness, and majority versus minority play out in the context of European nationalism. The birth of ethnic conceptions of nationalism has a common denominator in otherness: 'the position of Roma in European civilization from medieval times shows that, for Europeans, the Roma have always represented otherness' (Anděl 2013: 11). This otherness is manifest in tropes, myths and symbols that construct Roma not only as different but as potentially threatening to the social fabric of the nation. In this context, persecution in the form of expulsion or murder is acceptable in order to preserve the supposed coherence of the ethnic nation. In 1548, the Imperial Diet at Augsburg ruled that he who kills a Gypsy 'shan't guilty of any murder be' as Gypsies are 'profiteers, spies and traitors' (ibid.: 11). Roma or Gypsies were subject to special laws that reinforced otherness and confirmed their undesirability as an unwanted presence in the nation who could be removed with impunity. More

famously, in the Austro-Hungarian empire, Empress
Maria Theresa (1717–80) and her son Joseph II (1741–90)
pursued policies of assimilation whereby supposedly
unproductive Gypsies would be given land, resettled and
prohibited from speaking Romanes, and Roma children
taken away and given to non-Roma families in order to
learn how to be obedient and respectable. Legislative
interventions like these fuelled prejudicial attitudes and
legitimated discriminatory behaviour and left a legacy
of Roma otherness in contemporary European society.
While the experiences of Roma groups across Europe
were very distinct – particularly in how different nascent
nation-states addressed Roma groups within a sovereign
territory – the impact has been a demarcation between
Roma and the majority and hostile actions against Roma
in the form of ethnic cleansing, murder, discrimination
in education, employment and healthcare, physical and
symbolic segregation, expulsion and deportation.

Since the arrival of Roma in Europe, they have often
been represented as an unwelcome 'other' that threatens
the nation, creating a collective fear within societies. While
there exists plenty of evidence of Roma communities
and non-Roma cohabiting peacefully and successfully,
the dominant narrative of Roma presence in Europe has
been one of marginalization. Even though Roma groups
are recognized as constitutive of some states as national
minorities (as in Sweden, Romania, Germany and Serbia),
this has not created a perceptible shift in public attitudes
or, for that matter, compelled political elites to address the

socio-economic and political position of Roma communities within a given state. As the archetypal 'other' in
contemporary Europe, Roma communities frequently
continue to represent a threat that must be removed; in
the past this manifested as assimilation, where Roma or
Gypsy identity was phased out, but today, with the rise
of far-right and populist nationalism across Europe, we
are witnessing a determined effort to remove Roma from
the nation, justified in part by the representation of Roma
as a problem community. In modern Czech society, Roma
are regarded by the majority as unadaptable, boisterous,
overly fertile, temperamental and dishonourable, signifying everything that was problematic in the Czech nation.
Those participating in recent anti-Roma demonstrations,
such as those in Příbram and Duchcov, may not consider
themselves to be racist and argue that they want a normal,
civilized community with law and order. But what is so
civilized about intimidating a group of people, including
children, on a misplaced notion of what is considered to
be normal or appropriate behaviour in society? In their
eyes, it is they, the insiders, those participating in anti-
Roma demonstrations, who are the victims, not Roma.
The shifting of victimhood to favour the majority is
a tactic and a testament to the power of stereotypes by
presenting racists with one option – defence based on
fear – expressed as self-defence of the nation against an
unwanted intruder, or an enemy within.

'Gypsy' as an identity has implications for integration
and belonging. Identity is not just created by society but

is produced by the interplay between people and territory, meaning that our environment produces collective understandings of our place within that space, and invariably relates to the delineation of inclusion and exclusion. Both within and outside the community, the term 'Gypsy' continues to be used, particularly in Central and Eastern European states. Horváth (2012: 118) draws our attention to how identity, visibility and place intersect in one Hungarian village with the demarcation of place and roles along a Hungarian–Gypsy axis: 'in the village, the Gypsy was always allocated a place, but their positions (for example in remedial school), roles (for example, "the disabled") or possibilities for action ... were clearly distinguished and had an inferior status.' Interestingly, the delineation of roles played out in silence, in the sense that the Gypsy was not named or discussed in public discussions in the village; discussion of the appearance of the issue and the category was taboo. 'Gypsy' is an inferior and unchangeable status. It is a stigma. But in the Hungarian village where Horváth carried out her research, it is understood among Gypsies that the key to their separateness (in a classroom, in a work environment) is not their 'Gypsyness' but their behavioural characteristics, including a lack of education, poverty and a lack of civilization, all of which can be eradicated with effort (2012: 122). Kovai works with Horváth in the same village and argues that when the Gypsy began to appear in places where earlier he had not been allowed at all or entered only occasionally, the hierarchy between

Hungarian and Gypsy started to be questioned. As the Gypsy moved into schools and workplaces and stepped beyond his own 'kin' associations, 'he left behind the safety of the positions assigned by the order of not naming and exposed himself to the dangers of being named as Gypsy. As a result the "Gypsy" became visible because he left behind exactly those positions where his presence was covered up' (Kovai 2012: 289). An impact of this recalibration has been that the term 'Gypsy' has changed in meaning. It is still pejorative and oppressive but nowadays carries with it 'a sense of threat' and of 'place or space-grabber' (ibid.: 293) as Roma or Gypsies continue to make demands and claims to public space and public life: in short, to claim the rights to citizenship they rightfully possess. Fear drives the meaning of Roma identity, with Roma groups struggling to negotiate a public space for the inclusion and participation of collective identity.

BELONGING AND NATIONHOOD

Roma identity is not a cohesive tangible 'fact', and this has consequences for how individuals feel they belong with or to other people. The relationship between identity and belonging is one of mutual dependence. Group identity is based on the assumption that group members have a sense of solidarity with one another even if they have never met; this presumes that the sense of belonging is imagined. However, the social construction of identity means that members of the group may experience their group membership as particularly strong, defining who they are as a person and delineating core values, ideas and norms. Belonging to a community presupposes an understanding of 'them and us' as we cast our eyes beyond the boundaries of our community and become aware of cultural or community differences. At the risk of re-treading well-worn paths on Barth's conception of ethnic boundary maintenance (1969), it is worth high-lighting how identity and belonging are negotiated through parallel processes of boundary maintenance, often through the mediation of symbols, rituals, tradi-tions and values. Jenkins (2008: 135), reading Cohen argues that: 'Recognition of a "sense of us" and commu-nity stems from the awareness that things are done differently *there*, and the sense of threat that poses for how things are done *here* ... collective forms – such as "cultures" – are produced by the local sense of difference at the boundary.' It is here that we can unpick the rela-tionship between identity and belonging:

> The boundary symbolizes the community to its members in two quite different ways: it is the sense they have of its perception by people on the other side – the public face, or 'typical' mode; and it is their own sense of the community as refracted through all the complexi-ties of their lives and experiences – the private face, and 'idiosyncratic' mode.
>
> COHEN 1986: 13; CITED IN JENKINS 2008: 137

Roma identity is an internal gaze that comprises self-identification as well as the sharing of symbols, norms, traditions and cultural practices. Simultaneously, the majority gaze projects its own understanding of Roma identity with the sole purpose of maintaining the boundary between the two.

Like identity, belonging is negotiated by Roma individuals and communities and mediated by non-Roma in wider communities. We build up an understanding of where we belong and a sense of ourselves as belonging in a particular space and time as well as being nested in relationships and interactions with others. This provides a context in which our identity is expressed and understood. We might well ask if belonging necessarily creates inequalities between social entities, as one group attempts to assert communal power over another. For centuries, nationalism projects have sought to do so. Indeed, one could argue that nationalism is premised on the elevation of one group, the nation, over others, and this would suggest that there is no place for a minority ethnic identity in the nation other than as a stigmatized other. As stigmatized groups, such as Roma, have attempted to change the nationalism script and to assert belonging in and to the nation, we see appeals to foster group solidarity in the form of identity politics. Roma activists and advocates have sowed the admittedly extant seeds of domestic division and have demanded rights to redress inequality and stigmatization by drawing attention to the difference of Roma communities. I do not want to suggest that Roma activists or advocates want to reinforce their difference, but rather that the political power of Roma is premised on difference and this identity dilemma (McGarry and Jasper 2015) is one that must be negotiated.

According to Calhoun (2003), identities are not simply fixed or simply fluid but depend on circumstances. Identities can be benign when they are not perceived as threatening: nations have managed to accommodate different identities through multiculturalism with varying degrees of success in terms of integration. But when identities are fixed by political entrepreneurs seeking to acquire power, they often act as though all members of the group share the same interests and are more similar than they actually are. This is what Brubaker has termed 'groupism' (2002: 164), which he explains as the 'tendency to take discrete, sharply differentiated, internally homogeneous and externally bounded groups as basic constituents of social life'. He argues that it is better to regard groups as 'projects' that are made, usually by political elites from within but also for outside: Roma political elites have proclaimed Roma nationhood as a distinct transnational nation sharing a common culture, while non-Roma political elites encourage an understanding of Roma as a distinct ethnic 'other' residing in different states. Brubaker (2003: 554) warns that, in political struggles, different actors cast ethnic groups or nations as the protagonists or heroes, and thus 'reification is central to the *practice* of politicized ethnicity, as indeed to other forms of politics'. Vigilance is necessary when identity politics comes into play in order not to fall into the trap of assuming a fixed identity with clearly defined goals for any group because this approach is based on a groupist ontology and overstates the coherence of identity. The idea of a unified group is a 'political fiction' (ibid.: 554). The alternative to reified articulations of Roma or the nation as a distinct entity is to focus on Romaphobia as a dynamic interactive project constructed and sustained by events and institutional forums, as well as norms, rules and practices. Significantly, the key to understanding the root causes of Romaphobia is to be found in the intersection between identity and belonging.

The nation is one of the key organizing units in modern Europe and has been supported by the establishment of the sovereign state. Nations, like other identity-based groups such as class or gender, function to the extent that members feel solidarity with others based on the assumption of a common culture that can produce a sense of shared belonging (Calhoun 2003). The emergence of citizenship as a catalogue of rights attempted to establish a formal relationship between the state and those recognized as belonging to that state. The bestowing of rights is an expression of political power and the nation-state is the peak logic of political power: the nation-state determines who is in and who is out, who belongs and who does not. While difference can be accommodated through multicultural policies, usually difference is assimilated or expelled. Unity begets stability, and therefore citizenship, as an institution, attempts to unify disparate people under a common cause: the preservation of citizenship and the nation. But attempts to build a nation must continually fight otherness from within and outside – what Kristeva (1991: 191) calls 'the stranger within us'. This means that difference is accepted as part of collective culture, today realized in nation-state polities as well as in semi-autonomous distinct ethnic identities contained within states. This struggle is the result of centuries of dealing with foreigners and strangers (those who are not us) in our midst. The stranger can become familiar over time and can come to be seen as a fellow man or citizen, making them less strange. But they remain different, usually on the basis of self-ascribed identity categories such as religion or language. Roma communities across Europe often speak the dominant language of the state (many Roma are bilingual) and practise the official religion and possess formal citizenship rights, but this has not shielded Roma groups from processes of othering where the differences between Roma and non-Roma are highlighted. In practice, Roma identity (not Roma groups per se) is reified to negative stereotypes, usually behaviours and pathologies such as criminality, nomadism, inadaptability and secrecy, which creates an incessant narrative of difference. Rom scholar Ian Hancock (1994) argues that 'as foreigners everywhere in Europe, Romanies have no territorial, political, military or financial strength, no home in which to seek refuge; they continue to be the perpetual "outsiders"'. The designation 'foreigner' implies that Roma do not belong and have never belonged, even if Roma are citizens of the states in which they reside. The status of foreigner is ascribed and does not designate a formal status.

Romaphobia is more than simply the fear and hatred of Roma individuals and communities. The negative ascription of Roma identity should be understood as the internalization of cultural stigma driven, in large part, by the creation and maintenance of the dominant nation. Such a conceptualization helps us to look beyond belonging and fear as psycho-social conditions and instead view negative ascriptions and inferior status as a phenomenon sustained via culture rather than on an individual basis. Let us consider the 2015 Eurobarometer poll, which asked respondents how comfortable they would be if one of their colleagues at work belonged to one of fourteen different groups: 'Roma' came bottom with 54 per cent, behind 'Transgender or transsexual' (56 per cent), 'Muslim' (61 per cent), and 'Gay, lesbian or bisexual' (63 per cent) (European Commission 2015: 5). To understand why Roma are so discriminated against we must explore majority cultural power expressed through the hegemonic nation. The hegemonic nation will accommodate and even recognize difference in terms of minorities within the nation as long as that difference does not threaten the nation-state; this threat is usually understood as potential secessionist or irredentist elements. Roma are seen and treated as a distinct ethnic group and have come to understand themselves as an ethnic minority inhabiting various states. Calhoun maintains that ethnicity is not an attribute of individuals or a group but is 'a commonality of understanding, access to the world, and mode of action that facilitates the construction of social relationships ... people *participate* to varying degrees in ethnicity, rather than they simply are or are not members of ethnic groups' (2003: 560). This does not mean that ethnicity does not produce groups. Diverse agencies produce an ethnic group, from within and from outside, and the same holds true for nations (which are also ethnic groups). There can be no objective criteria for belonging to an ethnic group or for specific characteristics as these are created through social relationships in contexts of ethnic diversity. Occupying a non-dominant position means that minority ethnic groups must negotiate negative ascriptions and discrimination that can create the impression that groups are internally homogeneous and bounded or that an ethnic group identity becomes more salient or stable over time.

Forces conspire to deny the significance of ethnicity in creating Romaphobia, which is a potent source of continuing racism. Take, for example, the prevalence of governments maintaining that issues relating to ethnicity are actually social and economic issues. The Czech Republic argues that it is not racist when it permits the segregation of schoolchildren. The schoolchildren in these schools are socially disadvantaged, it argues, and the fact that these children share the same ethnicity, as Roma, is a coincidence at most or merely beside the point. By denying the existence of Romaphobia, national governments can shirk their responsibility to challenge racial discrimination, but they can actively sustain it too. Governments can also compound the matter by using ethnicity and culture as a means to justify inclusion: Roma children are *not ready* for general public schools and segregated schools are created to support Roma families and children, not to exclude them. Since when has segregation ever helped build a fair and inclusive society? Evidence suggests that Roma want to live, study and work together with the rest of society but are routinely excluded. If one requires evidence of the racist logic motivating exclusion then look no further than segregated settlements, schools and hospital rooms, which are not just physically separate but are generally much poorer in quality (Petrova 2004). Politicians in the Netherlands evoke sentiments of home and belonging in order to draw lines between citizens; those who belong and those who, despite their presence, do not (Duyvendak 2012).

Csepeli and Simon (2004: 130) believe that 'the strategies used by nation states were more or less uniform throughout Europe – Gypsies were by and large ignored'. Similarly, Stewart (2013: 415) argues that Roma have evaded the trap of nation-state/ethnic figurations but this ignores the importance of social relationships and cultural exchange, which have been harnessed, particularly by the state, to exclude Roma groups. How else can we explain research which shows that Roma are the most rejected of all minority groups (Csepeli et al. 2000)? France, for example, created a law in 1912 to stop vagrancy that provided the government with a legal means to control travelling professions, defined categories of itinerant merchants, and introduced a new identity card aimed specifically at Roma (Fogg 2009) in order to make iterant Gypsy sedentary, thereby encouraging assimilation: 'Lawmakers believed that those who chose to conform to French cultural norms, including having a permanent residence, could be integrated into society' (ibid.: 89). It is clear that a great deal of effort is required to construct and maintain difference, and this identity work is the basis of Romaphobia. Anthropologists have written much of the history of Roma communities, for better or for worse, concentrating on self-identification performed by Roma themselves and boundary maintenance between Roma and non-Roma by focusing on cultural difference. Here, Roma are active players in identity work. This approach imbues Roma communities with agency and the power to represent and articulate the meaning of identity. In contrast, studies that emphasize the role of the majority in oppressing Roma (Gheorghe 1997) demonstrate how the negative representation of group identity limits opportunities for socio-economic engagement and reinforces the image of Roma as a group lacking a voice.

Dutch scholars Willems (1997) and Luccassen et al. (1998) have drawn attention to the power of the state in constructing Roma difference, labelling Roma groups as potential sources of instability and insecurity. It is important not to jump from negative ascriptions of a group identity to the assumption of the de facto existence of that identity, and instead be attentive to the role of the majority in representing Roma identity, for example as a 'problem' community in Italy (Sigona 2005). It is tempting to argue that the maelstrom of negative ascription and discourse becomes internalized by Roma communities, who come to understand themselves as a targeted, despised community, and over time this shared experience becomes a collective identity. Roma activists and advocates seek to challenge the forces of populist nationalism across Europe by appealing to ideas of cultural belonging and distinctiveness in order to build social and political capital and to raise a collective consciousness among Roma communities. These efforts at political mobilization face a puzzle: how to build political capital without resources or traditional tools of nation-building such as a shared language that all Roma speak (even though a common language, Romanes, exists), territorial claims or a shared religion? Instead, political entrepreneurs appeal to a common experience as a despised and persecuted minority represented in the media and in the mainstream rhetoric of political elites as an impoverished, difficult community. So, identity is not a 'fact' but is constructed individually in the everyday and publicly by politics, political groups, the media, the public sector, public discourses and so on. Identity politics then rest on group formation that delineates belonging and creates boundaries of inclusion and exclusion. I want to shed light on the role of Roma in identity politics and will concentrate on the creation of the Roma nation.

THE ROMA NATION

The staccato elaboration of the Roma nation over the years has been pushed by Romani political elites and international organizations seeking to address the 'Roma issue'. 'Roma' has been used as common currency among academics since the 1970s and 1980s, when the elites determined that the use of 'Roma' was preferable to the exonym 'Gypsy', the latter being loaded with negative baggage. It should be noted that not all use 'Roma' and many continue to identify as 'Gypsy'. Since the arrival of Roma communities in Europe in around the fourteenth century, Roma have been labelled by established populations as *atsinganoi* (Greece), *Tsigani* (Bulgaria), *Tsigane* (France), *Zigeuner* (Germany), *Cigányok* (Hungary) and *Zingari* (Italy), as well as 'Bohemians' and 'pagans'. Today, 'Roma' as a self-appellation carries a normative power and is used by policymakers, journalists, activists, advocates and academics. It has been noted that today it might be more appropriate to conceive of Roma as a political project or phenomenon (Vermeersch 2006; McGarry 2014). At the first World Congress in 1971, a flag and anthem were created, laying the foundations for the elaboration of the Roma nation. Nationalism implies a challenge to the existing political order in a given space and so Roma nationalism has been interpreted as a threat: 'once invented, nations become intolerant of those who do not fit into their narratives of invention' (Isin 2012: 162).

Nationalism has been incorrectly described as 'collective action designed to render the boundaries of a nation congruent with those of its governance unit' (Hechter 2000: 7). Such a definition does not capture the Roma nationalist movement as no claims to territorial governance are made or implied. Anderson (1991) demonstrates that the presence of one or more imagined communities on a territory can lead to tension as different claims to self-determination collide. This might help to explain why Roma have faced economic and political marginalization as they do not belong in the narratives of history, origins and culture of national identities expressed across Europe. Roma communities reinforce difference vis-à-vis the majority with the use of '*gadje*' to describe non-Roma: 'an "us/them" opposition that has been historically reinforced by centuries of internalized oppression and isolation' (Petrova 2004: 7). The use of Roma and *gadje* acts as an adhesive for a disparate group; it creates a sense of belonging and community for a group that has been held at arm's length by the majority. When identities become struggles they require coherence so that people understand what it means to belong to an identity group, and from this political capital can be built. A key defining feature of an ethnic movement is that 'claims are made based upon particular identity or boundary, defined by the presence of racial or ethnic markers' (Olzak 2003: 667); these typically include skin pigmentation, ancestry, language, history of discrimination or other shared experiences. Mobilization is the ability to appropriate resources (such as loyalty, organization and material resources) in order to reach a common goal and requires solidarity:

that is, the conscious collective identification of a particular population (ibid.: 668). Identity is a key outcome of
mobilization yet it is required for mobilization to occur: it
is a product as well as a process (Flesher-Fominaya 2015).

Social movement literature has done much to help
develop our understanding of how and why groups
engage in collective action and the significance of identity
for mobilization. Since much of the work of nationalist
movements concerns the construction and expression of
collective identity, it is worth considering the processes
that underpin them. Collective identity is not a 'thing to
be studied' (Melucci 1995: 46) but rather a tool to capture
shared meanings and understandings, and the opportunities and constraints that such constructions engender:
'In the process of constructing a collective identity, challenging groups adopt labels for themselves ... draw lines
between insiders and outsiders, and develop interpre-
tive frameworks, a political consciousness' (Whittier
1995: 15). Using the case of the women's movement in
Australia, Maddison (2004) argues that collective action
is discursively constructed through movement participants' reflexive discussion and contestation over ends,
means and fields of action, and thus movement participants discursively create the movement itself from the
bottom up. She also points to moments when there is a
shared sense of threat from outsiders (such as the police);
this cements feelings of interdependence for movement
participants who in turn identify more strongly with
others who are similarly threatened. The goals of Roma

nationalism are multiple and shifting: to secure recognition; to change policy or law; to challenge Romaphobia; to politicize others to become active; to foster remembrance; and to build a collective solidarity. None of these goals can be addressed without negotiating the meaning of Roma identity, an identity that is highly contested.

The move towards Roma nationhood has been presented as part of a collective consciousness and a determination to address the very real problems facing Roma people across Europe. Roma nationhood has been the vehicle for the political mobilization of Roma in order to acquire power, to become visible and to address the relative weakness of Roma communities across Europe. Nationalism is then merely a strategy to unify disparate Roma groups and to become politically significant, a position that would temper Romaphobia by countering hostility, humiliation, resentment and oppression. Roma nationhood is fabricated for political ends, invariably articulated in the image of the political elite. Of concern is the meaning and content of Roma nationhood as articulated by elites and what this says about Roma identity, particularly for Roma communities. Mirga and Gheorghe (1997: 4) believe that the main challenge facing Roma political mobilization is defining its 'political space' and struggling for political status at the national and international levels. Additionally, for Fraser (1995), Roma mobilization means forging a collective agency in spite of the tendency among Roma to emphasize the differences between various Roma communities across Europe. The fact that many have rejected the umbrella term 'Roma' is testament to the lack of coherence in building a collective identity (Marushiakova and Popov 2004), never mind a political movement with clearly defined goals. As Simhandl (2009: 88) observes, 'not all the people who feel themselves covered by the term subscribe to its usage', with 'gypsy' and its variants persisting across Europe. For many, the birth of the Roma nation heralds an affirmation of a collective existence as well as a demand for recognition and the adequate redistribution of socio-economic provisions. But for others, it signifies a backwards step, and the creation of an ethnic boundary in society that supports differential treatment.

The claim to Roma nationhood was first clearly articulated in 2000 in the 'Declaration of a Roma Nation' at the fifth meeting of the Romani World Congress organized by the International Romani Union in Prague. The declaration asserts a right to self-determination as a non-territorial nation but makes no claims to territory. The declaration was made by International Romani Union President Emil Ščuka (Acton and Klímová 2001):

Individuals belonging to the Roma Nation call for a representation of their Nation, which does not want to become a State. We ask for being recognized as a Nation, for the sake of Roma and of non-Roma individuals, who share the need to deal with the nowadays new challenges ... We are a Nation, we share the same tradition, the same culture, the same origin, the same language;

we are a Nation. We have never looked for creating a
Roma State.

In line with international legal principles, any claim to
self-determination as a nation requires recognition by
others, usually states, that a nation exists. The Roma nation
is dialogically created (first articulated then recognized). If
the Roma nation is denied, denigrated or misrecognized,
then this has the potential to cause harm to Roma and it
is arguably this harm that the call for recognition seeks
to overcome (Goodwin 2004). However, some argue that
the declaration of nationhood can never be realized as it
is not based on territory or sovereignty and will always
require a state to act as guarantor; thus the declaration
simply confirms Roma as a minority (Isin 2012). Only
states can be signatories to international law, based on the
principle of *pacta sunt servanda*, and states have territorial
sovereignty to support nationalist claims to recognition.
I have argued elsewhere that 'the concept of a "nation"
as it is used in the European Westphalian tradition does
not apply to the Romani case' (McGarry 2008: 454), while
Mirga and Gheorghe (1997: 17) hold that the concept of
nation has more of a symbolic, moral and political value
than a legal one. Kapralski (2012: 66) argues that territory,
statehood and cultural homogeneity are not precondi-
tions of nationhood as identity projects or movements can
claim recognition and support in international or transnational institutions. Grattan Puxon has been a Roma rights
activist since the 1960s and is one of the key advocates

of Roma Nation Day, held on 8 April every year across Europe (the EU now refers to this as 'International Roma Day', removing the nation component and downplaying Romani ethnicity). He believes that loyalty to a state can be broken and, due to the persistent marginalization of Roma communities across Europe, this loyalty is under significant strain today. He argues that Roma nationhood is crucial for recognition in order to gain parity with states, with which Roma have to negotiate (personal interview, March 2015). International Roma Day acts as a focal point for Roma across the world to unite, to commemorate the Holocaust, to celebrate Romani arts and history, and for international organizations and NGOs to showcase their work on education, healthcare and poverty eradication. Zeljko Jovanovic (2016) believes that the purpose of International Roma Day is to express self-determination, as a nation, and international unity as core components of Roma political identity.

It has been argued that Roma identity is weak (Barany 2001: 288–90) and lacks a coherence that we find with other nationalisms, usually those tied to territorial claims or cultural preservation. But most nations retain a contested historiography and ideas of essentialist culture are usually as constraining as they are liberating. The promotion of Roma as a transnational minority without a kin state is useful to an extent in order to build political capital but it does reinforce the idea that Roma do not belong in or to any one state. The 2000 declaration circumvents the nation-state and appeals to the international political community for recognition and support. This is a bold move as it affirms that Roma are different and are not part of the majority nation, even though they have been living across diverse states and borders for centuries and enjoy citizenship status. On the eve of International Roma Day in 2016, Romani scholar Professor Ethel Brooks tied the claim to establish a European Roma Institute for Arts and Culture with the position of Roma as a European people: 'We have been organizing across generations and borders. Without resorting to violence or reclaiming a nation, we came up with a simple claim: our place is in the centre of European societies' (Brooks 2016). She points to Roma as a source of hope for Europe, as an example to others from which lessons can be drawn, which suggests a community becoming more assured of its place in European society.

Roma nationalism is 'intended to build an identity which exists over and above the ties and identities linked to and derived from the nations in which Gypsies are living' (Mayall 2004: 207). Since the 2000 declaration, articulations of Roma nationhood have been less vocal, with transnational activists and advocacy organizations continuing the identity work in multiple contexts. The international political community is widely acknowledged as holding the answers to problems facing Roma communities, due to the ineffectiveness of national governments, and currently generates the lion's share of attention for the so-called Roma elite. This reveals a tension in terms of the authenticity of the Roma voice (if authenticity is ever even possible) and who has legitimacy to speak on behalf of whom. If we cannot define who is Roma then it follows that it is impossible to determine a legitimate voice. One charge that is consistently levelled at the Roma elite is that many lack any sense of community with or understanding of the majority of Roma: if someone receives a wage from an international organization and spends time attending meetings with policymakers in Brussels, Strasbourg or Warsaw, then is it possible for them to understand what life is like for ordinary Roma people, irrespective of a shared ethnicity? Perhaps more significantly, since the 1990s, the increasing activism and advocacy of the Roma elite in the transnational political context has blunted the boundaries between different groups, including Sinti, Traveller and Gypsy, who are increasingly subsumed under the term 'Roma'. European policymakers and funding streams want to know who they are speaking to and who those people are speaking for.

For Roma, 'every country is a "foreign" country, a country of residence; there is no homeland to go back to' (Barany 2001: 142), and this conviction has certainly contributed to the minority status of Roma across Europe even when they are recognized as a national minority, thus belonging to the state. While some believe that the capacity to forge a common identity is based on common origins, culture and shared traumatic experiences in Europe (ibid.: 299), others see Roma nation-building as a recalibration of 'cultural heritage and past, a redefinition and construction of its own minority identity, and a rejection of its imposed and stigmatized name as well as the emancipation of Roma masses' (Mirga and Gheorghe 1997: 10). It does not matter if Roma identity is 'weak', relatively or not, notwithstanding the criteria on which such a claim can be made; what matters is how Roma identity is harnessed, by whom, and the impact that it has on the lives of ordinary Roma.

The impact of the declaration was symbolically important but also resonated with international organizations and those involved in the transnational Roma movement. It is important to note that the declaration of the Roma nation was driven by the elite and still lacks traction in the lives of communities across Europe. A key aspect of the declaration was the demand for representation that would be realized in 2004 with the establishment of the European Roma and Traveller Forum (ERTF) in Strasbourg as a partner organization of the Council of Europe, with the express purpose to act as a representative assembly for Roma groups across Europe. What makes the ERTF unique is the diversity of Roma groups which it brings together under its umbrella – these include Kalderash, Lovara, Sinti, Beas, Jenish, Resande, Pavee and Travellers – and the fact that it seeks to be a true expression of the wishes of Roma and Travellers (ERTF 2005). A key part of the problem facing ERTF today is precisely how to have a legitimately representative organization for a heterogeneous population not united by a common identity.

A Roma voice is being heard but its demands for equal treatment stand in opposition to the majority's

Romaphobia, meaning that efforts to maintain and develop a distinctive group identity perpetuate Roma inequality. This highlights a number of dilemmas facing Roma ethno-political mobilization: to be different and remain apart; to be indifferent to society and state; to assert difference and risk intolerance and exclusion; to demand recognition as a distinct group or to assimilate (Mirga and Gheorghe 1997: 33). Each of these dilemmas presents a choice for Roma and these choices require attention to the meaning and content of Roma identity, sometimes actively changing it in order to pursue a goal.

The issue of the gradual Europeanization of the Roma has been noted by Van Baar (2011b). In 1993, the Council of Europe asserted that Roma are 'a true European minority', seeking to anchor Roma communities in the domestic political context. In 2009, the first meeting of the European Platform for Roma Inclusion met in Brussels and outlined ten Common Basic Principles on Roma Inclusion. It acknowledged that 'Roma communities have been part of European societies for centuries, often marginalized and sometimes persecuted'. When the EU created the Framework for National Roma Integration Strategies in 2011, it signified a break with efforts to shift the responsibility of Roma issues to the European level. The European Commission effectively told member states that inclusion can only be addressed at the local and national level and stated that it would help support governments in addressing the integration of Roma communities. While this came as a surprise to Roma activists, who had hoped that the EU would take a more prescriptive and monitoring role, the Commission was unlikely to do so. In a staff working document to the European Parliament and the Council of the EU in 2008, it maintained that 'core issues of Roma inclusion – education, employment, public health, housing and infrastructure and the fight against poverty – fall mainly under the responsibility of Member States' (European Commission 2008: 4). The document specifically mentions that it has deliberately avoided the 'Europeanization' of the *problems* (the integration of Roma) lest it symbolically transfers responsibility to EU institutions. The EU maintains that policymaking can only be effectively implemented and monitored at the local and national level. The EU invokes citizenship rights, that approximately 10 million Roma are EU citizens, and so draws a line between belonging and responsibility and appeals to member states to do their duty by their citizens, emphasizing the economic benefits of including Roma and the economic disadvantages of not doing so. Roma may express identification with their country of citizenship and may not be interested in the forging of a collective Roma identity (Willems 1997), European or not.

The politico-cultural struggle for recognition of the Romani Holocaust in Europe reveals a number of fault lines and tensions within the broader Roma movement. The struggle began shortly after World War Two in Germany and was galvanized through the emergence of international networks of Roma activism in the 1960s and 1970s, gaining more prominence in the 1990s. Van Baar

(2015b: 152) discusses identity formation and the Roma movement through the lens of cultural memory by drawing attention to acts of memory that contest some prevailing notions of history and reveals a crucial identity dilemma in Germany: 'The German Roma wanted to be considered as equal members of society, while their memory politics stressed their distinctiveness as an ethnic group in order to be recognised at all as victims of Nazi genocide' (ibid.: 164–5). The effort to secure status as victims rested on the ability to prove that Roma were murdered by the Nazis because of the perception of racial inferiority, but this was out of step with prevailing identity work that advocated equality and rejected differentiated treatment. Gheorghe (1991) and Kapralski (1997) highlight efforts to foster ethnogenesis as an internally bounded and coherent group identity in order to promote Roma nationalism, which means that a coherent identity is important for political mobilization. Significantly, ethnogenesis is about bolstering the agency of Roma to determine who they are and the claims they make in the public sphere and is both inward looking and outward facing.

The institutions of a nation are never neutral but are 'implicitly tilted towards the needs, interests and identities of the majority group; and this creates a range of burdens, stigmatizations and exclusions for members of the minority group' (Kymlicka and Norman 2000: 4). For Roma, this is manifest in exclusion and discrimination. By demanding to be recognized as a nation, Roma are not claiming sovereignty or autonomy; instead they seek to exist alongside the majority nation and to enjoy equal rights as citizens of the state. Roma reside in the legal and political framework of the state, and so the exclusion and institutional marginalization that Roma endure at the hands of the majority are ruptured by claims of self-determination. Self-determination is not akin to an indigenous community making claims to recognition and/or territory, which is often treated as a desire to separate. Roma nationalism is an attempt to challenge the status quo and to facilitate the participation of Roma in the political life of the majority nation. It could be argued that the emergence of Roma nationalism is welcomed by the majority as it seeks to affirm the difference between Roma and the majority. Roma nationalism is not regarded as a threat: that is, it is not seen as undermining the cohesive fabric of the nation or indeed viewed as risky or divisive in terms of national unity (Robbins 2010: 270).

Demands for recognition of the Roma nation have waned since 2000, and the Roma elite has instead placed its faith in participating in European political institutions such as the Council of Europe and the EU. Transnational representation through the ERTF in Strasbourg was an invitation to the top table and a signal that European political structures were willing to address the situation of Roma due to the unwillingness of national governments to do so. Now, as enthusiasm for the ERTF dissipates, we are seeing the emergence of the most recent manifestation of Roma identity politics: the creation of the European Roma Institute, which places Roma ownership and participation front and centre, although questions remain about how the ERI will engage ordinary Roma and improve the socio-economic and political position of Roma. Social movements ebb and flow and Roma nationalism is one part of a broader political mobilization. But, like all movements, Roma must grapple with tensions and dilemmas concerning collective identity, tensions that are unlikely to be resolved anytime soon, if ever.

CHAPTER 4

AN EXPRESSION OF ROMAPHOBIA: SOCIO-SPATIAL SEGREGATION IN EASTERN EUROPE

Romaphobia is manifest in numerous actions by different actors in a range of fields. Roma face prejudice, discrimination and social exclusion in their daily lives, and this impacts on their ability to get a job and to access healthcare and education. Moreover, many Roma endure material deprivation and live in extremely poor socio-economic conditions, with research finding that 90 per cent of Roma are living below the poverty line (FRA 2012: 3). So, we can safely assume that Romaphobia impacts on Roma people's lives and opportunities. Thus far I have considered some of the key causes of Romaphobia and the forces that build and sustain it, but it is imperative to contextualize Romaphobia to understand how it is manifest. I could explore the marginalization of Roma women, the criminalization of Roma identity, or the continued exclusion of Roma from employment, and each would be a valuable exercise, not least as it would underscore the reach of

Romaphobia. With that being said, this chapter will focus on housing, particularly on socio-spatial segregation and what this means for territoriality, identity and belonging. I will draw upon theories of advanced marginalization, human geography and public policy in order to outline the parameters of the discussion, and what I believe is at stake. Then I will offer a comparative case study of two Roma settlements, in Skopje, the capital of Macedonia, and in Košice in eastern Slovakia, where Roma are in the majority. In both cases I will examine the role of the state in creating segregated communities and examine the impact of socio-spatial exclusion on belonging.

Segregation, whether in education or in housing, is a form of exclusion and reinforces division in society. It is based on the conviction that people are not the same, and are not equal. Segregated settlements, be they urban or rural, result in inadequate or interrupted access to schooling, and fewer opportunities to hear about work or to use public transport to get to work, and there is evidence that possessing an address known as being in a Roma neighbourhood means that job applications are rejected outright (FRA 2009: 5). In his study of poor African American communities, Wilson (1978) points out that socio-spatial segregation limits access to education and jobs independent of the direct discrimination that might generate segregation in the first place; this means that segregation is a process which actively nourishes racism, ensuring that people living in segregated communities are trapped by structural conditions that confirm their marginalization. For this reason, segregated settlements ought to be understood as outcomes of complex economic and social forces leading to exclusion and control (ibid.). The physical separation of communities also fosters distrust and hostility between Roma and the majority; over time a lack of interaction fuels misunderstanding, stereotypes and scapegoating. Symbolic boundaries between communities are mirrored in physical separation. Of course, we do see some communities deliberately choosing to inhabit segregated spaces, usually migrants living in major cities in the global North as a strategy for survival or to foster a sense of belonging and social cohesion. Communities also adapt to survive, to make the best of the environment they inhabit, which gives rise to associations of Roma communities wanting to live in segregated settlements, as if this were the result of an autonomous decision. Segregation is one component of a much larger housing issue for Roma across Europe; this includes security of tenure, which leads to frequent evictions, habitability, location, affordability, discrimination in accessing housing, access to public utilities such as gas, water and electricity, and the impact of housing on education, healthcare and employment. In a survey conducted by the Fundamental Rights Agency in 2011, it was found that 26 per cent of Roma lived in homes without piped water compared with 6 per cent for non-Roma and 30 per cent of Roma surveyed confirmed that the main reason they lived where they did was eviction or relocation (by the state) (FRA 2011). It should be noted that less segregation does not necessarily mean more contact or integration for marginalized groups (Bonilla-Silva 2013), as discrimination against Roma is rife no matter where Roma live.

EVICTION AND EXCLUSION

Before proceeding to a focus on segregation, it is necessary first to consider the issue that is generating the most attention today regarding housing and Roma: evictions. This aggressive punitive measure serves to further marginalize already vulnerable communities. In recent years there have been evictions of Roma in France, Italy, Bulgaria, Serbia, Slovakia, Spain, Romania and the UK, among others. To give two examples in Istanbul (Turkey) and Miskolc (Hungary), we have recently witnessed the deliberate wholesale destruction of neighbourhoods and homes, dispersing communities, families and people's way of life. The provision of housing falls to the state as only it can address the housing needs of Roma by adopting the necessary legislative, administrative, financial and social measures, but to date states have been unwilling or unable to address the housing needs of Roma, and, more worryingly, they have actively exacerbated the socio-spatial exclusion of Roma. Amnesty International and the European Roma Rights Centre argue that 'much state-sanctioned exclusion fuels anti-Roma discrimination within society, seriously jeopardizing any progress for Roma' (2015). When discussing agency with regard to social-spatial exclusion, I understand the state as comprising national governments as well as local authorities, police, municipalities and mayors, for these institutions are the arms of the state and implement housing policies. The eviction of Roma is possible because many Roma inhabit non-regularized dwellings or lack the documentation to prove that they are residents. Roma have been evicted and relocated in zones of exclusion; this is the case of Pata Rât, a rubbish dump in Cluj-Napoca, Romania, where eighty Roma families live – a total of 400 people living on the dump itself and another 2,100 in the surrounding areas, an estimated 1,500 of whom are children (http://www.small stepsproject.org/dump-projects/romania-cluj/). Pata Rât has been in existence for twenty years, but 50 per cent of the people who live there now have been previously evicted from Cluj proper at various times. The presence of Roma living on a rubbish dump is a telling metaphor for how Roma are viewed by the state: as detritus, waste, polluting, a stain that needs to be removed. Relocating Roma to a rubbish dump communicates a dehuman-izing effect to those who reside there, and evokes Fanon's argument of the depersonalization of colonized subjects, consigned 'to a zone of non-being' (1968: 2). At the same time, it demonstrates how social distancing is enacted and how interaction between Roma and non-Roma is made more limited, with any interaction reinforcing an already clearly defined power discrepancy between those who belong in society and those who do not. Residents and civil society complain about conditions and believe that it is stigmatizing to live in Pata Rât, which impacts on collective identity and understandings of belonging. Stefan Luca from the European Roma Rights Centre (ERRC) maintains that 'if we can apply this concept of citizenship in a city, to belonging to that city, that's clearly there and there's this discourse from the authorities that they're not our citizens essentially, they're not from this city, they came here from God knows where' (interview, Budapest, October 2015). So, if the assumption that Roma do not belong in or to a particular territory is accepted, then policies of eviction become justified and even acceptable.

There exists a raft of international political commitments on the responsibilities of states towards Roma in housing. In 2009, the Council of the EU called upon the Commission and member states to take the Common Basic Principles on Roma Inclusion into account when formulating social inclusion policies. It states: 'All inclusion policies aim to insert the Roma in the mainstream of society (mainstream educational institutions, mainstream jobs, and mainstream housing). Where partially or entirely segregated education or housing still exists, Roma inclusion policies must aim to overcome this legacy' (Council of the European Union 2009). The Organization for Security and Cooperation in Europe's (OSCE) *Action Plan on Improving the Situation of Roma/Sinti* (2003) requires participating states to 'ensure that Roma housing projects do not foster ethnic and/or racial segregation', and in 2008 the OSCE and the Office for Democratic Institutions and Human Rights (ODIHR) highlighted that

Roma are frequently pushed to the margins of society, which leads to residential segregation. The Decade of Roma Inclusion (2005–15) had four priority areas, one of which was housing, but it has failed to make substantial progress on this issue for various structural reasons including persistent Romaphobia in diverse policy fields. Local authorities are often influenced by prevailing anti-Roma prejudices and attitudes that inform decision-making on housing (FRA 2009: 50). But proving deliberate housing segregation is challenging, as it is not possible to mitigate against other variables including individual choice. Additionally, there are no specific laws prohibiting housing segregation on racial or ethnic grounds: laws centre on guards against non-discrimination by local authorities and private owners. Segregation translates as the grouping of individuals with similar social features within given geographical or social boundaries, and in essence means significant social isolation of one group from another. The need to address the segregation of Roma is recognized by many states, although insufficient resources coupled with inadequate political will has meant that there has been little change. However, interventions such as the *Strategy of the Slovak Republic for the Integration of Roma up to 2020* demonstrate that states acknowledge the problems relating to residential segregation even if they fail to deliver.

Voluntary segregation of a given group is defensive in its nature. It enables the group to survive in a foreign environment, maintain its language and culture. Forced segregation initiated by the majority society is tied to endangerment of such group, and often comes in a form of social exclusion and ghettoizing. Racial and ethnic segregation occurring on an informal level in various areas leads to inequality, differences in living conditions, gaps in the accessibility of services of the majority population on one hand and ethnically or racially different group on the other – in the field of education, housing and employment. Segregation results in inequality of opportunities and inequality in the access to basic services. Desegregation thus means the elimination of structural and institutional discrimination.

GOVERNMENT OF SLOVAKIA 2012

On the other hand, desegregation could mean that communities will disappear, and residents are resistant as it disrupts community cohesion as well as practical concerns such as schooling. Understandably, people are reticent about moving from their homes as they would have new neighbours who might be hostile to incoming Roma; they therefore prefer to stay in areas with a dense Romani demography. Desegregation could also be used to destroy Romani communities through dispersal and could be deployed as a tool to justify evictions. In Hungary, the Czech Republic and Slovakia there exist ghettos of social housing, often former workers' housing under communism, that have relatively large Roma populations; these have been systematically neglected by the authorities, which are the official landlords. Now these ghettos of social housing are dilapidated and the authorities want to relocate Roma in various ways, including by changing the rules of tenancy so that every minor infraction such as missing a payment for a month becomes a reason for eviction, or, in the case of Miskolc, the authorities essentially tried to bribe Roma to move out of the municipality. In towns across Transylvania, Romania, there are mayors who evoke the exalted status of citizens who are hardworking and productive and argue that Roma do not fit this vision, do not work, and are undesirable, and therefore their exclusion and expulsion can be justified – usually with overwhelming support from non-Roma locals (interview with Stefan Luca, Budapest, October 2015).

States are also compelled to counter local measures such as the unlawful expulsion of Roma as well as the placing of Roma in camps outside populated areas that are isolated and without access to basic services (UNCERD 2000). The United Nations Committee on the Elimination of Racial Discrimination (UNCERD) notes that complete or partial racial segregation may have been created in some states by governmental policies as well as by the actions of private agents, but it maintains that 'a condition of racial segregation can also arise without any initiative or direct involvement by the public authorities' (1995). The issues of eviction and segregation are intertwined due to the precarious position and tenuous claims to legally reside on a piece of land. Municipalities frequently evict Roma because the municipality needs to develop the land; a compact community of Roma is then told to move elsewhere, where they will be able to build another settlement, with the municipality often helping the process along by offering materials. So, local authorities deal differently with Roma than they would with non-Roma, treating Roma collectively rather than on a case-by-case basis, which means that the whole community is uprooted and moved. What is more, they are treated differently because of the informality with which they are treated: Roma are frequently not given legal residents' documentation by the state – which would be given to non-Roma who are moved – which would protect them from potential eviction in the future. Roma are simply told, 'Just go to that field,' as if it doesn't matter where they reside. Authorities in the future might move Roma again, arguing that Roma people are not from that locale, and a cycle of destabilized belonging continues unabated. Taken together, this will inevitably impact on perceptions of belonging and inclusion: Roma are seen as having no roots and no fixed position in society, and norms of 'home' are not extended to Roma or protected equally by the state.

SEGREGATION: A MODERN-DAY APARTHEID

Segregation refers to settlements or areas that are Roma-only or that have a predominantly Roma population. Non-Roma who live alongside Roma are typically on the margins of society too, often unemployed and suffering

discrimination due to their proximity to Roma populations. Segregated areas can be neighbourhoods in the
capital city, regional hubs, small towns and villages, as well
as informal settlements, halting sites and camps, and their
location can be very central, peripheral or remote (FRA
2009: 77). Roma living in segregated settlements may be
more susceptible to violent racist attacks: in 2008–09, nine
Roma were murdered as a result of fire bombs and shoot-
ings, evoking memories of the Deep South in the USA in
the 1950s (Vágvölgyi 2014). One of the central features of
these attack was that victims often lived on the edges of
Roma settlements, ensuring that the victim was Romani
and the perpetrators could make a safe getaway. Attacks
like this are not confined to Eastern Europe, as affirmed
by the racist attacks on Roma in Belfast, Northern Ireland,
where Roma were accused by locals, usually working-class
loyalists, of stealing scarce housing in a desirable location,
with hundreds of Roma having to seek refuge in a church
nearby (Clark and Rice 2012).

Nesime Salioska runs an NGO called ROMA S.O.S.
(http://romasosprilep.org/language/en/) in the town of
Prilep in Macedonia, in a Roma settlement called Trizla.
She outlines the issues facing isolated and segregated
Roma communities:

> Roma communities are always on the margins so road
> infrastructure, access to water supply, access to elec-
> tricity is not fixed. Transportation is a problem and
> urbanization is a problem in Roma communities, so if

you see all these problems it looks like society wants Roma to stay in this condition, in a cycle of problems where poverty is the main one. This is because of the prejudiced stereotypes, anti-Gypsyism that society still has against Roma.

INTERVIEW, PRILEP, JUNE 2015

Trizla is on the outskirts of town and the local authorities have not invested the area with the same resources and infrastructure as the rest of Prilep in terms of roads, healthcare and education. For example, in some parts the asphalt paving stops when the streets inhabited by ethnic Macedonians end and Trizla begins, and those roads that are paved are often blighted by potholes and uneven surfaces. Other streets and paths lack paving and have mud tracks instead, which residents, some elderly, have to negotiate to go about their daily business. Access to healthcare is tenuous because the nearest health facility to Trizla is 1 kilometre away; if an urgent ambulance is called from Trizla it can take up to an hour to arrive, compared with the 10 minutes it is supposed to take. This is due to poor access to the roads and the fact that there are no proper addresses: there are no officially registered street names or numbers and so healthcare providers cannot find those in need in order to deliver services. The nearest school to Trizla is just outside the settlement in an ethnic Macedonian neighbourhood, but when Roma children increased in numbers in the school, non-Roma Macedonian parents started pulling their kids out and sending them to schools in the centre of town, away from Roma. Now the school is up to 90 per cent Roma. This is segregation and it sends a clear message of belonging to the nation: 'Roma feel themselves as part of the Macedonian nation but the problem is that there is still so much marginalization from society which is why they feel so different and they don't feel like part of society' (interview with Nesime Salioska, Prilep, June 2015). A coordinated input from local authorities will ensure not only that Roma are better able to access institutions and services but that local government is doing its job in providing for its residents, because local government has the primary role and responsibility regarding these issues.

Figure 4.1 Street paving stops where the ethnic Macedonian street ends and Trizla begins

Segregation reveals how boundaries produce territory, while separation actively orders space and produces
hierarchies of belonging. Sack's definition of territoriality emphasizes the attempt by individuals or groups
to 'affect, control and influence people and relationships
by delimiting and asserting control over a geographic
area' (1986: 19). So, power is not a thing to be possessed;
rather, it is constantly produced and is a dynamic process
that generates discourses and creates attitudes, part of
which delineates belonging and identity (Novak 2011).
This process is negotiated at different scales, and, for
Roma communities, it is overwhelmingly characterized
by zones of exclusion in states and societies, and not just
by the geographic and material marginalization of Roma
communities but also by the active exclusion of Roma from
public life. Moreover, power is exercised not only over
the control of a space but through the capacity to create
space, because the application of territoriality reflects the
needs and values of those who design and maintain such
spaces (Penrose 2002: 280). When the mayor of Baia Mare
in Romania built a wall around a Roma settlement in
2013, this demonstrated how normalized the socio-spatial
exclusion of Roma has become and how latent Romaphobia informs policymaking decisions. It should be
noted that the spatial positioning of Roma is the territorial expression of social inequalities created by the state:
spatial exclusion is both a cause and a consequence of
social inequalities, and marginalization is created by both
social and spatial processes (Vincze et al. 2015: 5). Roma

do not possess the power to create spaces even if the majority views Roma as existing on the margins of society by choice. Paradoxically, Roma communities are highly visible even though they often reside on the margins of society and they are used by political entrepreneurs to generate electoral support. The segregation of Roma, in tandem with expulsion, deportation and eviction of Roma communities (not just Roma individuals), produces a sense of territorial belonging in which Roma come to be understood as inhabiting particular liminal spaces because they are Roma; this is a product of Romaphobia.

Neighbourhoods, villages, cities, states, nations and regions all give rise to a sense of belonging, partly because of direct personal experiences and partly because of mediated experiences as well as socially and culturally ascribed meanings (Anderson 1991; Gustafson 2009). Conceptions of belonging and home are built around static understandings of space and become tied to an identity that defines who belongs to a space and who does not (Kabachnik 2010a; 2010b). In her study of Roma in Russia, anthropologist Lemon maintains that 'Roma nevertheless are and speak of themselves as connected to local places and pasts' (2000: 3), while Gay y Blasco (1999) believes that Spanish Roma (*Gitanos*) do not have a strong connection to place partly because the authorities have constantly intervened through resettlement programmes and have not allowed Roma communities to establish roots (cited in Kabachnik 2010a). This suggests that Roma have little choice but to abide by local government decisions, but we should recognize that an absence of objection on the part of Roma points to structural inequalities in the realization of political decisions. A word on agency is in order when we discuss territory and belonging because 'when people create territories, they create boundaries that both unite and divide space along with everything that it contains ... *territories give physical substance and symbolic meaning* to notions of "us" and "them" and "ours" and "theirs"' (Penrose 2002: 280, emphasis added). That is to say, boundaries not only constitute the basis for material needs but also create an association with a specific space so that a people come to be associated with a territory. It follows that stigmatization of a people means stigmatization of a territory and vice versa. More to the point, inhabiting a territory possesses an emotional power, so people have 'deep feelings of belonging; of feeling "at peace" and secure, or "at home"' (ibid.: 281).

The potential depth of such emotional attachments can be seen when people are forcibly removed from their homes, as was the case in the Sulukule neighbourhood in Istanbul, which was home to a Roma community of 5,000. Sulukule is an area associated with immorality (due to its previous links with entertainment houses, prostitution and drugs) and became the target of an urban renewal project in 2005 when Prime Minister Erdoğan stated his intention of 'cleaning away the monstrosity' (Karaman and Islam 2012: 236). It is important to recognize how Romaphobia informs policies of eviction or segregation, and that interventions by state agencies are only possible due to the presence of narratives that construct 'them and us', which determine who belongs and who does not: 'the construction of boundaries at all scales and dimensions takes place through narrativity' (Newman and Paasi 1998: 195). In the case of Sulukule, the politics of boundary-making is informed by Romaphobia, an exclusionary discourse from outsiders that reinforces the community's introversion and boundaries by othering Roma as noisy, immoral, lazy and criminal, and that subsequently served as 'a pretext for urgent state intervention' (Karaman and Islam 2012: 242). Another discourse informed by Romaphobia relates to questions concerning integration or assimilation, whereby the residents of Sulukule are being saved from themselves through the benevolent intervention of a state in which these deviant subjects can be integrated. Suffice to say, how this result would be best realized through eviction is not exactly clear. The intention of the renewal project is to evict Roma, to clear this 'slum', to disperse a community with the hope that this will do the job of integration.

As a corollary, Romaphobia informs discourses on integration by justifying eviction and deportation in France, the state that evicts more Roma than any other (in 2013, the Human Rights League estimated that 21,000 Roma were evicted). Manuel Valls, then Interior Minister and now Prime Minister, said in a radio interview that 'those people [Roma migrants] have lifestyles that are extremely different from ours. For this reason, they should return to Bulgaria or Romania' (Amnesty International 2014: 15).

This view is supported by the majority, with 77 per cent seeing Roma as a separate group and 'not part of French society'. It is not surprising, therefore, that the state can act with relative impunity in evicting Roma communities en masse due to dominant narratives that construct an understanding not only of 'them and us' but also of belonging to the nation and to the state. The exalted national subject is protected by the state from unwanted elements who are not part of the nation.

Displacement of Roma communities in Eastern and Western Europe is motivated by Romaphobia and has had a similar impact. Under socialist regimes, states sidestepped a commitment to ethnic desegregation by removing Roma communities from city centres to spaces where they remained invisible and away from public services. However, after 1989 many former socialist cities became subject to neoliberal land and housing restructuring, which meant that many Roma were evicted due to the competition for desirable urban space. Ivancheva (2015) reveals how Roma in Sofia were historically segregated into ethnic *mahalas*; these contained Roma within a quarantined space where responsibility lay with the local mayor, meaning that majority representatives could ignore the issues facing Roma, which in turn were exacerbated by spatial segregation. Analysing the intersection between ethnicity and class, Ivancheva (ibid.: 51) demonstrates how mechanisms 'produced Roma as an abject group during and after state socialism ... [and] in the aftermath of state socialism, marginalized groups were increasingly dealt with as surplus populations residing on land of growing financial value'. The poor living conditions were understood by state authorities as being caused by ethno-cultural factors that would, in turn, conveniently justify the removal of Roma communities from urban spaces. A study of the gentrification of District VIII in Budapest, a predominantly Roma area known as Józsefváros, confirms that the intersection of Romaphobia and class, where the state withdraws welfare protection, scapegoats poor and marginalized communities, including Roma, and results in regulations that directly support spatial exclusion and the criminalization of poverty (Czirfusz et al. 2015). Those residing in Józsefváros are not seen as deserving the regenerated housing stock, new apartments and amenities, and are forced out by rising rent charges. Housing policies are elaborated that clear the way for neoliberal reforms: Roma communities are removed due to perceived ethno-cultural characteristics regarded as incompatible with neoliberalism.

IN THE GHETTOS

In order to better understand the interplay between territoriality, belonging, identity and Romaphobia, I conducted field research in two large Roma settlements, or ghettos: Šuto Orizari (Macedonia) and Lunik IX (Slovakia). 'Ghetto' is a term loaded with negative associations; it typically is understood as an area of ethnic homogeneity, spatial confinement and shared cultural identity, with residents of ghettos often retreating into the private sphere as opposed to investing in the community (Wacquant 2008; Powell 2013). The term 'settlement' is also problematic as it implies choice on the part of those doing the settling when the reality is that those residing in Roma ghettos or settlements lack the capacity to determine where they live. The purpose of the research was to explore the function of territory in the process of exclusion and the role that Romaphobia plays in the creation of socio-spatial arrangements for Roma. It was motivated by the conviction that where things happen is important in understanding how and why things happen (Warf and Arias 2009). This is not an ethnographic study comparing two Roma settlements and the lives of Roma who inhabit such spaces. I am more interested in how Romaphobia is manifest in state and societal practices, including segregation, and what the persistence of spatial exclusion of Roma reveals about understandings of belonging and identity. The state, acting through local authorities and agencies, elevates some spaces as it marginalizes others: Roma are removed from spaces where they do not belong, which is then populated by exalted subjects, and placed on the margins of society in out-of-sight, hard-to-reach spaces where they are considered to belong.

Šuto Orizari

Šuto Orizari is a Roma settlement in Skopje, the capital of Macedonia, and is one of the largest Roma settlements in the world; the official population is 22,000, but estimates suggest that 30,000 to 40,000 is more accurate. The number of Roma is underestimated; officially Roma number 52,000 in Macedonia but the actual number is over 200,000. The living conditions of Roma in Macedonia are very poor, with 95 per cent of Roma concentrated in urban areas and 28 per cent living in makeshift homes in poor settlements, often in illegal buildings (Skenderi 2014: 11). After an earthquake in 1963 destroyed Skopje's Roma quarter, Šuto Orizari emerged for displaced Roma on a site that the government selected in the north of the city, on a rubbish dump, away from the centre. In 1996, it became designated as a district and is now the only Roma-majority municipality in the world; Romanes is the official language. Šuto Orizari, known as Šutka by locals, has swelled and sprawled to include a variety of brick houses and apartments, some with gardens filled with hens, as well as ramshackle dwellings on narrow lanes on the outskirts of the settlement. The living conditions of residents are highly diverse and depend on a number of factors. There is a small park, a market, shops, government buildings and a TV station, and the area is dominated by a large mosque for the predominantly Muslim Roma community that lives there. Šuto Orizari is the product of a deliberate attempt by successive Macedonian governments to ghettoize the Roma community, an attempt that has faced little resistance from Roma themselves, particularly the Romani political elite, who are to some extent complicit in this spatial exclusion. But the ghettoization of Roma in Šuto Orizari is actually the result of gerrymandering that took place in the 1990s to curb the

political power of ethnic Albanians, who present a secessionist threat in Macedonia. Still, the fact that Roma own
the municipality and possess control of the governance
structures of the local authority represents an opportunity
to improve the lives of Roma living there, not least because
the political elite can focus on the needs and interests of
the inhabitants of Šuto Orizari. While the problems facing
the Roma community in Šuto Orizari are typical of those
of Roma across Europe, one political leader, Samka Ibraimovski, argues that poverty is the key issue and that the
unemployment levels of Roma are staggering (interview,
Skopje, June 2015). It is estimated that 90 per cent of the
residents of Šuto Orizari receive the €30 a month welfare
payment, and that they supplement this by selling goods
at the market, collecting glass, scrap metal and paper,
begging, and collecting plastic to recycle (Sudetic 2013).

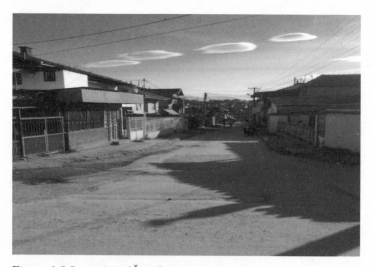

Figure 4.2 Street view of Šuto Orizari

Residents of Šuto Orizari have elected Romani political representatives to the governance structures administering the settlement. There have been efforts to increase commercial activities in the settlement and office space has been built, but much of the space remains vacant. Such initiatives have been undertaken by the current mayor, Elvis Bajram, who is the son of prominent political leader and MP Amdi Bajram. Residents I spoke to complained that the mayor is corrupt and does nothing for the people of Šuto Orizari, and that the same political elite is elected time and time again. The allegiance between Roma political representatives in Šuto Orizari and the mainstream political elite is highly problematic because Roma-elected representatives become dependent on the majority for support; this means that they are not as critical of successive inadequate policies as they ought to be. Mainstream parties select coalition partners from Roma political parties that they can control and manipulate, which means that mainstream (non-Roma) parties set the agenda in terms of what Roma politicians can actually fight for. Asmet Elezovski is the director of an NGO, the National Roma Centre, and argues that the state uses the status of a single Roma community to attract political and financial support for itself, but it does not act in the interests of Roma. He believes that Roma political representatives are complicit in supporting institutions that do not have the needs of Roma at heart (interview, June 2015). The upshot is that, even in areas where Roma constitute the majority and have political representatives in post, they do not possess power to control budgets or policies.

Political representatives have not managed to improve the employment prospects of Roma living in Šuto Orizari, resulting in a weak tax basis. Part of the issue is that all municipalities are controlled and managed by local self-governments, meaning that, in effect, Roma do not have control over decisions that affect them. Municipalities depend on income from utilities such as water and electricity but only a small part of this goes to the local municipality: Šuto Orizari is dependent on funds from central authorities that are controlled by non-Roma, and the lack of coordination results in poor planning and policy implementation – for example, the high school was built in Šuto Orizari six years ago but still doesn't function.

Nedjo Mehmed is an activist and vice president of a political party, Roma Alliance. He believes that segregation is a problem in Macedonia and is due to the actions of non-Roma: 'the reason why non-Roma want Roma to be segregated and confined to one place is because non-Roma want Roma to be poor and to be on a minimal employment; they want to have control over them' (interview, Skopje, June 2015). He argues that Roma feel that they are not a distinct nation in the Macedonian state, and because Roma are not on an equal footing with other communities, including ethnic Macedonians and Albanians, Roma are seen as second-class citizens. Roma may be recognized in the constitution as a minority but in reality this does not translate into appropriate policy provisions because, in the eyes of the majority, 'Roma do not belong to the majority nation'. This separation of Roma into settlements and other areas with a dense Roma demography is an expression of the spatialized power of the state: Roma are confined to Roma settlements with self-governance restricted by the very institutions that marginalize them. Roma are labelled according to name, area of residence, skin colour, poverty and how they dress, which provides the opportunity for discrimination: they are a visible minority removed from public life.

In 1996, Šuto Orizari was designated as an electoral district and Nezdet Mustafa became the first mayor of the largest municipality of Roma in Europe, serving two terms. In 2006, he began his first mandate as a member of parliament. He is now a minister of the government of Macedonia (albeit without a portfolio) responsible for the implementation of the national strategy and action plans on Roma, and as such is one of the highest-ranking Roma politicians in Europe. In a familiar refrain, he laments the fact that Roma citizens have not been active participants in society but have been only observers of the progress of other majority and minority (Albanian) communities. His intention, when he became mayor, was to harness the demographic strength of Roma and pivot this into a political movement by getting more Roma to vote, since he regards voting as a tool to achieve progress for the community. He argues that non-Roma representatives are afraid of the self-organization of Roma, the power that Roma could generate, and therefore do not support efforts at self-governance. In 1996, when the first Roma-controlled municipality was established, where Roma could govern their own lives, an opportunity emerged to show that Roma could manage a budget and use that budget for useful actions, for example to improve the education system in Šuto Orizari. The intention here was to send a message: 'With one goal I wanted to extinguish the stereotype that Roma are not able to care for themselves' (interview with Nezdet Mustafa, Skopje, 15 June 2015). His aim was to 'transform the Roma community from one which begs for help to one who would take control of their own destinies and use their votes and political authority to take the official and legal status which they deserve in Macedonia'. He concedes that Roma problems persist, notably high levels of unemployment, and that 'Roma still do not live in very good, urbanized municipalities and we are still facing the stereotypes, discrimination and humiliation in certain instances'. While changing this perception is difficult, it is hampered by persistent Romaphobia. Interestingly, he points out that 'Romaphobia is a product of the inactive participation of Roma in politics and government'. Roma are citizens and so possess a right to vote; this should translate into political power but many Roma do not engage in politics, which is in line with Anne Phillips' (1998) argument regarding the politics of presence: if you are present and visible in public life then your interests are less likely to be ignored or assumed by others. But this stance sidesteps Romaphobia within the political institutions of the state, which conspire to suppress the needs of Roma communities and actively mark Roma as second-class citizens.

Minister Mustafa argues that Roma should not be subject to ghettoization processes that result in very poor standards of living, although he points to the affected and practical dimension of community living in Šuto Orizari:

> This community where Roma live, or what other people might call a ghetto, it's the soul of our community, this is where people are raising their children and this is an important place for them. And if someone tries to disperse or evict them to another place, then this community will lose their historical value. Living in such communities helps us to preserve our culture and we must resist assimilation efforts.
>
> INTERVIEW, SKOPJE, JUNE 2015

The state should improve the conditions in Šuto Orizari, invest in new schools, open new kindergartens, increase the employment levels and 'instead of building walls and separating the citizens they should give them the opportunity to actively participate in the political race to create a better future for the whole country'. He sees the improvement of the position of Roma as beneficial for Macedonia, not solely for Roma communities, and links this objective to the realization of full citizenship for Roma, and European citizenship, while destabilizing the power of Romaphobia:

It is not true that Roma are not interested in being integrated, this is vocabulary which non-Roma use. The
main point is to give this community a real chance for
integration and improve the situation that they are
living in to become an equal partner in society. Crucial
to this is to minimize the stereotypes of the majority
towards Roma.

Territorial governance is mediated by a range of other
factors, including the interplay between space and
belonging. Clearly there are arguments that advocate the
conditions for a liveable life, which, according to Tyler
(2013: 12), involve 'being able to lay down roots, feel safe,
to create a family and home, to belong to a community
and to have some sense of a better future'. She argues that
'what disenfranchised people actively desire is not *flight*
but *anchorage*' (ibid., emphasis in original). But segregated
settlements and spatial marginalization are an expression of state power and absolutely reinforce the social
abjection of Roma communities, even if they provide
a context for a community to develop. With its market,
media centre, and kids in the street playing sport, Šuto
Orizari certainly conveys the impression of a community,
and for the various residents I spoke to, it is still home to
all intents and purposes. I interviewed the imam of the
mosque in Šuto Orizari, Ali Berat, who argued that people
living there do not want to destroy the community; they
want to improve it with better infrastructure and services,
jobs and education. They want to stay and make it better

because it is their home and where they belong (interview, Skopje, June 2015). Roma settlements allow communities to survive and self-sustain through the appropriation and demarcation of territory, but they also entrap and isolate communities through Romaphobia. Residents of Šuto Orizari generate feelings of solidarity and belonging from inhabiting this space but this comes at a price: the majority 'others' Roma as not belonging to the nation precisely because of this communal existence confirmed by physical exclusion.

Politically, Roma participate as Roma and are invariably represented by other Roma, which suggests that mainstream political architecture (including political parties) is not for them. Roma issues are dealt with by Roma representatives, as if Roma are not subject to the same curriculum in school or are not competing with non-Roma in the job market. Integration is both a carrot and a stick. Roma communities certainly have the right to inhabit parts of the city or the state they choose because they are citizens, but equally they have the right to be different, to attend to cultural norms and foster Roma identity, irrespective of how the majority views such efforts (Karaman and Islam 2012). Having a mayor or control of a municipality is only empowering if the needs and interests of Roma in Šuto Orizari are being met: the continued exclusion and stigmatization of Roma, coupled with rampant unemployment, poverty and a lack of opportunities, means that Roma continue to be oppressed (interview with Ali Berat, Skopje, June 2015). The Network for Protection from

Discrimination (NPD), an alliance of NGOs in Macedonia, notes that because Roma in Macedonia are often victims of discrimination and prejudice, 'they do not feel safe in ethnically-mixed environments and are often prone to self-segregation' (NPD 2015: 3). Engaging in a political system that supports Roma exclusion may appear as if Roma are indirectly supporting mechanisms of oppression but in fact accentuates the paradox of segregation and how belonging and identity are negotiated within and across different scales of the state.

Lunik IX

According to the Roma ATLAS project, which mapped the Roma population of Slovakia in 2013, out of the estimated 403,000 Roma, 24 per cent live in settlements on the outskirts of municipalities while 17 per cent live in segregated communities (ATLAS 2014). That means that over 40 per cent live in areas with little interaction with the majority, which is fertile ground for the growth of stereotypes and scapegoating. The most notorious Roma settlement in terms of news coverage and international attention is Lunik IX, a district of the city of Košice in eastern Slovakia, which was built in 1979 and began as a desirable area for the state elite under the socialist regime. Initially, it was used to house army and police personnel as well as a limited number of Roma and was regarded as a modern suburb with a shopping centre and two kindergartens; even then, the area was segregated between Roma and non-Roma (Magdonelová 2003). Many of the Roma who now live in Lunik IX used to inhabit town houses in the city centre, but the city officials of Košice initiated a 'social experiment' in 1987; this was the turning point for Roma living in the city centre, and they were relocated to Lunik IX in huge numbers. Due to the modernization of the city centre it became more desirable to live there, and so Roma were relocated (Hušová 2010). Roma were crammed into flats, sometimes with several unrelated families sharing an apartment, and the number of Roma inhabiting Lunik IX swelled to approximately 6,000 people. Roma were taken from other parts of the city where they were not wanted and put into Lunik IX, so local authorities actively created this Roma ghetto. In 1997, Košice city council, led by Rudolf Schuster (who would later become the President of Slovakia), announced a lucrative $50 million public–private partnership to gentrify and beautify the city. Part of the plan was to evict some 25,000 Roma from the centre and move them to segregated areas, including Lunik IX; housing in this area would be substandard and specifically for Roma (Farnam 2003). The drive to segregate Roma was thus a product of state intervention and public–private partnerships, with the latter then privatizing the housing sector: the visible presence of Roma in the centre of the city was not the image of Košice that officials wanted to project.

One of the main housing issues has been the rapid deterioration of Lunik IX: Roma have no stake in the district because many don't own their apartments, they don't feel they belong there, they have no investment in fostering a community, and many simply seek a way to get out. Some have managed to do so and have moved into other accommodation around the city or have been able to move abroad. I visited three apartment blocks dotted around the city, sites where a select number of Roma have been moved on from Lunik IX due to overcrowding. All of these blocks are much more desirable than living in Lunik IX as they have heating, water and electricity, which many residents of Lunik IX do not have. Facilities and services in Lunik IX are limited: there is a kindergarten; a high school that trains pupils in vocational qualifications such as construction work and tailoring; some grocery shops; a police patrol vehicle but no police station; no post office, although postal workers do deliver; and a group of Salesian monks who have been present in Lunik IX for years and attempt to improve the living conditions (and faith) of residents. The church owns several of the apartments, and these are typically in better condition as they are maintained by the church. As the city has now officially condemned and demolished some of the apartment blocks of Lunik IX, a question remains over where the residents will be moved to.

Lunik IX has been created by Romaphobia, which structures living conditions, exacerbates marginalization, and precludes any opportunities to make a better life. One former resident of Lunik IX is documentary filmmaker Artur Conka, whose family moved to the UK in the 1990s and who returned to make a film about the lives of the residents. He notes that Lunik IX:

turned into an unrecognizable ghetto with no way out
for those who live there, trapped by poverty and prejudice. Some blame the collapse of communism. Although
lacking in freedom, communism was like a sticky glue
that bound everyone together, and my mum and dad
said they would never have left had it not collapsed,
because everyone had jobs and decent housing, and
there was better integration between Roma and ethnic
Slovaks, who shared the same houses, schools and jobs.
In the 1990s the local factories closed, and since recruit-
ment methods for smaller employers were relaxed,
old prejudices against Roma resurfaced and Romani
inhabitants of Lunik IX found it much harder to get
work than their Slavic neighbours. As unemployment
rose, debts mounted and one by one, utility companies
cut off services to the local area for everyone, whether
they were able to pay or not. The council did not treat
the problem as a priority, reducing the waste collection
services instead. Promises were made to find the local
population work but they never materialized.

So, Lunik IX traps people in a cycle of poverty and
exclusion, one that fuels anti-Roma prejudices. A social
worker who works at Lunik IX believes that negative
stereotypes impact on people who live in Lunik IX:
'They are seen as lazy, dirty, uneducated.' But there are
serious problems such as housing quality and a lack of
employment and money. The lack of interaction between
Roma and the majority is an issue because there are no

constructive relationships, meaning that distrust and mutual suspicion often characterize the two communities. Slavka Macakova, the Director of ETP Slovakia, an NGO that focuses on housing issues of Roma, argues that when Roma and non-Roma live alongside one another they can develop common housing projects that benefit the whole community in the locality, but when Roma and non-Roma are segregated, they lack interaction and Roma are frequently excluded by the majority and by local government from participating in projects as well as in community life (interview, Košice, November 2014). She notes that Roma are increasingly segregated, living separate lives from the majority, even as new housing and construction projects are built and as attempts to improve social housing by the government are implemented. In Lunik IX, segregation is not considered the most pressing housing concern; the issue is the quality of housing as the flats are in poor condition – many are uninhabitable – and people do not have wages that they can put into improving their homes. This is made worse by the lack of amenities and services. Only one block, whose residents pay rent, receives electricity and water; the vast majority of the 6,000 people live in flats with no electricity, running water or heating. The outside of the apartment blocks are blackened due to soot from makeshift chimney flues that residents construct in the winter to heat their apartments, something that has serious health ramifications. Water is only accessible for most residents through a number of strategically placed taps that are turned on twice a day:

Figure 4.3 Uncollected rubbish and soot-covered apartments in Lunik IX

in the morning for one hour and again in the afternoon. For those residents of Lunik IX who are working or go to school, sharing a communal tap for an allocated amount of time is highly inadequate and the type of conditions you might expect in the global South. Slovakia has been an EU member since 2004 and Košice was the European City of Culture in 2013.

Non-Roma stay away from Lunik IX and actively contribute to further socio-spatial marginalization. Surrounding districts have tried to remove Roma from sight by erecting a 2 metre high wall; this is ostensibly to protect children from the nearby road, but the effect is to keep Roma out of other districts and confined to Lunik

IX. There have been fourteen concrete walls erected in the city in the past decade, but this is only one of the visible signs of socio-spatial isolation in Slovakia: 'the development of Roma settlements is relegated to the periphery of towns and town life segregated by more "discrete" barriers including distance, empty fields, roads, rivers and police stations' (Filčák and Steger 2014: 239). The erection of walls exacerbates spatial exclusion and even securitizes Roma settlements as a risky area, with unwanted and threatening people living there who are likely to rob and steal, given the opportunity. People who live in such areas are often blamed for their exclusion: residents of a ghetto are there either because of poor choices they have made or worse, in the case of Roma, due to cultural pathology because Roma do not want to integrate, they want to live separate lives. One social worker I interviewed believes that Lunik IX, as a place, stigmatizes residents:

> Most people from the city have never been here but they imagine that it is a disaster. On TV, they make it out like it's a black hole and usually they focus on children playing on the rubbish dump. This picture of Roma from the majority is really wrong. A lot of the stereotypes are about money; they think that every Roma gets something for free, and get special treatment from the state, getting better treatment, they get these super apartments from the social [laughs].
>
> INTERVIEW, LUNIK IX, NOVEMBER 2014

That anyone could believe that Roma get special treatment in Slovakia, or indeed in Lunik IX, seems remarkable. Lunik IX is an abject, desolate place that traps and stigmatizes residents, and where the state is not interested in addressing the housing, health and employment needs. 'Governmental agencies too have stereotypes of what Lunik IX is like and the people who live here: they think all the residents here are glue sniffing, dirty, not living in a normal way, and that they steal.' An elderly resident confirms how the association of Lunik IX stigmatizes people: 'No matter how nice you are dressed and clean, when some government office comes to see you and they see you are from Lunik IX, you are not respected. They don't talk to you like they would if you were from another city district' (interview, Lunik IX, November 2014). One Romani government worker maintains that change must also come from within the Roma community: 'They need to show the majority that we can be integrated because, right now, the majority is scared of them' (interview, Lunik IX, November 2014).

According to another social worker, the lack of community cohesion in Lunik IX is jarring: 'There is no solidarity, no community spirit because everyone is fighting for themselves, to get food, money' (interview, Lunik IX, November 2014). Many Roma who live in Lunik IX come from different family clans, cities, districts and villages; there are sometimes tensions between them and so 'there is no one community'. This is confirmed by one older female resident who had lived in Lunik IX for ten years: 'There is no community spirit. Some people who come and live here don't care about this place, they break windows and don't fix them. People here are kind of lethargic – when they see something wrong, they don't say anything' (interview, Lunik IX, November 2014). She argues that 'this was a really nice area, and a nice part of the city, so it would be OK if normal people who want to live in a community come here so they defend it and make it nice'. It is hardly surprising that people with so little compete over scarce resources. The social worker expresses disbelief that people would choose to live in Lunik IX – 'People are staying here and I don't know why' – but perhaps it is easier for an educated state worker who is not Roma to see routes out of the ghetto. Many Roma choose to stay because they cannot imagine an alternative: if someone has been brought up in Lunik IX, without an education, with parents who do not work, then it is difficult to envisage a life beyond Lunik IX where things could be better. I am not entirely clear if this constitutes choice or resignation about life opportunities.

One Roma leader, who works for the state department on Roma, points to the importance of electing representatives who can formulate a strategy for Lunik IX and can try to solve the various social problems that people who live here endure. The key focus, he argues, should be on addressing poverty, because without money people cannot afford to pay rent and cannot get electricity, heating or water. At the moment, people do not have any hope or any dreams of a better future:

If I was a child living here and my parents were unemployed, my grandparents are unemployed too, and
we are living thirty-six people in one flat. And for two
hours a day we get water, how can I have a dream
about a better life? If someone asks me what I want to
do when I grow up I will say I hope to be able to help
cleaning the street. So, people need to be able to dream
about a better future.

INTERVIEW, LUNIK IX, NOVEMBER 2014

The government does not appear to understand the acute
problems facing Lunik IX as it does not engage with the
area, treating it as a problem environment, and does not
see any potential in terms of investment. The authorities in the city of Košice do not demonstrate any desire
to improve the conditions of Roma who live there. One
resident believes that the government is centralizing
Lunik IX as a social problem by relocating people who are
not paying their rent elsewhere, putting them in Lunik
IX, and these people don't care 'because when they live
in Lunik IX, all they see is dirt and nothing to help them
to improve their lives'. It should be said that many Roma
living in Lunik IX do not show much interest in addressing
the dire conditions there and appear somewhat resigned
to their fate: there are no community organizations, for
instance. When ghettos are neglected and maligned, we
usually see the emergence of NGOs to fill the gaps where
the state has failed, providing much needed services
and community support, but this has not happened in

Lunik IX; here the only real presence of the state is social workers and the police. The only ray of hope in Lunik IX is the kindergarten, which sits like an island in the middle of the ghetto; all 120 children who attend the school are Roma, and around fifty parents also work at the school as support and auxiliary workers, receiving social benefits from the state for this work. Anna Klepacova has been head of the kindergarten for nineteen years and believes that parents are more involved now because they see the benefits of education in terms of accessing employment in the future (interview, Lunik IX, November 2014). For her, education is emancipatory and the only viable option for improving the lives of Roma; the state needs to support such initiatives and contribute to the improvement of Roma lives. At present, Lunik IX is a ghetto that constricts the capacity of its residents, offers no hope or opportunity, and actively stigmatizes those who reside there.

DISCUSSION

Roma are subject to policies of social control activated by the state (either by the government or by local authorities). Stigmatization and socio-spatial isolation motivate these interventions with the result that Roma communities live in segregated settlements that limit their opportunities to access employment and basic services. The state orchestrates socio-spatial segregation as a solution to the Roma 'problem', with Roma physically removed and isolated from mainstream society in settlements that are ethnically homogeneous. These segregated communities are entrapped by economic and other structural forces, which conspire to inhibit mobility out of the ghetto. Attempts to escape are thwarted by the challenges of accessing affordable housing elsewhere, with no guarantee that life somewhere else will be better. What I have argued is that state agents have made a series of housing policy interventions that deliberately encase Roma and actively deny them access to adequate housing in ethnically heterogeneous spaces. One of the crucial impacts of continued marginalization is that 'large segments of the workforce in segregated spaces are simply perceived as being no longer needed by the outside "superior" world. Hence, ghettoization results from a decline in the economic function of an isolated social segment of society' (Filčák and Steger 2014: 232). As a further step, Filčák and Steger (ibid.) convincingly argue that ghettoization is characterized by stigmatization and entrenchment, and in turn is linked to the problem of environmental justice, meaning that communities who are segregated are less likely to have access to clean water and air, which they maintain is a form of environmental racism. The fact that Roma settlements have limited or no access to basic utilities would suggest that such settlements are viewed as not warranting the effort of infrastructural investment, particularly if Roma are unemployed and unable to pay for utilities.

The fact that Šuto Orizari and Lunik IX are ethnically homogeneous and are spatially segregated is important in terms of how the space becomes stigmatized, which means that the residents living there are stigmatized too. The problem is that a false image is built up of Roma as a secretive and secluded community that wants to be isolated, and this image becomes difficult to challenge. Hegemonic discourses emerge of Roma as a problem community on the margins of society who frequently become the scapegoat for various societal ills, but also become understood as the author of their own perceived failures. Roma are seen by the majority to exclude themselves as a strategy for survival and to resist assimilation: they become a relatively closed community, and this fuels suspicion and distrust due to a lack of societal interaction. The state has managed to pull off a great trick: relegating Roma to zones of exclusion in decomposing neighbourhoods and stigmatizing them for choosing to live there. Through spatial marginalization, Roma are 'included through their exclusion'; as the state oscillates between inclusion and exclusion, it produces waste populations but cannot fully expel that waste, since it requires this surplus both to constitute the boundaries of state sovereign power and to legitimize this power (Tyler 2013: 20). The state enforces particular categorical boundaries to help it make sense of its population and understand its potential power, with some populations becoming gradually absorbed into the dominant nation; 'those who do not remain "unassimilated" and coalesce in ethnic enclaves or descend into the urban underclass ("segmented assimilation")' (Wimmer 2013: 30). Perhaps I am overstating the degree and ubiquity of systemic discrimination, but I understand it as absolutely necessary and universally the defining feature of the historical relationship between European states and Roma.

Šuto Orizari and Lunik IX are two of the largest Roma settlements in Europe in different political contexts. Macedonia is not a member of the EU while Slovakia is, but this has not helped curb the activities of the state in delineating socio-spatial exclusion and attendant associations of identity and belonging. While both settlements are ethnically homogeneous and are the product of deliberate interventions by the state, Lunik IX is certainly more abject. Here, the state has simply relieved itself of any responsibility towards the residents (who are EU citizens, it should be noted); there is almost no visible sign of state presence (including the provision of basic services). The most alarming aspect of this has been the hopelessness that characterizes the settlement: residents want out but are forced to stay as they lack the material resources and opportunity to escape. Unlike Lunik IX, Šuto Orizari is a vibrant community with services, activities and opportunities and where people feel invested in their community. Although Roma are contained here, there is still significant interaction with the majority community in markets and a semblance of political representation at different levels. While residents may not feel that they can control the decisions of the municipality, Roma are at least represented.

Socio-spatial segregation of Roma is motivated by Romaphobia, which reinforces societal exclusion. Segregation reveals power dynamics at play in society, with the state possessing the authority through different agencies to exclude and to evict; this is possible because Roma are not regarded by the majority as belonging to a given space, and therefore territory is a crucial factor in determining the subordination and exclusion of Roma in society.

CHAPTER 5

OPRE ROMA!
CHALLENGING
ROMAPHOBIA
THROUGH PRIDE
PROTESTS

So far, I have explored the underlying causes of Romaphobia as well as the impact of anti-Roma prejudice in
segregation policies. Now attention is turned to Roma
agency to demonstrate how Roma are not a helpless
group that acquiesces in the face of persistent persecution but that Roma are actively participating in struggles
to challenge negative associations of Roma identity. This
chapter explores collective mobilization through the
nascent Roma Pride movement. The purpose of Roma
Pride is to improve visibility of Roma in the public sphere,
raise group consciousness, challenge negative stereotypes
and stigmatization, and resist persecution. It is too soon
to determine the impact of recent Pride protests, but such
activities reveal interesting insights about challenging
Romaphobia and raise questions about identity, belonging

and territoriality. Roma Pride also reveals a number of issues for Roma activists. On the one hand, Roma are extremely heterogeneous, with even the endonym 'Roma' being contested, thus building solidarity is difficult; on the other hand, how do activists transform the meaning and content of a group identity which is so vilified? Pride parades concern visibility and presence in the public sphere but Romaphobia is so prevalent that activists must change how the majority understands Roma group identity. Roma Pride is inward-looking, seeking to build solidarity among Roma, and outward-facing as it attempts to challenge how the majority perceive Roma. This chapter addresses conceptual issues concerning the stigmatized identity and persecution of Roma, and focuses empirically on how Roma activists and advocates have begun to mobilize against negative ascriptions of group identity, at the same time as they appropriate public space to improve their visibility (and the narrative of that visibility) in public life.

While Roma experience discrimination as individuals, there is a clear collective dimension to this stigmatization and, more recently, this has become acutely felt by Roma communities across Europe. In a recent survey by the European Commission (2012: 111), 75 per cent of EU citizens believed that Roma are at risk of persecution. Roma are now the target of right-wing rhetoric, which frequently stigmatizes them as thieves, beggars and parasites (Stewart 2012). Political party discourse across Europe has constructed Roma as a 'problem' community, even going as far as to conflate criminality with Roma identity; thus crime is widely regarded as endemic to Roma culture. In response, Roma activists and advocates have mobilized at the national and transnational political levels to challenge how governments are treating Roma communities within their territories (McGarry 2010). However, such reactive interventions have fallen short of the mark because they have failed to substantively address stigmatization, overwhelming negative attitudes towards Roma, and the root causes of Romaphobia. Policy and legal interventions such as anti-discrimination legislation certainly have their place, but dealing with stigmatization requires the transformation of the meaning and content of Roma group identity. Unless Romaphobia is addressed, symbolic boundaries between Roma and the majority will remain intact through active boundary policing (Wimmer 2008). Responses to Romaphobia can weaken symbolic boundaries between groups (by downplaying difference), but they may also result in greater rigidity (when group membership is affirmed and defined in opposition to that of out-groups) (Fleming et al. 2012).

It is in this context that the importance of devising strategies for dealing with Romaphobia becomes more pronounced. De-stigmatization strategies are ways of debunking stereotypes that fuel discriminatory behaviour in order to rebut 'the notion of inferiority' (Lamont 2009: 151). As with other groups who have experienced stig-matization of group identity, such as women, disabled, LGBTIQ and Jews, among others, Roma have a number of options in order to challenge stigmatization. These options are not mutually exclusive. Firstly, a group advances claims regarding their moral worth, membership and even superiority to majority group members (Lamont and Mizrachi 2012). Attempts to integrate and belong will draw upon aspects of group identity which the majority finds positive or acceptable, thus Roma will emphasize their skill as musicians or celebrities with Romany heritage. Again, a positive image of the group is projected to challenge prevailing negative ascriptions of Roma group identity. Secondly, a group confirms its difference by emphasizing its cultural specificity and demands recognition as being equal to the majority. Here, the image of the group is rehabilitated through an articulation of victimhood and injustices (ibid.); Roma activists have emphasized traumatic events in their past, notably the Holocaust, in order to draw attention to ongoing persecution. Finally, the group develops a de-stigmatization strategy based on the affirmation of a collective identity that becomes the basis for collective action, and attempts are made to change the status of the group (Gamson 1995; Bernstein 1997). Such action is inward-looking and attempts to transform affective understandings of group identity by turning shame into pride, but also outward-looking by changing how the group is recognized and understood by the majority. It is in this context that Roma Pride protests have sprung up across Europe, and this is where this chapter will focus. A group is much harder to stigmatize if it is proud of itself and is confident of its place in society. However, Roma Pride is a manifestation of identity politics that has a tendency to essentialize a movement into a bounded block of unified actors, which glosses over the heterogeneity in and across Roma people.

COLLECTIVE IDENTITY AND THE ROMA COMMUNITY

Identity is more than a resource to forge a political consciousness. Jenkins (2008: 106) argues that 'group members, in recognizing themselves as such, effectively constitute that to which they belong'. We can see here that Jenkins is suggesting a self-replicating relationship between identity and belonging. But self-ascription and understanding do not carry much weight without the recognition of others, namely non-group members, that you exist and you are distinct for whatever reason. This is consistent with what we know of identity as both a social process and a product of intersubjective relations. There are two issues with regards to Roma identity. First is the internal incoherence of Roma group identity in terms of what actually constitutes that identity (language, religion, employment, a shared experience or memory of persecution, poverty, etc.), notwithstanding elite efforts to foster a group identity, meaning that no objective criteria exist to determine who is Roma and who is not. Group identification is based on the conviction that group members will see themselves as similar in some ways even if they have different experiences of language, religion, employment, persecution or poverty. Secondly, and more importantly in the context of Romaphobia, the meaning of Roma identity is overwhelmingly constructed by non-Roma, including those hostile to Roma. This chapter will move on from the problems associated with the external classification of Roma discussed elsewhere (McGarry 2014) and the subsequent stereotypes linked to this exercise of power, and will draw attention to the way in which Roma are mobilizing through Pride parades to assert their belonging to broader society.

The emergence of a Roma Pride movement in the last few years reveals a number of identity dilemmas which Roma protestors and activists must negotiate. One is that Roma are too dispersed and too heterogeneous to mobilize into a coherent protest movement. However, diverse groups in the past, including women and LGBTIQ, have mobilized on the basis of their group identity, notwithstanding how fragmented and contested the idea of a 'community' actually is. Structural barriers such as widespread poverty, poor intra-group communication and low levels of education also conspire to impede mobilization efforts and mean that the Roma voices being heard are those who are the most educated and well connected, but this is true for all movements. Moreover, most movements must grapple with the challenge of building solidarity across a heterogeneous group. Another more pertinent dilemma facing Roma activists is that Roma must draw attention to their difference vis-à-vis the majority. This difference is the basis of oppression, negative stereotyping, exclusion and segregation. Activists must change the meaning and content of their group identity, debunk stereotypes, and project a positive image of themselves that will resonate with the majority. It is not enough for Roma to demand fair treatment or equal rights because such claims are likely to be ignored. Pride protestors are publicly celebrating and making visible a group identity that is stigmatized and attempting to change how this group identity is under-stood by Roma themselves and by the majority.

Identities come into being through a process of ethnogen-esis (Roosens 1989), whereby people come to understand themselves as a distinct ethnic group and then sustain this identity over time. Individuals will react to a threatened identity in different ways (Jaspal and Cinnirella 2012), but this chapter is concerned with how the group responds and so the focus is on Roma agency. Roma activists and advocates deploy strategies and develop tactics in order to attain goals or secure interests, usually in the political context (McGarry 2010). As noted in Chapter 3, the elabo-ration of the Roma nation has generated the most attention on this front. Identity is constructed through and against representations held by others in particular socio-political contexts: it is irrelevant whether these representations are 'true' or not. Certainly, they are the product of power relations, but what is important is how the stigma-tized group responds. While research has explored the social-psychological impact on individuals belonging to communities that are stigmatized as deviant or criminal (Howarth 2002) and the strategies developed by these individuals (Lamont 2009), less is known about how identity is 'managed' by the group. Hall (1996: 6) maintains that identity requires a 'process of becoming rather than being: not "who we are" or "where we come from", so much as what we might become, how we have been represented and how that bears on how we might represent ourselves'. There is a danger that stigmatized groups accept the representations projected onto them, which, in turn, can become self-fulfilling prophecies. However, time and time again stigmatized groups have actively challenged these representations and in the process have negotiated their collective identity and symbolic boundaries (Lamont and Fournier 1992), changing how they are seen by others and how they see themselves. Failure to present a united front or some sense of solidarity can mean that movements are ignored or not taken seriously. Public bodies and state institutions demand to know who legitimately constitutes the group and speaks on their behalf so that appropriate policy can be formulated and implemented. So, attempts to fix the content of identities occur exogenously as well as endogenously.

It is not entirely fair to say that Roma are not present or visible in the public sphere, the issue is that this presence is owned and controlled by others such as political parties (mainstream and extreme) and the media, which by and large paints an unfavourable portrait of Roma. Phillips (1998) maintains that presence is enough to ensure that minority groups will be listened to or at least that their interests cannot be ignored, but this presumes causality through mere presence, which is not supported by research. The nascent Roma Pride movement certainly seeks to address the presence and visibility of Roma across Europe, but it also aspires to provide Roma with a voice, something that is conspicuously absent at present. Roma Pride is not simply an attempt to ensure presence in the public sphere: it signifies an effort to resist exclusion by the majority and to affirm cultural validity. But it is unclear how Roma Pride will help improve the very real socio-economic and political marginalization that Roma experience in every state.

VISIBILITY AND PUBLIC SPACE

Not all those who identify as Roma engage in activism, with actual numbers quite small. Those who advocate or engage in activism do not seek to represent their communities as such because defining the parameters of heterogeneous communities is a task fraught with diffi-culties, setting aside the thorny issue of representation for a porous group. Activists and advocates attempt to foster solidarity internally by uniting the group around a common cause but also seek to draw attention exter-nally to the multiple and inter-related socio-economic and political issues facing Roma communities. Suffice to say, even if someone identifies as Roma, it does not mean that they will be an activist, even though they are likely to benefit from any legislative concessions and changes in societal attitudes. One key motivation for activism is to promote visibility, based on the argument that those who are present in public life are less likely to be ignored or have their interests assumed by policymakers acting on their behalf (Phillips 1998). A lack of visibility is the product of fear, oppression, violence, humiliation and internalized prejudice. It could also point to self-censorship in the elaboration of identity or the invisibilizing of Roma through a lack of representation in political and policy debates and a marginalized socio-cultural status (Ross 2008; see also Ayoub 2016). For Roma, the issue is that visibility is not on terms of their own choosing: nationalist parties and other groups construct Roma as a plague, a disease and a parasitic community threatening the fabric of the nation, and negative attitudes are fuelled by relentless negative coverage in the media. Thus, Roma communities are certainly present in the public sphere but they have been placed there by others (including the media and politicians) in order to serve political ends.

Visibility requires a presence in public life and recognition of existence, and is only possible through citizen participation. Ross (2008: 244) argues that 'coming out into the light and demanding social recognition entails a process of self-affirmation, self-identification and the assumption of a political stance'. I am not concerned with self-affirmation or self-identity but how and why Roma use public space to promote visibility and the impact they hope to have. Visibility alone is not enough: the *content* of visibility is important, as the case of stigmatized Roma communities attests. Underwood (2011: 44) notes that visibility is important for fostering acceptance, although it can heighten intolerance as marginalized communities attempt to assert their presence in a public space. If visibility is a strategy for acceptance, then Pride could be counter-productive if it stirs up Romaphobia, at least in the short term. When communities take control of the visibility process and affirm their status in public, it signifies a performance of group identity that carries with it a declaration to be tolerated, understood and accepted. We can speak of visibility as a process which seeks to challenge the cultural codes and discourses that constrain and denigrate Roma communities. Invisibility suggests a refusal of recognition within broader social, cultural and political discourses which could mean that a community does not exist – indeed, that it is actively denied existence by the majority.

The process of visibility is mediated through public space; this can refer to material space, such as a city, or a virtual space such as social media platforms. Space is something that is 'folded into' social relations through mundane and dramatic activities (Harvey 1996). Communities attempt to appropriate public space in order to control the process of visibility, meaning that space is a resource harnessed and transformed through political action. To be clear, visibility brings communities and identities into the open and requires others to take notice, but, more than this, the interaction between people and space shapes social identities (Massey 1998). Space does not function as an actor or a political subject but is used by individuals and groups to claim, sustain or propagate power, usually the state's (Painter 2010). In post-socialist Europe, public space is used by the state to affirm national and ethnic identity belonging, but other identity groups then struggle to organize publicly. Using space as a medium is a power strategy (Sack 1986) to exert influence; Roma do not seek to control public space in the same way that demonstrators in Istanbul in 2013 appropriated Gezi Park to challenge the government (Akcali and Korkut 2015). Rather, Pride parades are attempts to use urban spaces to influence cultural codes and discourses in order to affirm a group identity. Visibility here as a process is episodic rather than sustained – it usually occurs once a year in the capital or a regional city – and brings together a diverse range of individuals. The idea that public space belongs solely to the state or government has been challenged by successive social movements across the world so that increasingly public space is regarded as an interpersonal sphere of sociability (Loftland 1998), which is, in theory, accessible to many different people for a range of activities (Kärrholm 2007). The appropriation of public space is relatively non-controversial in states that uphold human rights, including freedom of assembly and freedom of speech, until groups that heretofore have been invisible attempt to use public space to demand recognition. Pride is a celebration of the community as an outward-looking intervention, a moment of rupture that challenges the shackles of invisibility.

Space has been recognized as vitally important to marginalized groups as they attempt to ensure a sense of security to assuage perceived vulnerability. For example, Pickering et al. (2011) show that young people, lacking their own spaces, are present in public spaces such as shopping centres, parks, city squares and streets and through habitual presence these spaces foster a sense of identity. Similar to young people, when Roma are present in public space they are described as being unsightly, unwanted and undesirable, and perceived by the majority as potentially dangerous. Marginalized communities often appropriate or inhabit a space for cultural and material production: for example, gay bars, cafés or saunas, where members can meet in a 'safe space' in which activities are out of sight and, in theory, the possibility of hostility is precluded. Protection is ensured through invisibility. For Roma communities living in ghettos, settlements, villages, towns and apartment blocks surrounded by other Roma, some protection is provided in numbers. But spaces that are considered as Roma only can be targeted by those hostile to Roma communities, as the spate of murders of Roma in Hungary in 2009 and 2010 confirm. Invisibility is a strategy for some but sits uncomfortably with others. Roma are frequently visible, deploying cultural tropes and aesthetics such as clothes to signal to others within and outside the community who they are. This could be interpreted as an act of defiance or simply an embracing of one's identity.

I will now examine how Roma Pride in Prague (2014) and Budapest (2015) use public space and promote visibility, and I address some of the tensions inherent in visibility as well as the simultaneous mobilization and transformation of a stigmatized group identity. Pride parades are deliberate and public acts by marginalized communities who appropriate public space to become visible, to foster a collective sense of solidarity and identity, and to declare belonging to the polity.

THE ROMA PRIDE MOVEMENT: ORIGINS AND OBJECTIVES

In the last five years, a phenomenon has emerged that, while new, has the potential to debunk stereotypes and transform the meaning of Romani group identity as well as to forge a political consciousness for Roma across Europe. It should be noted that Roma Pride is part of a broader political movement occurring in local, national and transnational contexts. It is difficult to isolate movements within movements, but Roma Pride is a collective mobilization centred on public space, belonging and identity; for these reasons it warrants particular attention. There are a number of criticisms levelled at Roma Pride, not least the fact that it was initiated by non-Roma, the European Grassroots Antiracist Movement (EGAM), and also that it cannot easily capture those who do not identify specifically as Roma. It is questionable whether it is possible to measure any successes of Roma Pride given its infancy, but a cursory glance at the longer-established gay rights and Gay Pride movement, which Roma Pride is styled on, reveals that it takes years of collective effort for significant changes – such as changes in the law and/or shifts in public attitudes – to take effect in society. The key point is that it can be done. That being said, Roma Pride is getting bigger each year, with more participants and more Pride events taking place in more states, and it garners more media attention. Pride is inward-facing and attempts to raise Roma consciousness, but it is also explicitly outward-facing and aims to challenge dominant discourses and narratives held by non-Roma, a much more difficult task given the prevalence of anti-Roma attitudes and deeply entrenched social and political structures in European societies.

The Pride parades that have taken place since 2011 across Europe are not the only expression of Roma pride. 'Barvalipe' (Pride) programmes have been organized by the Open Society Foundations (OSF) with the purpose of bringing together Roma graduates who want to pursue careers in public leadership and develop the dignity and pride of Roma people through their actions. The express objectives of Barvalipe are to articulate a collective narrative by 'building pride in belonging to the Roma community' (OSF 2015) as well as establishing a sense of collective purpose among various communities, local cultures and political orientations, while understanding that Roma are a heterogeneous group. The focus of Barvalipe is on the next generation of activists, scholars and leaders and attempts to curate a collective understanding of pride in Roma identity.

The research in this chapter is based on interviews I conducted with Roma activists and advocates between

September 2013 and December 2015, including participant observation at two of the largest Roma Pride events in Prague (October 2014) and Budapest (October 2015). Before attending the two Pride marches I interviewed seven Roma Pride organizers from the 2013 Pride events in Bulgaria, Moldova, Norway, Denmark, Czech Republic, France and Austria. Pride takes place in East and West Europe but usually has a distinctive local flavour, meaning that it is not always a parade but can be a seminar or a speech or a campaign. Local activists, usually Roma NGOs, individuals and anti-racist NGOs, have autonomy in creating the Pride event so they tailor Roma Pride to suit particular circumstances and to address pertinent local issues.

Benjamin Abtan is the Director of Paris-based transnational NGO EGAM, which established Roma Pride in 2011 in response to the speech delivered by President Nicholas Sarkozy in Grenoble, France in 2010. In this speech, Sarkozy highlighted 'the problems posed by the behaviour of some of the travelling people and Roma', using racist language to argue that Roma were a security threat in France in order to justify the expulsion of thousands of Roma from France to Romania and Bulgaria. Abtan (interview, October 2013) argues that the purpose of Roma Pride is to create a mainstream movement by pushing human rights and anti-racism onto the agenda and regards it as a 'way for Roma to get involved in public life and integration in society'. From the outset, then, Roma Pride was set up by non-Roma to develop Roma agency, and he acknowledges that 'mobilization of Roma and non-Roma is necessary as it creates cultural links and a celebration of diversity in society'. He notes that there are stereotypes linked to Roma identity and that the majority 'fear this identity'. Ultimately, he maintains that the goal of Roma Pride is to stop discrimination and violence against Roma across Europe. Abtan recognizes the reluctance of many Roma to mobilize publicly because they are fearful of the consequences. He argues that through participation in the public sphere, everyone has the opportunity to be included, and that this can have an educative effect on the majority who learn more about Roma culture in the process. The assumption is that the more the majority knows and understands of Roma, the less prejudiced they are likely to feel. So, Roma Pride is intended to have a transformative potential by bringing Roma issues into the purview of the majority, to highlight rights and integration, and to challenge negative stereotypes of Roma identity through societal interaction.

The first Roma Pride was a loosely organized series of events across Europe on 1 October 2011 led by EGAM. Events included speeches, lectures, exhibitions, public awareness campaigns, concerts, gatherings in public spaces and open access to an illegal Roma settlement and were held in Belgium, Bulgaria, Croatia, Denmark, France, Italy, Norway and Romania (EGAM 2011a). Two Pride marches occurred, in France and Romania. The march in Bucharest was called the 'Dignity March' and was a celebration of Romani heritage and culture; participants dressed in colourful traditional clothing but political slogans and messages were not prominent. In a message of support from George Soros (who established and continues to fund the OSF) played to those assembled he argued: 'You do not seek to disappear into the general population but want to retain your identity as Roma. That is the best way to challenge the mistreatment to which you are subjected and to shatter the negative stereotypes which prevail about you in the general public' (Soros 2011). On the eve of the first Roma Pride, EGAM published a manifesto signed by representatives from Roma NGOs and anti-racism NGOs from twenty-one states entitled '*Dosta!*' ('Enough!'). The manifesto notes the current climate of fear and violence suffered by Roma across Europe and draws parallels to the experience of the gay community in the USA in the 1960s, who also endured demeaning representations, marginality and being denied the same rights as other citizens, and who frequently suffered violence at the hands of individuals and the police because of who they were (EGAM 2011b). The creation of Roma Pride is clearly based on the persecution that Roma are facing and draws upon the victim status of Roma across Europe: 'We will march at the heart of the main European cities to raise awareness about and to denounce the racism and the racial discriminations Roma people are today victim of all over Europe' (ibid.).

By 2013, Roma Pride had become more established across Europe. In Prague, one activist from anti-racist NGO Konnexe said that the parade was held in the city centre with participants carrying placards stating 'We are Roma', 'Black/White, Lets Unite!' and 'Roma Pride' (interview with Miroslav Bros, November 2013). There were banners drawing attention to specific local issues including the failure of the social inclusion policy in the Czech Republic as well as the continued existence of a pig farm on the site of Lety concentration camp, which was used for Roma internment during World War Two. In Bulgaria, the goal has not been to hold a parade but to 'show Roma presence, to show what we have contributed and that we are proud of Roma identity' (interview with Deyan Kolev, October 2013). He argues that 'Roma Pride is a tool to change attitudes and anti-Roma stereotypes and also a tool to express our identity and our presence'. In Moldova, one organizer maintains that the purpose of Pride is not clear and asks, 'Pride in what?' He argues that it should be linked to demands such as combatting discrimination, but this is impeded because 'there is no solidarity amongst Roma here' (interview with Nicolai Radita, October 2013). He believes that Roma Pride is not a priority because there are other more pressing matters, such as social cohesion, education, health and improving the material life conditions of Roma, and he does not see the potential of Roma Pride to act as a vehicle to achieve these goals. While the Pride organizers I interviewed in Central and Eastern Europe were all self-declared Roma, those in Western Europe were not but regarded themselves as advocates, usually working for anti-racist NGOs. In Norway, for example, the main organizer was the Norwegian Centre Against Racism, which works with various minority groups, including Roma. Many Roma in Norway are recent migrants from Romania and the focus of Pride was on the day-to-day challenges facing migrant Roma. One organizer believes that the purpose of Roma Pride in Oslo was to bring Roma and non-Roma together, to help counteract negative stereo-types with positive images, and to facilitate the creation of a platform for Roma to cooperate (interview with Rune Berglund Steen, October 2013). Similarly, in Austria 'Roma is understood as a begging issue' and there is a lack of interaction between Roma and non-Roma; this means that people do not know about Roma and thus 'stereotypes are strong'. While 'pride' does not trans-late easily into Austrian, organizers focus on 'dignity', which they argue shifts the focus onto the attitude of the whole society rather than just on Roma themselves. At the 'Respect for Roma' event in 2013, there were a number of speakers and 'only a few stressed pride while most asked for respect' (interview with Andreea Haerle, October 2013). Roma Pride has taken a variety of forms and this flexibility allows local activists and advocates to promote collective consciousness, raise awareness and improve visibility in the public sphere.

ROMA PRIDE IN PRAGUE IN 2014

In 2014, Roma Pride was held in sixteen different coun-tries across Europe. It is usually held on the first Sunday of October, unlike Gay Pride events which are spread across

several months. I attended Roma Pride in Prague and interviewed two of the key organizers. Roma are a relatively
small population in the Czech Republic, with approximately 200,000 people considered to be Roma although
self-identification in the national census is much lower
(13,000); this is a common phenomenon across Central
and Eastern Europe, as Roma communities are reluctant
to declare their ethnicity for fear of discrimination. The
number of Roma living in and around Prague is quite low,
with most Roma living in the north and east of the country.
However, the organizers believed it was important to have
a presence in the capital city to draw attention to the issues
facing Roma. Buses were hired to bring Roma individuals
from the north of the country to Prague for Roma Pride in
2013 and 2014 (interview with Miroslov Broz, November
2013). Anti-Roma prejudice is high in the Czech Republic
despite the relatively small Roma population, so Roma
Pride is taking place in the context of rising fascism and
neo-Nazism, including regular demonstrations against
and intimidation of Roma communities.

The Director of Roma Pride in Prague is Ivanka
Mariposa Čonková. She believes that the main purpose
of Roma Pride is to promote solidarity among Roma
but she is not confident that Pride can address the
problems facing Roma communities across Europe (interview, December 2013). The event was co-organized by
Konnexe, a Czech anti-racist NGO, which is made up of
Roma and non-Roma. Significantly, while Pride events
were held across Europe on the first Sunday of October,

the organizers decided to reschedule as they wanted to be present at a neo-Nazi rally targeting Roma communities on the same day, so the Pride event was held the day before. Roma Pride in Prague in 2014 was a series of events and performances held in different parts of the city. The events ran from early morning and started in the Old Town; after the Pride parade, a religious service was held in a church, and that was followed by a party at a different venue. Several hundred people were in attendance in the Old Town Square (Staroměstské náměstí), including many Romani women dressed in traditional clothing as well as a woman dressed in traditional Indian clothing. The event attracted a range of media, including TV, radio, blogs and newspapers, with Ivanka, in traditional clothes, giving interviews. Many of those present were not Roma but were drawn to the dancing and singing of different Roma and non-Roma groups. A series of speeches closed the first part of Pride before the participants gathered behind a horse-drawn carriage that led the Pride parade as it snaked through the Old Town. A Roma band played music from the carriage while participants chanted slogans such as 'We are human too' to people watching in the streets and along the Charles Bridge. The organizers know that the Old Town Square, Old Town and Charles Bridge are frequented primarily by tourists and that not many 'locals' were there to witness the parade. While this has obvious drawbacks in terms of visibility, it does mean that those hostile to the presence of Roma – such as neo-Nazis – are themselves less visible, the police being unwilling to permit an incident to occur in such a high-profile public space with so many tourists. The presence of the police on the parade was minimal and the whole event passed without incident. There were a few calls from the sidelines from a few people who registered their dissatisfaction with the parade but they were quickly silenced by other people in the crowd, who appeared to enjoy the celebratory atmosphere of the music played by the Roma band. Many of those watching may not have registered the significance of what was happening: a vulnerable group standing together demanding recognition. And the fact that those watching were tourists for the most part meant that the visibility of the parade was negated somewhat and recognition ruled out. However, Roma Pride had the advantage of amplifying the voice of Roma, raising consciousness, and gaining international media attention.

Figure 5.1 The lead procession for the Roma Pride parade in Prague (2014)

The goal of Roma Pride is to stand up for victims of oppression and discrimination. Roma Pride is the 'freedom to say we are oppressed, that we are not equal citizens, so Roma Pride is a celebration of this freedom' (interview with Ivanka Mariposa Čonková, December 2013). Ivanka is more circumspect about the potential of Pride and believes that 'it cannot change anything. It cannot change the attitude of people but it can give people information' concerning who Roma are and the issues they face. She suggests that agency is important but it will not necessarily change the hearts and minds of the majority; instead, she emphasizes the transformative potential of Pride for Roma: 'The first step is for people to believe that they can be part of this. They feel that they are powerless so Pride can bring power to people to help them stand up. Roma Pride is new because it is asking Roma people to stand up. It is an act ... it is a new experience.' When they return home from Prague, they feel better as Roma because 'we have created a beautiful space and pride as Roma so they feel more empowered' since 'it shows that space is also here for us'. While Roma Pride occurs on just one day and in one place, the key is to inspire people so that they feel empowered to make a difference in their own communities. One of the main reasons why Roma Pride is so important is that many Roma 'have fear', particularly in the face of rising far-right demonstrations that target Roma, but this fear can and should be harnessed: 'Roma Pride is a celebration that we are fighting against discrimination and neo-fascism in our times' (interview with Miroslav Broz, Prague, October 2014). Finally, on the day of the Pride parade, Ivanka told me that marching in public 'has a huge impact on building solidarity between Roma and non-Roma and between Roma themselves' (interview, Prague, October 2014).

ROMA PRIDE IN BUDAPEST IN 2015

Budapest Pride was held on 17 October 2015, the third time it was held. Participants gathered in the early afternoon at Madách Imre Tér, a centrally located square. The organizers had made 500 small hand-held Roma flags and distributed these to participants. Organizers and participants spoke to the news media who had assembled. There were placards bearing the faces of famous individuals of Roma heritage as well as signs showing the names of places participants had come from, including Miskolc, Albania and Sweden. Some of the participants were not Roma but were allies who live in Hungary as well as representatives from NGOs. The atmosphere was celebratory and welcoming. Unlike Prague Pride, not many participants were dressed in traditional clothing.

While waiting for people to gather and the parade to start, I spoke with a group of young students from Romaversitas, an NGO that supports Roma students attending university by helping them to acquire books as well as to secure scholarships, which means that students can focus on university and not have to take another job. The students were male and female, aged 19 to 21 years old, and wore T-shirts with slogans such as 'I am Roma, I am studying medicine' and 'I am Roma, I am studying sociology'. One student pointed out the difference between a private and public dimension of identity: 'I am Roma. I am Gypsy. I am Roma with my family and it's OK but Pride is different because it is public. If someone asks me, I say, "Yes, of course, I am Gypsy," but now everyone can see it.' Visibility is a key issue that came up when students explained why Roma Pride was important to them. Another student said: 'It is really important to build identity and how we identify. I am a Gypsy woman studying at university and I am proud of it. It really is important for Gypsies to be proud of themselves.' For her, 'the march is really important because the people [the majority] will see that we are here and that we are not the people who they think we are', highlighting the prevalence of negative ascriptions and stereotypes of Roma communities in Hungary and that a public affirmation of group identity can help combat such stereotypes by showing that Roma are lawyers, doctors and kindergarten teachers. One male student, studying medicine, told me that Pride was a good event at which to meet new people like him and to make connections with other people.

The parade itself passed without incident and moved through Budapest city centre, proceeding through main streets such as Rákóczi út, stopping traffic and making noise, while participants chanted 'Opre Roma!' ('Wake up, Roma!' or 'Let's go, Roma!'). Some members of the public

Figure 5.2 Roma Pride in Budapest (2015)

stood on the footpath and watched impassively – not hostile, just curious. Other members of the public joined in the parade while many asked for some of the Roma flags that were being handed out. There were approximately 800 people by the time the parade arrived in the 8th district (Józsefváros) where a stage had been erected. The 8th district is an area historically associated with Roma but gentrification has meant that the price of rent is rising and many Roma have had to leave or have been forced out (Czirfusz et al. 2015). The area now has renovated housing projects and new paving on the roads but there are still Roma living there. In the square in the 8th district, there was a series of performances from singers and dancers as well as speeches from a range of activists, politicians and allies. Key issues that arose during the speeches included the commemoration of the Holocaust, forging alliances with other marginalized communities, amplifying political voice and building solidarity, and securing jobs for Roma that were not just in public works (road sweeping and cleaning, for example). In 2014, Roma Pride asked for the inclusion of Roma history and the Roma Holocaust in public education and in the national curriculum. In 2015, the message of Roma Pride was to demand that every public institution employ Roma workers and for the employment rate of Roma to reach the national average. The reason for this is to argue that Roma should not be employed solely in public works programmes but also in other public bodies, as civil servants, teachers and so on. In the square there were stalls where people could sign petitions to support demands to improve the employment position of Roma. One speech was delivered by a Rom politician, the Mayor of Ács, who argued that 'there is no one else to stand for us, we must stand up for ourselves' and 'the biggest victory for the other side is if we are ashamed of ourselves. We have to get rid of stigma because this burdens all of us.' The speeches covered a range of issues and had both national and transnational dimensions as participants sought to build solidarity across borders.

Roma Pride was organized by dozens of Roma with support from non-Roma activists. The organizing committee of Budapest Pride was large, inclusive and highly heterogeneous. One organizer points out that activism on Roma issues usually takes place with a small group doing some work in their local communities and that 'there has not been this coming together of people at a national level until now' (interview with Lakatosne Dano Zsuzsanna, Budapest, October 2015). One of the key goals of this Pride parade was to bring Roma from different areas across Hungary to make Pride a larger and more inclusive event. The role of Pride is to create a positive image of group identity, one that resonates internally in the form of pride and dignity while also challenging stigma of Roma in the eyes of the majority. One of the main organizers, Setét Jenő, argues:

> Whenever the majority thinks of Roma or Gypsy, people just think about criminals or very deep poverty or inhuman living circumstances, so outsiders have prejudices about Roma and these prejudices are internalized by Roma themselves, resulting in a negative identity in the Roma population. But we think that every people builds their identity up from positive elements. It is our job to demonstrate Roma excellence to everyone and to teach people about Roma history so that we can counteract this negative image that has been created. Because the worst way of oppressing a people is to disassociate them from their own identity.
>
> INTERVIEW, BUDAPEST, OCTOBER 2015

So, by creating a positive public identity, Roma emancipation is possible. He believes that Roma Pride allows the majority to see Roma through their presence in the public sphere, and through this presence 'we will speak with our own voice'. Being Roma impacts on practical issues such as employability, and the 'real tragedy is [that] Roma people who are educated become assimilated and do not recognize anymore that they are Roma, because they have to get ahead and it is really hard to get ahead as an "out" Roma' (interview with Lakatosne Dano Zsuzsanna, Budapest, October 2015). The parallel language with Gay Pride of being 'out' is significant, as publicly affirming one's Roma identity could harm one's employment prospects. Several of the students I spoke to did not want to be named as they were worried about not getting jobs in schools and hospitals simply because they are Roma. One of the potential benefits of Roma Pride is that it challenges the trend for assimilation so that people can be proud of their identity and heritage.

While other Pride events across Europe, including in Prague, have a distinctly 'cultural' dimension in that they focus on music and dance, the organizers of Budapest Pride maintain that they are not interested in putting on a cultural event. For them, 'Pride is political, exclusively political' (interview with Setét Jenő). It is a vehicle of political voice, as Jenő explains:

> We cannot actually change the decisions that affect our everyday lives unless we are many who speak with the same voice and demand the same things. And Roma Pride for me is such a political movement where

we build a base upon which we can speak with our own voice and create our own goals that we want to achieve. At the same time as we say that it's good to be Roma and we are proud to be Roma and talk about our identity, we always have political messages that we want to disseminate, or political goals that we want to achieve. Last year our main goal was to get Roma history taught in schools and to put them, put Roma history, into school manuals. And this year we will have as a goal that in every public institution there will be Roma employees working. Roma Pride doesn't just mean bringing identity and values to people but also goals that they can fight for.

A crucial dimension of Pride is visibility in public space:

At the same time that we build our own identity within the Roma community, we challenge the negative identity that has been given to us by the majority population. That's why we will march to be visible on the most populated streets of Budapest. We don't want to hide and go into a cultural institution where we do our own things. Because in Hungary for the last ten years people have got used to hiding when the far-right demonstrations happen so we have, you know, as a people been trained how to hide, so now what we are going to do is challenge that and take back the streets and that's why our demonstration is going to be as loud as possible, as visible as possible and as open as possible.

Zsuzsanna concurs:

> For me the other important thing about this being a
> wider movement is that when we do activism and
> advocacy and sort out problems in our community with
> five, six people in one small place you can't actually
> have a media coverage, nobody knows what you are
> doing, but when you have a big event like this then
> everybody notices that the Roma are marching. And
> also it's important then for the Roma to say, 'Yes, look,
> there is such an event that brings us all together, not for
> a political party, not in a particular political platform
> but just for our community.'

Zsuzsanna believes that Pride signifies an invocation
of the citizenship rights of Roma and an opportunity to
declare belonging to the state: 'Roma Pride is an international movement so actually in each country people are
saying that they are also citizens of that country at the
same time as being Roma.' The intersection between
national belonging and citizenship is outlined by Jenő:

> The majority don't even let us be part of the Hungarian
> identity. And could I not be proud as a Roma if I don't
> have to prove all the time that I'm also Hungarian? There
> are many Roma who say that 'If the majority hates me
> so much then I would rather not be Hungarian, I will
> just be Roma.' The organizing team of Budapest Roma
> Pride feels that both are important but Pride is about

the Roma identity and what we want is that the society also notices that Roma identity. And women also have different identities; women are also Hungarian or Roma, or doctors or public workers. But on International Women's Day we focus on what the women's identity means. And on the Roma Pride Day we focus on what is the situation in society of Roma and what the Roma want to say in their own name.

Another element of Pride is the power of networking: if people experience similar problems in many different places, coming together to discuss and share those experiences allows for the potential to solve common problems, and when Roma mobilize again some of these issues can be brought to the fore. It is important to remember that Roma Pride is building on years of Roma activism and advocacy that have advocated for self-respect and identity as well as for the human rights of Roma. Like all movements, Roma Pride is derived from a heterogeneous population that includes different Roma groups and non-Roma. Jenő clarifies this situation:

We don't choose our friends depending on their background and we have a lot of non-Roma friends. Many other people have to work very hard for this. For us it's absolutely natural that we have non-Roma as part of the organizing team because we have non-Roma allies and non-Roma friends. And we also go to their events. We go to LGBT Pride, we go to the remembrance day for the Jewish community, for the Holocaust Remembrance Day. We are against domestic violence. We always go to protect the homeless if the powers come and annoy them ... We will actually speak up against the fascists if they go against the left wing, left movement. We also raise our voices if the left uses racist language and we also speak against the right wing if they are racist. We have values and principles.

Roma Pride is intended to be inclusive because the organizers recognize that Roma and the majority need to live together, and so a strong message of welcome is sent out to non-Roma. Everyone apart from the far right is welcome. However, the organizers are careful not to court the support of politicians, and so they do not invite politicians to participate – but, of course, many political representatives do attend. The organizers never request money from the government to support their activities as they are wary of accusations that they are not autonomous or can be co-opted, which they believe would undermine their activities. Roma Pride is intended to galvanize the activist community: 'Our main goal is to bring people ... out from their silos and our goal is to bring together the biggest Roma civil movement. So we are painfully aware and painstakingly try not to give anybody the opportunity to bring our movement into one or the other political party umbrella' (interview with Setét Jeno", Budapest, October 2015).

DISCUSSION

Roma Pride is a recent phenomenon, which means it is
not possible to determine how effective it is in challenging
Romaphobia and changing the perception of Roma, if at
all. The history of gay rights and emancipation suggests
that Pride parades were crucial in building solidarity and
raising consciousness of the LGBTIQ community as well
as in transforming the affective content of public identity
from shame into pride. Since the first Gay Pride in 1970,
laws criminalizing homosexuality have been revoked
across the world and progressive legislation enacted to
protect LGBTIQ people, and support for gay marriage
and adoption and non-discrimination is strong in many
Western states. We can safely argue that Gay Pride played
a significant role in gay emancipation, but the fruits of
this labour take time to ripen. There is no good reason
why Roma Pride cannot serve the same emancipatory
tool for European Roma. Roma are citizens of the states
in which they reside, for the most part, and are protected
by non-discrimination legislation, so Roma already have
the legal tools in place. The key role for Roma is to forge
a collective consciousness and to build internal solidarity
as well as to project a positive image of Roma identity and
to challenge deep-seated Romaphobia. Roma are not just
a public issue that must be dealt with, as a nuisance or as
an unwanted group, but become a public through agency,
through the appropriation of public space by rupturing
conventions of belonging. Roma Pride builds solidarity

and fosters a collective identity, and sends a message to non-Roma and Roma that they belong to the city, the nation, and the state. It is the appropriation of urban space that is the most important element of becoming visible because Roma become a public through performing their identity and rights as citizens, a theme developed in Chapter 6.

In the short term, Roma Pride empowers Roma communities through the appropriation of public space and by declaring their presence in the public sphere – a clear signal to the majority that Roma are constitutive of the nation. Roma Pride is certainly outward-facing and seeks to challenge dominant negative cultural codes and discourses which maintain that Roma are deviant, criminal parasites who do not belong to the majority nation. But changing these narratives is challenging and one unlikely to be achieved solely through public parades. The meaning and content of Roma group identity need to be expressed by Roma in the form of dignity and pride, which can only be fostered by challenging internal prejudices. Roma Pride is an attempt to stem the tide of internalized Romaphobia whereby some Roma come to accept the stereotypes prescribed by others, which in turn limits the parameters of what is possible with regard to work and education, among other areas. The Pride parades I attended were efforts to bolster collective dignity by celebrating Roma cultural heritage and to project this positive image internally and externally. It is difficult to draw a line between cultural and political mobilization. While both parades drew on cultural tropes and symbols, such as dress, they articulated political statements and demands. There is a fine line between what is considered political and what is cultural, and the history of the Roma movement has been characterized by such debates. I would argue that Pride is political: it is more than a cultural intervention or celebration. It seeks to challenge the status quo and disrupt dominant understandings of Roma identity and represents an attempt to declare belonging to the polity: this is politics.

While Roma Pride is a transnational movement, each parade had a clear local flavour: in Prague, participants criticized the government's social inclusion policy; in Budapest, organizers sought to harness the power of the parade to highlight unfair working practices in the public sector. However, there was a clear sense of being part of something larger. The flying of the Roma flag is a testament to that, as were participants stating that they were Roma standing together, not Hungarian Roma or Czech Roma. They saw themselves as Roma united in a collective mobilization, one that cut across state borders and was based on a more complex national identity. At the same time, it was not just Roma who participated in or helped organize the events. Many of the organizers were non-Roma who wanted to challenge what they perceived as state or societal racism against Roma communities. EGAM started the movement and acts as a common reference point, but Roma Pride in Prague and Budapest was led by Roma with support from national non-Roma activists and advocates, relations and colleagues who want to live in a society that refuses to tolerate Romaphobia. In Western European states, especially those with a smaller Roma population or without much of a history of Roma activism, we see NGOs led by non-Roma emerging to organize Pride events, although not necessarily a parade, as part of a broader anti-racist and anti-fascist strategy.

Pride is important because it promotes visibility, which means a group cannot be ignored. It is much harder to oppress, exclude or marginalize a community that is proud of itself and confident; Roma Pride seeks to build confidence through visibility. Historically, Roma have been excluded from mainstream society, physically segregated and kept out of sight, physically excluded from public institutions such as education, the media, state services and political representation. This invisibility has a disastrous impact on understandings of Roma belonging, with some Roma believing that they do not belong in public institutions. Sometimes this is a strategy for survival whereby Roma seek to stay out of public life as they fear repercussions. Roma Pride is a direct challenge to this. It is also a direct challenge to the idea that Roma are accepting a world built by non-Roma; through empowerment, voice and presence, Roma are beginning to create opportunities and discourses and to make demands to shape society. More recent generations of Roma activists and the contemporary Romani movement are creating a world that makes space for the inclusion of Roma in all facets of society. Pride participants claim urban public space and use this space to promote visibility and presence. This act of visibility is a collective 'coming out' and seeks to stem the tide of marginalization, and represents an affirmation of belonging to the polity, to the state and to the nation.

CHAPTER 6

ROMA CITIZENSHIP IN THE EUROPEAN UNION: A QUESTION OF BELONGING

Migration within the EU is one of the most pressing matters facing the Union today; a project that was intended to bring the citizens of Europe together in 'ever closer union' according to the preamble of the founding Treaty of Rome (1957) might end up tearing it apart. For citizens of the EU, migration has unleashed new kinds of anxieties about security, identity, rights and belonging, at the same time as it offers social and economic benefits. For some Roma, migration signifies an opportunity to secure a better future and to leave behind discrimination, stigmatization and persecution. But the mobility of Roma from East to West Europe is challenging due to inadequate material resources, language provision and institutional support. Opportunities to move elsewhere to improve one's life chances or those of one's family are severely inhibited by structural conditions even if the supposed privileges of EU citizenship exist on paper.

And for those Romani citizens who do migrate, it is not the panacea hoped for, with Western European governments responding with varying degrees of heightened securitization, exclusion and even expulsion. A focus on citizenship reveals the tension of belonging for Roma who are EU citizens (approximately 8 to 10 million). Despite possessing EU citizenship, Roma are not equal because endemic Romaphobia nullifies affective bonds of solidarity as 'Europeans', extending belonging to some and not to others. It is argued that EU migration has destabilized understandings of belonging, which are already tenuous for many Roma across Europe, who are perceived to have no homeland or kin state, even as it offers opportunities to perform citizenship through migration.

This chapter will tease out some tensions regarding the duality of belonging between national and transnational or supranational spaces. The EU is founded on inherent tensions regarding sovereignty and authority and a constant battle between member states and supranational institutions, which pull in different directions. The EU is a political space that is constituted by member state governments and EU institutions, and is built on principles of territorialized belonging and contested sovereignties. Certainly, the EU offers Roma new opportunities and means to develop forms of belonging that potentially transcend those of national belonging and citizenship. The creation of EU citizenship and the fulfilment of the internal market require this duality to function. The EU represents a political space where rights to citizenship are guaranteed but are neither completely national or transnational. The performative dimension of citizenship discussed here opens up new horizons for Roma to declare belonging to the EU polity.

This chapter examines how Roma communities declare belonging to the EU through acts of citizenship. It seeks to challenge the ascription of negative stereotypes across and through political narratives and discursive interventions that characterize Roma as a hopeless and helpless unwanted community. It explores how mass protests in the wake of the expulsion of Roma migrants from France in 2010 offered an opportunity to perform an act of citizenship through which Roma declared their belonging across national and transnational political contexts. But acts of citizenship can have negative implications resulting in further stigmatization, which can operate 'as a form of governance which legitimizes the reproduction and entrenchment of inequalities and injustices' (Tyler 2013: 8). I will start with a caveat: I do not address asylum seekers or internally displaced persons in the EU, which includes Roma from Kosovo who now reside in West European states, particularly Germany and France, because citizenship as status is withheld from those individuals.

Migration of Roma within the EU has not created Romaphobia but has provided opportunities for Romaphobia to manifest, particularly in terms of how the media and politicians delineate belonging within the sphere of rights. The EU migration regime is an exemplary institution through which to examine Romaphobia and the relationship between identity, belonging and territoriality. The introduction of EU citizenship was intended to facilitate the movement of people as well as goods and services and to eliminate barriers and borders within the internal market in order to create a de-bordered political and economic space. It was hoped that attachments of identity and belonging would become more fluid and less fixed to the national political context through the creation of a cosmopolitan space underpinned by liberal norms.

Mobility, sedentarization and perceived nomadism (in Eastern Europe under socialist regimes) have informed Romaphobia. In the past, policies have attempted to regulate Roma mobility, and have also attempted to eradicate or substantially limit the movement of Roma. In the former Czechoslovakia, for instance, the majority of Roma lived sedentarily when, in 1958, the programmes of sedentarization were introduced to deal with Roma. Rather than seeing these policies exclusively as attempts to reduce so-called Roma 'nomadism', as many scholars have discussed them, Van Baar (2011a) suggests that we consider them as means to differentiate Roma mobility from other, regularized forms of mobility. Through what he calls 'nomadization' – problematizing Roma as eternal nomads and thus irregularizing their citizen status – states have institutionalized differential treatment vis-à-vis other citizens and have legitimized substandard housing, education and other public services. We can see a clear continuation of Roma nomadization in terms of how

Roma were treated in the immediate aftermath of the fall of communism, during the Yugoslavian crisis, and, most recently, in the context of the ongoing expulsion of Roma from France.

CITIZENSHIP AND BELONGING

The state is the institutional guarantor for the obligations and prerogatives of citizenship. States that are members of the EU possess an additional layer of citizenship created by the Maastricht Treaty (1992) to facilitate the realization of the internal market, a fundamental principle of which is the freedom of movement of people. The state is often considered the source of affective bonds of belonging, usually fostered through national and sub-national identity affirmations. In this sense, the state holds citizens together, but, at the same time, it can exclude those who do not fit into the preferred vision of the nation; therefore, 'it also unbinds, releases, expels, banishes' (Butler and Spivak 2007: 4–5). This exclusion is not necessarily emancipatory on the part of the state nor welcomed by the citizen. I argue that some Roma communities are susceptible to such practices in the context of EU migration. As Roma avail themselves of the freedom of movement principle and move elsewhere (usually from Central and Eastern Europe to Western European states) in search of a better life, they can become dislodged from already tenuous affective bonds of solidarity with the home state. It is a stretch to argue that EU citizenship has produced an enforced sense of statelessness – an extreme form of dispossession – for EU Roma citizens on a par with refugees and asylum seekers. At the same time, migration offers the opportunity to perform acts of citizenship through which Roma visibility and agency are expressed, as well as a concomitant declaration of belonging to a political community (the EU polity), strengthening claims that Roma are a 'true European minority' (Council of Europe 1993). It is important to note that increased visibility of marginalized communities can lead to a backlash from society to 'put them in their place', as is shown by the hostile reactions to LGBTIQ Pride marches across Central and Eastern Europe and to a lesser extent in Western Europe. Part of the issue with Roma migrants is that some are highly visibilized: washing car windows at traffic lights, begging in busy shopping areas, inhabiting prominent places in major European cities. In these instances, visibility antagonizes the majority and can stoke 'social insecurity' (Wacquant 2010: 197).

In 2010, tens of thousands of protestors, led by Roma alongside non-Roma supporters and advocates, took part in mass demonstrations against the French government that had targeted and deported Roma migrants. Prior to the expulsions, Roma communities had been constructed as a security threat who engaged in criminal activity by the French authorities. The government systematically destroyed temporary homes and settlements of Roma communities across France and deported thousands of Roma migrants (who are EU citizens) back to Bulgaria and Romania. The protests drew attention to the precarious citizenship status that Roma people retain; although Roma possess formal citizenship and can avail themselves of the freedom of movement principle, the state and society conspire to withhold core tenets of citizenship, notably belonging. The mass protests of Roma migrants are a performance of citizenship in which Roma declare their belonging to a political community, the EU, but also draw attention to overt racist practices whereby a community can be targeted for special treatment by the state. This act of citizenship challenges the idea of the citizen with a singular loyalty and belonging. Citizenship is traditionally understood as membership of a state, thus citizenship is rooted in the sovereignty of the nation-state. Post-national conceptualizations of citizenship are predicated on national citizenship, which if removed or revoked would undermine the post-national institution. However, such an understanding obscures intersubjective relations and how actors negotiate belonging to a community. The protests signify an act of citizenship to draw attention to the tenuous belonging of Roma communities in national as well as transnational social, economic and political contexts. I will return to the 2010 French Roma crisis later, but first it is necessary to address the relationship between citizenship and belonging and the challenges and opportunities generated by EU migration.

Research on citizenship has tended to focus on rights (Turner 1990), participation in citizenship (Lister 1998), and identity (Delanty 2000), while the creation of EU citizenship heralded cosmopolitan ramifications (Soysal 1994) for member states as well as citizens. Citizenship is therefore presented as a framework of rights and responsibilities and is relatively silent on conceptualizations of belonging. Roma individuals across the EU are citizens in theory but when they attempt to invoke said rights – by migrating within the EU polity, for example – a situation unfolds which reveals that Roma do not enjoy equal citizenship rights. Roma are included in the EU as citizens, meaning that they retain a formal citizenship status and some fundamental rights, but they do not *belong* to the EU because the everyday reality of citizenship as practice is unequal and highly restricted by governments and societies. Eric Fassin (2015b) argues that this is due to neoliberalism, which means that governments regard Roma as 'useless' in that they are unable to contribute to the economy, and so they are superfluous to requirements and certainly not worth the energy of investment or integration. Here I will explain how Roma individuals and communities perform acts of citizenship, staking their belonging to the EU through instances of collective mobilization that affirm group identity and visibility in the public sphere. Opportunities for mobilization have emerged in the context of successive repressive interventions by national governments seeking to assert sovereign power over recently arrived Roma migrants. It reveals a tension between formal citizenship status, the rupturing capacity of migration, and belonging in the EU. Roma agency is demonstrated on two fronts: by the autonomy of migration and through performing acts of citizenship such as protesting against unfair and discriminatory treatment on the basis of ethnic origin. I will explore these dynamics by focusing on the targeting and expulsions of Roma in France in 2010 and the subsequent mass protests that took place in France and beyond.

A reading of Badiou (2005) highlights how the EU is a meta-structure that is unconcerned with belonging yet is consistently concerned with inclusion. Discursive interventions and policies on Roma refer to inclusion and integration but are silent on belonging; thus 'belonging carries no promise or guarantee of eventual inclusion' (Prozorov 2008: 192) but remains significant for communities who have historically been excluded, marginalized and persecuted, as Roma communities have been. Citizenship is an instructive example of Roma people's participation in the EU meta-structure: citizenship is a framework to actively maintain an ideology of liberal capitalism. By performing acts of citizenship, Roma engage in political action that at first glance can be regarded as liberating but actually serves to recreate the power of the EU to delineate belonging and inclusion. Rancière (2004) and Badiou (2005) present a definition of politics of disruption and continuous disequilibrium that offers the possibility of accommodating disruption by creating political subjects (Van den Hemel 2008). This would suggest that citizenship rights are meaningless until they are invoked and they serve as a tool to critique the allocation of power and belonging. This disruption is political and helps challenge prevailing notions of political community, particularly who belongs and who does not. Roma migrants walk the tightrope between visibility and invisibility in a political community that polices the boundaries of belonging and inclusion. Roma migrants are usually highly visible (targeted by government and the media) but the autonomy of migration reveals a silent agency through the mobility of bodies. I argue that autonomy of migration is not enough to declare belonging to the EU political community; for this to occur, acts of citizenship must be performed that draw attention to unequal citizenship status and the withholding of belonging. The increased presence of Eastern European Roma inhabiting temporary (sometimes illegal) spaces in towns and cities across Western Europe highlights the concurrent potential and shortcomings of the EU's migration regime. As Roma migrate from east to west, their status as citizens is declared, but belonging, a central tenet of citizenship, is either deferred or refused.

The nation, regarded as singular and homogeneous, is couched in claims to a common homeland, a shared language or a common culture. Minority groups often do not fit the nation-equals-state framework, are recognized as being different, and sometimes require special rights or protections – this all serves to confirm their differential status vis-à-vis the nation. For example, in many European states, such as Romania, Roma are formally recognized as a national minority (or, in Hungary, as an ethnic minority), but in other states they are not recognized as constituting a minority at all. For Roma communities, who now inhabit every state in Europe, political status is further regulated by perceptions of belonging. The historical exclusion of Roma from societies in East and West Europe is partly justified by the perception of Roma as ethnogenic nomads who possess no ties to a specific territory in Europe. Roma have become a target of the rising tide of right-wing populism across Europe, whose success can be attributed partly to capitalizing on the dominant narrative that Roma do not belong in the host state (McGarry and Drake 2013). EU citizenship offers the promise of hope and a better future but it can reinforce the view that Roma do not belong; this conundrum is realized as 'cruel optimism' (Berland 2011), encapsulating unfulfilled hope, a promise that can never be kept.

The last decade has witnessed a steadily creeping advance of nationalism with the result that xenophobic discourse is no longer solely the preserve of the far right – it is increasingly incorporated into mainstream party discourse (Korkut et al. 2013). Public attitudes towards migration have hardened as political elites have embraced a return to a 'purer' national identity, which is invariably defined by those on the extreme. At outlined in Chapter 3, nationalism alone cannot be used to explain the changing faces of Romaphobia over time. Romaphobia existed before the creation of the nation-state, but increased concern over borders and belonging has left many Roma vulnerable to stereotypes and scapegoating. The distinctive feature of modern-day populism in Europe is its ability to determine membership, especially who belongs and who is excluded. This exclusion is justified by the supposed threat posed by minorities and migrants to the stability and fabric of the nation. This is what marks it as different from the older manifestations of nationalism, which usually tried to include as much of the population as possible in the national political community (Ignatieff 1994). It is the product of fear, insecurity and discontent and is concerned with preserving differences (Delanty 2000). While politicians and the media can whip up fervent emotions and convince a fearful public that they are under attack, the actions of the state are carried out in bureaucratic exercises which target communities such as Roma for special treatment. The impact can be expulsion (being physically removed from the state), the destruction of property, increased segregation and containment, surveillance, and societal vigilance, among others. All this is extended to EU citizens who are Roma.

What is at stake is whether Roma are members of a political community, and, if so, how Roma experience that community. Belonging is expressed through Pride marches but also through migration. Citizenship is a political community that is realized in everyday practices, work, when using public services, voting, and engaging in social and cultural life. In *Homo Sacer*, Giorgio Agamben (1998) maintains that there is a difference between membership and inclusion in a political community, but this is determined exclusively by the sovereign power. The inability of Roma communities to access citizenship on equitable terms does not mean that Roma are not members of the political community but it does mean that they are abandoned by the state. A reading of citizenship as status cannot capture the dynamics of Roma exclusion across the EU because Roma are not outside the law or even banned from the juridico-political spaces, but they are *not included* either. Thus the status of Roma is not comparable with, say, migrants from sub-Saharan Africa on the one hand or an ethnic Polish person on the other. Indeed, there are many Roma who remain outside the EU in Balkan states such as Serbia and Macedonia, and in Russia and Turkey, among other nations, and the absence of formal EU citizenship has a huge impact on rights and opportunities. For example, in recent years hundreds of Roma have been prevented from leaving Macedonia as border officials are concerned that they will attempt to claim asylum in the EU; rising numbers of asylum claims would jeopardize the visa liberalization arrangements for Macedonia and so Roma are racially profiled and prevented from leaving by the state (Kacarska 2012). Let me be clear: Roma do not lack rights; indeed, most of the rights that Roma retain are provided and guaranteed by international human rights standards. Citizenship rights delineate membership of a political community that is guaranteed by a sovereign power, usually a state – or, since 1992, a supranational polity: the EU.

ACTS OF CITIZENSHIP

Citizenship can be understood as acts: 'how people constitute themselves as political subjects by the things they do, their deeds' (Isin 2012: 110). Isin (2009) is careful to distinguish between acts and actions, arguing that acts have a performative quality because actors choose to perform the act while an action can occur independent of actors. Citizenship acts encompass voting and taxpaying but they also provide for moments of contestation over the meaning of citizenship, a disturbance or challenge to the existing norms that changes how citizenship is understood, such as the invocation of rights through protest and collective mobilization. Therefore, acts make a difference because they break routines, understandings and practices; indeed, 'acts are ruptures or beginnings' (ibid.: 379). So, people make themselves by the things they *do* and these things are acts and actions performed by an actor. At stake in acts of citizenship are the tensions between exclusion/inclusion and belonging/not belonging. Crucially, the acts through which claims are articulated and claimants are produced 'create new sites of contestation, belonging, identification and struggle' (ibid.: 370), a moment of rupture that changes the political community. Performing an act of citizenship reaffirms the sovereignty of the EU polity, but when those who are excluded perform an act of citizenship they disrupt the status quo and make a declaration of belonging.

For an act to occur, an actor must exist – this actor can be an individual or a group. Two acts of citizenship can be considered that reveal the tension between individual and collective agency. First, some Roma retain an additional status as members of the Roma nation, a transnational community, which may impact on belonging and inclusion in different nation-states. In the 2001 Declaration of the Nation, the International Romani Union affirmed the status of Roma as a 'nation without a territory'; but, more than that, this collective act of citizenship confounds and simplifies post-national citizenship because in this instance Roma ask to be recognized as 'we, the people' (Isin 2012), a 'people' that is very deliberately not part of a particular nation-state. The Roma nation exists through self-determination and is not tied to any nation-state, nor does it challenge the sovereignty of any state. Of course, we must be wary of such claims because, like most groups, Roma do not all speak with the same voice and lack a collective agency to 'represent' this heterogeneous group. Roma elites have declared nationhood without asserting claims of sovereignty, or tying the Roma nation to a territory. As the EU has slowly become more involved in Roma issues from the 1990s onwards, that involvement accelerating during accession negotiations and in response to the persecution of Roma communities within the EU polity from 2008 onwards, there has been a perceptible shift in scale from the national to the 'European' level; one that many activists and advocates have embraced. The EU is keen to stress that Roma issues ought to be addressed exclusively by member states with support from the EU institutions, as the state is where education, health, housing and employment policies can be implemented. This intervention is an attempt to ensure that member states do not shirk their responsibilities regarding Roma communities within their borders, with Roma becoming increasingly regarded as a 'European problem' that national governments do not have to address.

Secondly, political subjectivity is performed through acts of citizenship where the individual challenges norms and rules by affirming their citizenship status, or by drawing attention to unequal citizenship provisions. Roma become political subjects through the action of migration. The mobility of bodies – legal and illegalized – across borders demonstrates subjectivity through a deliberate and autonomous action, and it is through this action that Roma migrants have the potential to take ownership over the structures and institutions of citizenship. Investigating acts of citizenship means drawing attention to acts that may not, on the face of it, be considered political (Isin 2008). Furthermore, acts of citizenship require a third party to react through recognition, affirmation, or denial. The formal status of Roma as citizens is recognized by the mobility of Roma across borders and the presence of Roma migrants across the EU polity, but belonging is collectively conferred or withheld by the host state and society.

Roma, a diverse and geographically dispersed group, are under-represented in formal political life, which inhibits efforts to challenge the narratives that create and sustain discrimination and persecution across Europe. It is the nation and the state which determine who belongs and who does not. A refusal to participate in formal forms of politics may itself derive from a critique of the whole political system: in short, a rejection of any and all forms of Roma participation in 'mainstream' politics as potentially catastrophic, inasmuch as the whole European socio-political order has been arguably predicated on Romaphobia. In other words, what might at first glance appear to be disinterest or disregard for politics may in fact be the expression of a profound and radical critique of the existing socio-political and economic order, which has consistently and deliberately excluded Roma. Acts of citizenship then offer a viable opportunity to participate in the political community by simply declaring belonging to the EU polity, rather than, say, the nation or the state, by circumventing those institutions and structures hostile to Roma (although one could argue that the EU itself is hostile to Roma communities as it permits Roma to be persecuted).

For the purposes of this discussion, it does not matter where Roma feel at home or believe they belong. Attachments can arise in a variety of social milieu through work, relationships and cultural practices, and this is the basis of multiple and fluid identity formation. I argue that the majority (in the form of the nation or state) is crucial for the recognition of one's own belonging because the state delineates formal attachments of membership to a political community through citizenship. Jones and Krzyzanowski (2011: 47) maintain that 'belonging is to some extent based on an exclusion of the other'. At some point, belonging must be recognized by those who already belong to the group one aspires to be a part of, and a refusal to recognize can lead to marginalization. Moreover, the refusal to recognize is a denial of access to participation, identity and rights as well as belonging. This unequal citizenship status reveals that citizenship is not a given, automatically bequeathed to those who carry an EU member state passport, because belonging needs to be declared and demanded and is, in turn, either withheld or delineated. Indeed, Tyler (2010) notes that states have attempted to manage their populations more rigorously by passing laws that seek to naturalize specific populations within the state through the scaling of citizenship: processes such as securitization, segregation, deportation, exclusion and incarceration suggest that the state in twenty-first-century Europe is seeking to restrict citizenship, with the result that guarantees of protection and inclusion are seemingly gone. Many Roma are not seeking new political status or seeking to change their nationality but are seeking acceptance in the host state and the ability to participate in the economic, social and political life of the host state. But it is exactly in this context of securitization and restricted citizenship that the political agency of Roma *through* migration has emerged.

ROMA MIGRATION IN
THE EUROPEAN UNION

A Roma migrant occupies a precarious position even if her rights are guaranteed by EU citizenship as she is perceived as belonging neither 'here' nor 'there', which leads to a questioning of both her culture of origin and the newly encountered culture. Roma migration should be understood in the context of historical movement and settlement across Europe at different times and in different spaces with varying degrees of 'success' recognized in terms of adaptation and integration into the host culture. Stråth (2011: 35) argues that migrants risk 'getting lost' by falling between two cultures. While for some migrant communities this liminality resonates with experience, for some Roma the perception is that they have never really belonged 'there' in the first place. Roma communities have been integrated sometimes forcefully through assimilation under socialist regimes, as well as integrating strategically by taking on the dominant language or religion in a particular socio-political context in an attempt to fit in and avoid persecution. However, nations have consistently, and to varying degrees, sought to exclude Roma communities, treating them as an unwanted presence who refuse to adapt to the dominant culture. The nation has the power to include and exclude, and therefore Roma remain the perennial outsiders who are increasingly constructed by the political elite and the media as a threat or menace (Stewart 2012). Even as generations of Roma have resided and reproduced in the same sovereign state and have remained to all intents and purposes loyal to the state through residence, full citizenship – understood as inclusion in the body politic – has been consistently denied for many, while the majority residing in the same territory have been rewarded with full citizenship. EU citizenship offers hope and the opportunity to change the socio-economic and political reality of everyday life for those who have the resources, opportunity and will to migrate.

As we have explored previously, across Europe Roma often possess no defined social status, beyond that of the deviant 'other', and are regarded as lacking material, economic and intellectual utility. A common refrain in West European states is that Roma do not 'fit' because Roma culture is somehow incompatible with British or Italian or Swedish culture. The responsibility to adapt lies with Roma, but no substance is ever added to such claims. For instance, in 2013, former Home Secretary David Blunkett, an MP in the large industrial city of Sheffield in the north of England, said that 'we have got to change the behaviour and the culture of the incoming community, the Roma community, because there is going to be an explosion otherwise' (Bowers 2013). Roma culture is presented as a threat that could lead to inter-communal violence, thus Roma are a group to be fearful of. He further elaborated that there were already tensions with the local community because of aspects of Roma behaviour, such as congregating on the street in the evening, which local residents found intimidating. The image of Roma as the 'folk devil' is nothing new, but the conflation of Roma culture and security has emerged prominently in the context of EU migration. EU citizenship and migration have not caused this; rather, they have served to create a context in which binaries of wanted/unwanted and belong/do not belong are built.

Roma are increasingly treated as a policy issue that political elites and media outlets can target with impunity because Roma lack sufficient weapons to combat prevalent negative ascriptions of group identity. Roma are feared because they represent, for the exalted national subject (Thobani 2007), an unknown, chaotic, anachronistic 'other' from the East. They are feared because they do not fit in their home states – 'Even Romania doesn't want them!' – and now seek to belong here. Their intentions are not known but are assumed: to take what they can get, to *disrupt*, to scrounge, and to commit criminal acts. As Bauman (2004) observes, 'immigrants embody – visibly, tangibly, in the flesh – the inarticulate yet hurtful and painful presentment of their own disposability'. EU migration allows member state governments to play on security concerns (Van Baar 2011a) as well as threats to social services, which legitimizes their own position in protecting the nation and the state from interference from the unwanted, deviant 'other'. The grateful national subject is appeased and reassured. If we look at the actions of authorities in Italy in 2008 (McGarry 2011), the government at the time created a security threat in the guise of recently arrived migrant Roma, whipped up an atmosphere of criminality and disorder, and then unleashed the full power of the state in the form of expulsions and deportations while asserting a reassuring form of sovereign power. This is significant because it means that determining belonging is in the hands of the state, which can recognize and delimit belonging formally and informally.

In a statement in response to the mass expulsion of Roma migrants from France in 2010, the European Commission against Racism and Intolerance denounced the fact that Roma have been 'singled out for abusing EU legislation on freedom of movement' (ECRI 2010). The freedom of movement principle has generated the most attention from European politicians and the media, which have sought to capitalize on the fear of waves of unwanted migrants arriving at borders, leeching off the state, overwhelming services such as health, education and housing, taking jobs from more 'deserving' nationals, and demanding social assistance, all the while obstinately refusing to integrate. The key point here is that citizens are able to migrate across the EU, but some migrants are seen as undesirable and find themselves stigmatized and targeted for special treatment. It is in this context that it is particularly instructive to explore the migration of Roma in the EU and its implications for citizenship, given that Roma face persecution and stigma in their home state, which often prompts the desire to migrate westward in the first place, as well as in the state to which they migrate.

Recent years have witnessed a dramatic spike in acts of violence, property destruction, and the intimidation and murder of Roma across Europe. Roma communities have been the target of right-wing extremism in recent years in France, Hungary, Bulgaria and the Czech Republic, among others. Because of this, many Roma have been forced to leave their homes and claim asylum elsewhere: for example, in 2012, 448 Hungarians, overwhelmingly Romani, were granted refugee status in Canada, a figure up from three in 2009 (in 2009, five applications were rejected, whereas 2,151 applications were rejected in 2012) (Levine-Rasky et al. 2013: 85; see also Vidra 2013). Some Roma opt to apply for asylum in another EU member state, but EU law maintains that all member states shall be deemed 'safe countries of origin' in terms of asylum and that complementary protection on humanitarian grounds shall be available only for persons coming from non-EU member states and stateless persons. For example, Hungarian Roma who applied for asylum in France in 2009 were turned down. In 2010, a group of Roma arrived in Berlin in Moritzplatz and sought asylum even though they were EU citizens. The question then emerges as to whether an EU citizen ought to be able to seek asylum in another member state. But there is a more pressing question: how can an EU citizen be treated so badly in their home state that they seek asylum, rather than availing themselves of the freedom of movement principle (which comes with a number of legal, economic and bureaucratic hurdles to clear before the fruits of EU citizenship can be enjoyed)? The claim to asylum of the Roma in Berlin demonstrates the shortcomings of EU citizenship by flagging up the diverse living conditions and realities of being Roma in different parts of Europe. It also raises a prickly issue of belonging for Roma asylum seekers from Kosovo who were granted asylum status in the late 1990s in France and Germany, among other states, and are now expected to return to Kosovo, where the position of returning Roma is still precarious and many still reside in neighbouring Serbia and Macedonia in refugee camps and retain a de facto statelessness. In 2013, the French authorities arrested and deported 15-year-old Leonarda Dibrani and her family to Kosovo, a country she did not know; this led to widespread criticism and protests in Paris by schoolchildren and adults against her inhumane treatment. Her family lacks documentation but maintains that they are Italian (EU) rather than Kosovar (non-EU). When the authorities subsequently relented due to the mass protests and granted her the right to return to complete her education, she maintained that she would not do so without her family. The fact that a French schoolgirl could be removed from the only life she knew highlights the precarity of many Roma in the EU, where formal status matters and can determine belonging.

Attention on citizenship focuses on the legal recognition by the state and on how individuals participate in citizenship institutions, but 'citizenship, in its formal and informal senses of social belonging, is also an affective state where attachments that matter take shape' (Berland

2011: 163). Significantly, in the context of EU migration, it is *all* Roma whose belonging is negotiated by the host and home state and nation. This extends to Roma who do not migrate and have no intention of migrating, because they are treated as potential migrants and thus as potential problems. Roma communities have responded to historical exclusion by seeking out reciprocal bonds, including with friends, family, the nation and ethnic groups, which all have the capacity to deliver a sense of belonging and worth. Belonging arises through participation in social and cultural life in different contexts, from local to transnational. The social density of citizenship with its rights and responsibilities acts as a network of linkages to guarantee social reciprocity and the forging of affective bonds of belonging, but it can also dislodge a sense of belonging for those on the margins of society, the very people whom citizenship as status ought to protect.

Research on migration focuses on the subjective experience of migrants in terms of lived experiences and their reaction to a new environment, and how the host state manages the various issues presented by migration in terms of service provision, attitudes towards migration or migrants, and the governmental policies in place (Babacan 2010). In the EU context, we are not dealing with 'conventional' migration, which is movement from one state to another. The reality for migrants across the EU is that migration is, in theory at least, less restrictive, and this is certainly true for the educated and/or skilled. EU citizens belong to the political community when accessing the benefits of membership by migrating elsewhere in the EU. Acts of citizenship stretch across borders and territories to involve multiple and overlapping scales of contestation, belonging, identification and struggle (Isin 2009: 371). Bearing this in mind, it is instructive to understand how EU citizenship has changed in the context of migration and how it has impacted on Romaphobia.

THE PERFORMANCE OF CITIZENSHIP: FRANCE IN 2010

The previous sections have outlined the nexus between migration, belonging and citizenship in the EU polity. Most accounts frame Roma as helpless targets of the calcifying populism sweeping across Europe, but such frames fail to capture how citizenship is performed and enacted in this context. By portraying Roma as victims, we deny Roma migrants the position of active social subjects. Citizenship has a formal institutional component but also houses social practices that can challenge the formal institutions. Mezzadra and Nielsen argue that the meaning of citizenship can be changed: 'there is an autonomous space of subjective action that can force significant institutional transformations' (2004: 228). To develop this understanding of subjectivity, the focus is on migrants because they are not formal citizens within a particular political space and their subjective demands usually relate to changing or acquiring formal citizenship and legally belonging to the host state. But this is not true of

Roma, millions of whom possess EU citizenship, so how is agency realized for Roma migrants in the EU through migration? Furthermore, the argument could be made that the mere desire to 'desert' or 'escape' (Mezzadra 2003) from contexts of deprivation and marginalization or socio-political regimes of persecution is already a political act, even if it may not necessarily adhere to normative or customary gestures of politics. Migration is an action that facilitates the performance of acts of citizenship. Here it is helpful to draw attention to the tension between the subjective action of migration and the intersubjective performance of citizenship. When individual Roma migrate east to west, they are recognized by the state and society as a collective, usually a 'problem' community that upsets the cohesive fabric of the nation.

Unlike most other EU migrants, Roma are attempting to escape extreme poverty, widespread societal marginalization and persecution. Roma or *gens de voyage* have been present in France for several hundred years and are thought to currently number approximately 400,000. Around 10,000 to 12,000 of these are estimated to be migrants, 80 per cent of whom are thought to come from Romania or Bulgaria (Council of Europe 2010: 4). More recent Roma migration to France began in the 1990s from Central and Eastern European states and accelerated after the removal of the Schengen visa requirement for Romania and Bulgaria in 2001, which paved the way for a three-month stay as a tourist. Upon election as president in 2007, Sarkozy fuelled an already highly politicized debate on ethnicity and identity in the context of EU migration. Sarkozy initiated a security discourse with the 'Declaration sur la sécurité' on 21 July 2010, in reaction to events that had conspired to diminish the popularity of the government. A campaign targeting Roma migrants followed, which constructed Roma as a security threat and provided a context in which deportations of Roma (primarily to Romania but also to Bulgaria) could be carried out. He announced that the government was going to dismantle 200 illegal Roma sites, which he described as being a source of illegal trafficking and the exploitation of children for the purposes of begging, prostitution or crime (ibid.: 5). In a now infamous speech at Grenoble on 30 July, Sarkozy lumped together 'gens de voyage (travellers), Roma immigrants and French citizens "of foreign origin" and linked, at the same time, crime and migration' (Nacu 2011: 148). The French authorities maintained that Roma camps would be 'systematically evacuated' and some Roma would be given small stipends or would be 'voluntarily' flown home: estimates suggest that between 8,000 and 12,000 Roma were sent back to Romania and Bulgaria by the summer of 2010.

Most accounts of the French Roma crisis have focused on the use of the security discourse and the diplomatic fallout between France and the EU (Parker 2012; McGarry and Drake 2013). However, in reaction to events during the French Roma crisis, Roma citizens performed acts of citizenship that declared belonging to the EU while demanding an end to Romaphobia, particularly the destruction of homes and deportation. In early September 2010, marches were held in Paris, Bordeaux, Marseilles, Toulouse and other French towns as well as solidarity demonstrations in London, Brussels, Madrid, Rome and Barcelona and also in Serbia and Hungary. The march in Paris was led by Roma migrants whose camp was bulldozed in order to protest against the government's security crackdown and had support from human rights groups, unions and left-wing parties, while protestors outside France gathered at French embassies. Protestors paraded through Paris to the sound of drums and whistles. Organizers estimated that approximately 50,000 people took part in the demonstrations and included Roma migrants holding placards saying 'Je suis Européen' and 'Ne nous expulsez pas'. One protestor, Antoinou Jimenez, said, 'It is a right for us to take part in this demonstration, because if we let them crush us, one wonders where this will go.'

The mass protests in France reveal the uneven and tenuous position of Roma migrants in the EU, where Roma citizenship does not protect migrants from racist treatment at the hands of the state. Formal status as citizens did not protect Roma from securitization, the destruction of homes and mass deportation. The message sent by France was clear through its continued and accelerated deportation of Roma: Roma do not belong in France and Roma are not welcome. Such an intervention undermines the principles of EU citizenship and led to a severe diplomatic fallout between France and the EU Commission and Parliament. The mass protests that emerged after the expulsions highlight Roma agency and the potential of Roma migrants to perform acts of citizenship by declaring their belonging to the EU polity as Europeans. Protests took place not just in France but across the EU. They reveal the tension between multiple identities for Roma, as members of the Romani community, as Romanians, Bulgarians, Europeans, as migrants, as parents, and so on, who occupy diverse national and post- or transnational socio-political spaces. Significantly, the protests demonstrate that EU citizenship does not seamlessly map onto the EU migration regime.

The treaties of Schengen (1985) and Maastricht (1992) created a Europe of citizenship and migratory flows to support a particular brand of neoliberalism that promotes a dialectic of exclusion and inclusion: those citizens belong because they retain a citizenship status that is exalted. So the potential demands of Roma migrants could be to acquire that which has been denied: for example, participation in the labour market, or emancipation from societies that discriminate against Roma, or performing one's belonging to the EU polity. In this respect, migration is an action that can bring access to employment and can service neoliberal norms but also performs the multifarious rights and responsibilities of citizenship. The constitution of Europe is not fixed but is highly contested and in flux, with actors and institutions reorganizing and adjusting: migrants are key players in this contestation and change the meaning of citizenship by destabilizing understandings of belonging in a post- or transnational space. The Roma migrant sheds the threadbare cloak of national belonging and affirms agency and visibility, and through this action declares a belonging to the EU polity. This declaration is significantly different from those asserting Roma nationhood and heralds a crucial moment in Roma identity construction.

Migration within the EU has the potential to articulate political demands such as belonging, rights and sovereignty through the mobility of individual bodies, although migration is not just about the movement of physical entities making rational choices about their lives; it is about inclusion and belonging to a political community. Migrants are between 'here' and 'there', belonging and not belonging. For Roma communities across Europe, they have been historically excluded from the nation and the state and are then greeted with familiar negative ascriptions of group identity when they migrate, as David Blunkett's comments verify. Because 'here' and 'there' are regulated by sovereign powers that allocate belonging, by policing the boundaries of belonging/not belonging, the political community that holds particular potential for Roma, especially Roma migrants, is the EU. Migrants act together and remake the social reality of their existence by being visible and performing their belonging through acts of citizenship. The outcome is not a welcoming embrace from the host state, but that is not the point. De Genova (2010: 115), reading Rancière, maintains that we should see the autonomy of migration as '*political* enunciations precisely because they do *not* seek inclusion within the existing order of rights, privileges and entitlements'. Roma are not asking to be welcomed or to belong by migrating but are declaring their presence in the EU polity, actively producing and transforming the political community through what De Genova (2009: 450) calls 'the insubordinate act of making themselves visible', and, in doing so, they draw attention to their legal and material interests as well as to their affective needs. By declaring belonging, Roma migrants affirm their presence in a supposedly equal citizenship regime, calling attention to their marginality across EU member states.

A performance of citizenship is a moment of contestation over the meaning of citizenship, representing a disturbance or challenge to existing norms, and it has the potential to change how citizenship is understood. The invocation of rights through protest and collective mobilization in the summer of 2010 revealed the precarity of EU citizenship for Roma, and how formal citizenship status does not guarantee protection or equality. The application of the freedom of movement principle, available to all EU citizens including Roma, demonstrates that acts of citizenship break routines, understandings and practices; indeed, acts of citizenship are declarations of belonging. For Roma, EU citizenship is a resource to negotiate belonging to national and transnational political communities. As Roma migrate from east to west, their status as citizens is declared, but belonging, a central tenet of citizenship, is either deferred or refused. The horizons opened up by the performative dimensions of citizenship are significant for Roma because they allow Roma to declare belonging to national and transnational political spaces. This duality is not problematic from any legal or cultural perspective but requires Roma to negotiate belonging – if they do not, others, including national governments in the West, will do it for them, as the increased evictions of Roma in France and elsewhere demonstrate. Migration of Roma from Eastern to Western Europe reinforces the inadequacies of national governments in the east to address the needs of Roma communities residing on their territories and the unwillingness of Western states to include Roma. The EU provides the political framework for Roma to perform citizenship through migration, but this presents Roma with questions of belonging that tend to be answered by Western European states in the form of repressive measures.

Acts of citizenship are a rupture, a challenge to the existing order, which might have unintended consequences and are not always beneficial for Roma. It is worth highlighting how the majority has reacted to the Roma migrants' declaration of citizenship: a fortification of impediments to mobility; exaltation of the national subject; a concomitant restriction on belonging for outsiders, including those outsiders already within the citizenship regime; and, finally, Roma who have not migrated and perhaps have no intention of migrating are seen as potential and unwanted migrants who represent a threat. The act of citizenship is dialogical and requires recognition. The Roma migrant is regarded as unsettling because she 'belies the figure of the citizen with singular loyalty, identity and belonging' (Isin 2009: 368). Roma migrants have been targeted for special treatment including expulsion and deportation, which reveals the uneven application of EU citizenship and the disjuncture between formal status and belonging.

UNDERSTANDING THE CAUSES OF ROMAPHOBIA: BETWEEN TERRITORIALITY, IDENTITY AND BELONGING

This book has explored the causes and consequences of Romaphobia and points to the role of the state and nation in creating anti-Roma prejudice. It is motivated by the conviction that only by understanding the causes of Romaphobia can meaningful solutions be found. I have placed the blame for Romaphobia squarely at the feet of nation-states, which have consistently excluded Roma communities from equal citizenship and actively constructed Roma as a deviant 'other' that threatens the fabric of the nation. The negative ascription of Roma identity as criminals, parasitic, thieves, untrustworthy and dirty has stubbornly persisted due to deliberate identity work on the part of the state. The impact of this on Roma has been devastating; today, there are wholescale evictions of Roma from their homes, Roma are targeted by the far right, and Roma children are segregated in schools. Roma are widely understood as outsiders who do not belong to the nation. Fear alone is not enough to explain the level of anti-Roma prejudice and attitudes, which are on the rise in Europe, so this book has sought to train our sight on the nexus between territoriality, belonging and identity, and how states have harnessed the outsider status of Roma to consolidate their own material and symbolic power. What I have shown is that Roma have never lived separate from the majority, in spite of claims to the contrary. Indeed, Roma have served as a foil for the interests of the majority through the elevation of the exalted subject; the national subject is venerated and exalted above all others as the embodiment of quintessential characteristics and the personification of the nation's values and ethics (Thobani 2007: 3), while the outsider provokes anxiety as well as outright hostility. Exaltation is demanded by the nation and confirmed by the state, which becomes the cumulative expression of this community of belonging. Roma enjoy a qualified inclusion within the state that translates to a precarious position as second-class citizens. As claims to the contours of the nation are advanced, a paradox of exclusionary inclusion creates a subordinated identity through which Romaphobia grows and belonging to the political community is withheld.

One of the goals of *Romaphobia* has been to address the 'splendid isolation' (Willems 1997) of Romani studies by drawing on concepts and ideas from a variety of disciplinary perspectives, including politics, sociology, public policy, humanities and urban geography, in order to better grasp processes that conspire to supress Roma communities across Europe. To this end, I have explored the intersection between territoriality, belonging and identity as well as examined issues such as migration, citizenship, mobilization, participation, representation, spatialization, stigma and marginalization. As more scholars emerge to develop research projects highlighting under-researched or misunderstood phenomena, we will gain a better understanding of the complex issues facing Roma communities and determine how best to address these. In order for the lives of Roma to be improved, we need to address Romaphobia in policy interventions and in societal attitudes. As academics, we have a role to play and this ought to be done in the spirit of collaboration and constructive dialogue. After all, we have the same goals in mind: an improvement in the socio-economic and political position of Roma across Europe.

Romaphobia is the last acceptable racism in Europe: acceptable in the sense that it is tolerated and justified. Policy interventions that exclude and persecute Roma, such as ethnic profiling, are justified by the state and society due to the discourses of abjection which reify Roma populations. It is often perfectly acceptable for people to talk about Roma in ways they would never use for other communities. Romaphobia is both covert and overt: it is found in everyday conversations, at work, in public spaces and in public statements by politicians as well as when state authorities target Roma for segregation or eviction or take Roma children away from their families. The capacity and willingness to survive, and in some cases thrive, characterizes the history of Roma in Europe in the face of constant expulsions and persecution: what is more surprising is that European societies, whose own histories are characterized by survival in the face of adversity, do not respect Roma communities more, and, for the most part, do not regard Roma as belonging to the nation.

The power to cultivate and convert social anxieties into fear is a political function, with Roma frequently scapegoated by the state (such as in Italy in 2008 and France in 2010). We are usually drawn to the overt and dramatic manifestations of Romaphobia, but it is important to understand the impact of inaction by the majority, who accept the status quo and allow instances of Romaphobia to go unchecked. It is the tacit acceptance of Romaphobia that allows it to survive. In the past, we saw efforts to assimilate Roma communities by the state, to dilute Roma identity to the point where Roma lost their cultural specificity, but today we see Roma communities targeted by populist forces who spotlight the presence of Roma as being unwanted or threatening. Across a continent still reeling from economic collapse, Roma communities are a convenient scapegoat for social and economic problems, but more participation and visibility, I argue, not less, is the answer. The mobilization of Roma communities in fields of culture, politics and economics is the best way to declare belonging to society, to change the narrative of Roma stigmatization, and to demand rights to be included in society as equals.

The conviction that Roma are Europe's perennial outsiders has become a trope, and, while useful in order to understand the historical exclusion of Roma, it does not preclude the possibility of Roma agency and change in the future. The mobilization across Europe for Roma Pride or for International Roma Day signals a claim of belonging in Europe, to European polities. By articulating demands for equal rights, it challenges the notion of Roma as the archetypal other and enacts the citizenship of Roma across Europe. The EU offers a space for Roma identities to be negotiated and for Roma to declare their belonging to national and transnational polities. Roma do not have to belong in *either* the Roma nation or the majority nation, *nor* are they just citizens of the states in which they reside; Roma are EU citizens as well, and they must enjoy the rights, responsibilities and recognition that national and post-national citizenship demands. It is clear from the discussions that Roma have been historically persecuted and excluded and the only viable means to challenge Romaphobia is to bolster Roma agency. Roma agency is revealed through the declaration of Roma nationhood, through Roma Pride parades and through the performance of Roma citizenship as EU citizens. Agency must negotiate often contradictory ideas of identity and belonging, such as how different nations can (co-)exist on the same territory, that Roma nationalism does not undermine the majority nation, nor does it mean that Roma do not belong to the majority nation. Differential ideas of belonging can be declared and enjoyed in the same political space at local, national and transnational levels.

I want to emphasize that this is not about the exclusion of Roma from any one nation but from *all* nations in Europe. To be clear, Romaphobia is found in every state in Europe. We often see that stigmatized identities become so fixed in everyday practice that changing stereotypes is incredibly difficult. More worryingly, the heavily stigmatized Roma identity can become self-perpetuating: Roma are seen as beggars, which means they cannot get a job and may have to resort to begging to get by. The problems facing Roma communities are interrelated: social issues such as accessing healthcare, education, employment and adequate housing impact on one another. If a Rom is not educated, she is less likely to be able to afford a decent place to live or to get a job, and in turn this means that she has less money to invest in her child's education, and so on. This Romaphobia 'loop' is fuelled by distrust and a lack of understanding between the majority and Roma communities. Any interaction between Roma and non-Roma plays out in the context of the exalted subject who holds all the cards and decides on the rules of the game. This being said, I am careful not to over-emphasize the role of non-Roma in ascribing Roma identity, as it suggests that Roma are a category of people constructed only through 'othering', and this would negate the identity work that goes on within and across Roma communities. The purpose of *Romaphobia* has been to reflect upon the ways in which the state and the nation create differences that subordinate Roma, marginalize their presence in society, and limit their capacity to participate in socio-economic and political life.

The appropriation of territory by the state and society is a significant political accomplishment, undertaken so that states can make subjects and citizens more intelligible. Territoriality is a component of how societies and institutions organize themselves in space with respect to the social and material world. We have seen how this is acutely relevant for Roma as the organization of space is in the hands of the state, which often excludes Roma from particular spaces: Roma frequently are consigned to liminal, dangerous, marginal, polluted spaces that are separate from the majority. This is an expression of the socio-spatial power of the state, asserting its sovereign authority over a given space and people. The majority nation polices the material and symbolic boundaries of the nation and ensures that territoriality is expressed in ways that constitute the norms, principles and discourses of the majority. Seeing territory as a strategy is important but one needs to consider how territorial arrangements impact on group identities and shape group consciousness. Identities are produced and negotiated through the interactions between a group and the space it inhabits: communities produce space and vice versa. The Roma settlements in Slovakia and Macedonia discussed in Chapter 4 have an impact on the residents not only due to their inability to access public services but also in terms of affective bonds of belonging/non-belonging and inclusion/exclusion. Territories are meaningful because they delineate belonging and constitute markers that are intelligible to groups who understand their position in relation to others.

The key to understanding why Roma are marginalized across Europe lies in our conception of territory and space as well as in processes of identity construction and maintenance. This identity work includes European state nationalism as well as articulations of Roma identity and, importantly, the negative ascription of Roma identity by the majority. One example of the latter is the stereotype of Roma as itinerant 'nomads' who have no home or fixed roots; this serves to justify their exclusion today because Roma are not regarded as 'one of us'. The migration of Roma from Central and Eastern Europe to Western European states confirms their lack of commitment to a specific territory or nation due to perceived cultural traits, but the truth is that the socio-economic and political marginalization of Roma motivates migration. Roma seek a better standard of living at a minimum and want to escape persecution, but through migration I argue that Roma perform an act of (transnational) citizenship and belonging to the EU polity.

Changing the hearts and minds of the majority is made more challenging by the presence of Romaphobic statements made by political representatives, the persistence of entrenched negative associations of Roma or Gypsy identity in everyday discourse, and the inability of Roma communities to effectively break these stereotypes. However, there are signs of Roma mobilization in diverse contexts including the Roma Pride movement, which seeks to challenge the negative ascription of Roma identity, to raise consciousness of Roma communities, and to increase the visibility of Roma in public life through the appropriation of public space. Roma Pride, as a movement, is inclusive, involving different Roma communities across Europe and bringing together Roma and non-Roma in a collaborative effort. It dispels the myth that Roma are a helpless community that does not adequately participate in public life and reveals creative ways of challenging Romaphobia. While relatively new, we can see the successes gained by LGBTIQ communities in the global North through Pride movements stretching over fifty years. It may take a generation to start to see significant results, and it is unclear exactly what these successes will look like, but Roma communities are determining their future through participation and representation. The public voice of Roma is often ignored or silenced, and Romaphobia can stifle this voice or distort its message. That is why efforts at Roma mobilization at the local, national and transnational level need to be supported. It is only through the mobilization of Roma communities that manifestations of Romaphobia can be challenged, institutions underpinned by Romaphobia broken, and political practices motivated by Romaphobia halted.

REFERENCES

About, I. (2014) 'Unwanted "Gypsies": The Restriction of Cross Border Mobility and the Stigmatisation of Romani Families in Interwar Western Europe', *Quaderni Storici*, 146/a.XLIX(2): 499–531.

Achim, V. (1998) *The Roma in Romanian History*. Budapest: CEU Press.

Acton, T. (2016) 'Scientific Racism, Popular Racism and the Discourse of the Gypsy Lore Society', *Ethnic and Racial Studies*, 39(7): 1187–204.

Acton, T. and Klímová, I. (2001) 'The International Romani Union: An East European Answer to a West European Question?' in Guy, W. (ed.) *Between Past and Future. The Roma of Central and Eastern Europe*. Hatfield: University of Hertfordshire Press, pp. 157–219.

Agamben, G. (1998) *Homo Sacer: Sovereign Power and Bare Life*. Stanford CA: Stanford University Press.

Agnew, J. (2005) 'Sovereignty Regimes: Territoriality and State Authority in Contemporary World Politics', *Annals of the Association of American Geographers*, 95(2): 437–61.

Akcali, E. and Korkut, U. (2015) 'Urban Transformations in Istanbul and Budapest: Neoliberal Governmentality in the EU's Semi-periphery and its Limits', *Political Geography*, 46: 76–88.

Allport, G. W. (1954) *The Nature of Prejudice*. Cambridge MA: Addison-Wesley.

Amnesty International (2014) *'We Ask For Justice': Europe's Failure to Protect Roma from Racist Violence*. London: Amnesty International.

Amnesty International and the European Roma Rights Centre (2015) 'Romani Community is Fighting Against Forced Evictions and Housing Segregation in Romania'. Public statement, 17 December. AI Index: EUR 39/3100/2015.

Anděl, J. (2013) 'Out/Insiders in Making' in *Krzysztof Wodiczko: Out/Inside(rs)*. Prague: Centre for Contemporary Art, pp. 1–29.

Anderson, B. (1991) *Imagined Communities: Reflections on the Origins and Spread of Nationalism*. London: Verso.

Andreotti, A., Le Galès, P. and Moreno-Fuentes, F. J. (2015) *Globalised Minds, Roots in the City: Urban Upper-Middle Classes in Europe*. Chichester: Wiley.

Appadurai, A. (1991) 'Global Ethnoscapes: Notes and Queries for a Transnational Anthropology' in Fox, R. (ed.) *Recapturing Anthropology: Working in the Present*. Santa Fe NM: School of American Research Press, pp. 191–210.

ATLAS (2014) 'ATLAS of Roma Communities in Slovakia 2013'. http://www.romadecade.org/cms/upload/file/9653_file2_atlas-romadecade.pdf (accessed 29 April 2016).

Ayoub, P. (2016) *When States Come Out: Europe's Sexual Minorities and the Politics of Visibility*. Cambridge: Cambridge University Press.

Babacan, H. (2010) 'Immigration, Nation State and Belonging' in Babacan, A. and Singh, S. (eds) *Migration, Belonging and the Nation State*. Newcastle upon Tyne: Cambridge Scholars Publishing, pp. 7–30.

Badiou, A. (2005) *Being and Event*. London: Continuum.

Barany, Z. (1998) 'Ethnic Mobilisation and the State: The Roma in Eastern Europe', *Ethnic and Racial Studies*, 21(2): 308–27.

Barany, Z. (2001) *The East European Gypsies: Regime Change, Marginality, and Ethnopolitics*. Cambridge: Cambridge University Press.

Barth, F. (1969) *Ethnic Groups and Boundaries: The Social Organisation of Cultural Difference*. Boston MA: Little, Brown.

Bartolini, S. (2005) *Restructuring Europe: Centre Formation, System Building and Political Structuring Between the Nation-State and the European Union*. Oxford: Oxford University Press.

Bauman, Z. (2004) *Wasted Lives: Modernity and its Outcasts*. Cambridge: Polity.

Berland, L. (2011) *Cruel Optimism*. Durham NC: Duke University Press.

Bernstein, M. (1997) 'Celebration and Suppression: The Strategic Uses of Identity by the Lesbian and Gay Movement', *American Journal of Sociology*, 103: 531–65.

Bhopal, K. (2011) '"This is a School, it's not a Site": Teachers' Attitudes Towards Gypsy and Traveller Pupils in Schools in England, UK', *British Educational Research Journal*, 37(3): 465–83.

Bíró, A. (2013) 'The Price of Roma Integration' in Guy, W. (ed.) *From Victimhood to Citizenship: The Path of Romani Integration. A Debate*. Budapest: Kossuth Kiadó, pp. 10–39.

Bonilla-Silva, E. (2013) *Racism without Racists: Color-Blind Racism and the Persistence of Inequality in America*. Langham MD: Rowman and Littlefield.

Bourke, J. (2005) *Fear: A Cultural History*. London: Virago.

Bowers, J. (2013) 'David Blunkett is Feeding Romaphobia',

The Guardian, 13 November. http://www.theguardian.com/commentisfree/2013/nov/13/david-blunkett-romaphobia-slovak-roma (accessed 29 May 2016).

Brooks, E. (2016) 'Europe Can Learn from its Largest Ethnic Minority', *OpenDemocracy*, 7 April. https://www.opendemocracy.net/can-europe-make-it/ethel-brooks/europe-can-learn-from-its-largest-ethnic-minority (accessed 5 May 2016).

Brubaker, R. (2002) 'Ethnicity Without Groups', *Archives Européennes de Sociologie*, XLIII(2): 163–89.

Brubaker, R. (2003) 'Neither Individualism nor "Groupism": A Reply to Craig Calhoun', *Ethnicities*, 3(4): 553–7.

Brubaker, R. (2004) *Ethnicity Without Groups*. Cambridge MA: Harvard University Press.

Butler, J. and Spivak, G. (2007) *Who Sings the Nation? Language, Politics, Belonging*. Chicago IL: University of Chicago Press.

Calhoun, C. (2003) 'The Variability of Belonging: A Response to Rogers Brubaker', *Ethnicities*, 3(4): 558–68.

Ciorou, I. (2009) 'Some Geographical Aspects of the Gypsy Population from Moldovia in the 19th Century', *Seminarul Geografic 'D. Cantemir'*, 29: 151–6.

Clark, C. (2004) '"Severity has often Enraged but Never Subdued a Gypsy": The History and Making of European Romani Stereotypes' in Saul, N. and Tebbutt, S. (eds) *The Role of the Romanies: Images and Counter-Images of 'Gypsies'/ Romanies in European Cultures*. Liverpool: Liverpool University Press, pp. 226–46.

Clark, C. and Rice, G. (2012) 'Spaces of Hate, Places of Hope: The Romanian Roma in Belfast' in Stewart, M. (ed.) *The Gypsy 'Menace': Populism and the New Anti-Gypsy Politics*. London: Hurst, pp. 167–90.

Clark, M. (2015) 'Don't Call them Gypsies and Everything Else You Need to Know about Roma Women', *Refinery 29*, 16 December. http://www.refinery29.com/2015/12/98355/roma-women-activism-europe#slide (accessed 5 May 2016).

Cohen, A. P. (1986) *Belonging: Identity and Social Organization in British Rural Cultures*. Manchester: Manchester University Press.

Cohen, R. (1986) 'Diasporas and the Nation-State: From Victims to Challengers', *International Affairs*, 72(3): 507–20.

Connor, W. (1986) 'The Impact of Homelands upon Diasporas' in Sheffer, G. (ed.) *Modern Diasporas in International Politics*. London: Croom Helm, pp. 16–45.

Council of Europe (1993) *Recommendation 1203 Parliamentary Assembly*. Strasbourg: Council of Europe.

Council of Europe (2010) 'Recent Rise in National Security Discourse in Europe: The Case of Roma'. Doc. 12386, 5 October. Strasbourg: Council of Europe, Political Affairs Committee.

Council of Europe (2012) *Descriptive Glossary of Terms Related to Roma Issues*. Strasbourg: Council of Europe.

Council of the European Union (2009) *The 10 Common Basic Principles on Roma Inclusion*. Brussels: Council of the European Union. http://www.coe.int/t/dg4/youth/Source/Resources/Documents/2011_10_Common_Basic_Principles_Roma_Inclusion.pdf (accessed 29 April 2016).

Csepeli, G. and Simon, D. (2004) 'Construction of Roma Identity in Eastern and Central Europe: Perception and Self-Identification', *Journal of Ethnic and Migration Studies*, 30(1): 129–50.

Csepeli, G., Antal, Ö. and M. Székelyi (2000) *Grappling with National Identity: How Nations See Each Other in Central Europe*. Budapest: Akadémiai Kiadó.

Czirfusz, M., Horváth, V., Jelinek, C., Pósfai, Z. and L. Szabó
(2015) 'Gentrification and Rescaling Urban Governance in
Budapest – Józsefváros', *Intersections: East European Journal
of Society and Politics*, 1(4): 55–77.

De Genova, N. (2009) 'Conflicts of Mobility, and the Mobility
of Conflict: Rightlessness, Presence, Subjectivity, Freedom',
Subjectivity, 29: 445–66.

De Genova, N. (2010) 'The Queer Politics of Migration:
Reflections on "Illegality" and Incorrigibility', *Studies in
Social Justice*, 4(2): 101–26.

De Genova, N. (2013) '"We are of the Connections":
Migration, Methodological Nationalism, and "Militant
Research"', *Postcolonial Studies*, 16(3): 250–8.

Delaney, D. (2005) *Territory*. Oxford: Blackwell.

Delanty, G. (2000) *Citizenship in a Global Age: Society, Culture,
Politics*. Milton Keynes: Open University Press.

Duyvendak, J. W. (2012) *The Politics of Home: Nostalgia
and Belonging in Western Europe and the United States*.
Basingstoke: Palgrave.

ECRI (2010) 'Statement on the Situation of Roma
Migrants in France'. European Commission against
Racism and Intolerance (ECRI), 24 August. http://
www.coe.int/t/dghl/monitoring/ecri/Library/
PressReleases/70-24_08_2010_Roma_Migrants_en.asp
(accessed 21 May 2016).

EGAM (2011a) *Roma Pride 2011: Overview of Initiatives
Throughout Europe*. Paris: European Grassroots Antiracist
Movement (EGAM). http://egam-eu.blogspot.
com/2011/09/roma-pride-2011-overview-of-initiatives.
html (accessed 21 May 2016).

EGAM (2011b) *Roma, Racism, Europe: 'Dosta!', and Roma
Pride*. Manifesto. Paris: European Grassroots Antiracist

Movement (EGAM). http://egam-eu.blogspot.
com/2011/09/roma-racism-europe-dosta-and-roma-pride.
html (accessed 21 May 2016).

ERRC (2014) 'Hungarian City Set to "Expel" its Roma',
European Roma Rights Centre (ERRC), 25 June. http://
www.errc.org/article/hungarian-city-set-to-expel-its-
roma/4293 (accessed 10 May 2016).

ERRC (2015) 'Municipality of Rome Condemned for La
Barbuta Camp: For the First Time in Europe an Official
Roma-Only Settlement Ruled Discriminatory', European
Roma Rights Centre (ERRC), 10 June. http://www.errc.
org/article/municipality-of-rome-condemned-for-la-
barbuta-camp-for-the-first-time-in-europe-an-official-
roma-only-settlement-ruled-discriminatory/4369 (accessed
10 May 2016).

ERTF (2005) *First Annual Report*. Strasbourg: European Roma
and Traveller Forum (ERTF), Council of Europe.

Essed, P. (1991) *Understanding Everyday Racism: An
Interdisciplinary Theory*. London: Sage.

European Commission (2008) 'Commission Staff Working
Document. Roma in Europe: The Implementation of
European Union Instruments and Policies for Roma
Inclusion – Progress Report 2008–2010. Brussels, 7.4.2010.
SEC(2010) 400 final'. Brussels: European Commission.

European Commission (2012) *Special Eurobarometer 393.
Discrimination in the European Union in 2015*. Brussels: DG
Communication.

European Commission (2015) *Special Eurobarometer 437.
Discrimination in the European Union in 2015*. Brussels: DG
Communication.

Fanon, F. (1968) *Black Skin, White Masks*. London: Pluto.

Farnam, A. (2003) 'Slovakian Roma Forced to Ghettos', *Christian Science Monitor*, 3 January. http://www.csmonitor.com/2003/0103/p04s02-woeu.html (accessed 15 May 2016).

Fassin, É. (2015a) 'The Roma Question: The New Politics of Race in Color-Blind France and Neoliberal Europe'. Lecture given at UCLA Centre for European and Russian Studies, 7 December.

Fassin, É. (2015b) 'Why the Roma?', *Theory, Culture, Society*, 7 October. http://www.theoryculturesociety.org/eric-fassin-why-the-roma/ (accessed 29 April 2016).

Filčák, R. and Steger, T. (2014) 'Ghettos in Slovakia. Confronting Roma Social and Environmental Exclusion', *Analyse and Kritic*, 2: 229–50.

Fleming, C., Lamont, M. and Welburn, J. (2012) 'African Americans Respond to Stigmatisation: The Meanings and Salience of Confronting, Deflecting Conflict, Educating the Ignorant and "Managing" the Self', *Ethnic and Racial Studies*, 35(3): 400–17.

Flesher-Fominaya, C. (2015) 'Autonomous Social Movements and the Paradox of Anti-Identitarian Collective Identity' in McGarry, A. and Jasper, J. (eds) *The Identity Dilemma: Social Movements and Collective Identity*. Philadelphia PA: Temple University Press, pp. 65–84.

Fogg, S. (2009) *The Politics of Everyday Life in Vichy France: Foreigners, Undesirables, and Strangers*. Cambridge: Cambridge University Press.

Fortier, A. M. (1999) 'Re-membering Place and the Performance of Belonging(s)', *Theory, Culture and Society*, 16(2): 41–64.

Foucault, M. (2007) *Security, Territory, Population: Lectures at the Collège de France 1977–78*. Basingstoke: Palgrave.

FRA (2009) *Housing Conditions of Roma and Travellers in the European Union: Comparative Report.* Conference edition, October. Brussels: European Union Agency for Fundamental Rights (FRA).

FRA (2011) *Data in Focus Report: Multiple Discrimination. EU Minorities and Discrimination Survey.* Brussels: European Union Agency for Fundamental Rights (FRA).

FRA (2012) *The Situation of Roma in 11 EU Member States: Survey Results at a Glance.* Luxembourg: European Union Agency for Fundamental Rights (FRA).

Fraser, A. (1995) *The Gypsies: The Peoples of Europe.* Oxford: Wiley.

Freire, P. (2004) *Pedagogy of Indignation.* Boulder CO: Paradigm.

Gamson, J. (1995) 'Must Identity Movements Self-Destruct? A Queer Dilemma', *Social Problems*, 42(3): 390–407.

Gay y Blasco, P. (1999) *Gypsies in Madrid: Sex, Gender and the Performance of Identity.* Oxford: Berg.

Gellner, E. (1983) *Nations and Nationalism.* Ithaca NY: Cornell University Press.

Geschiere, P. and Nyamnjoh, F. (2000) 'Capitalism and Autochthony: The Seesaw of Mobility and Belonging', *Public Culture* 12(2): 423–52.

Gheorghe, N. (1991) 'Roma-Gypsy Ethnicity in Eastern Europe', *Social Research*, 58(4): 829–44.

Gheorghe, N. (1997) 'The Social Construction of Romani Identity' in Acton, T. (ed.) *Gypsy Politics and Traveler Identity.* Hatfield: University of Hertfordshire Press, pp. 153–63.

Gheorghe, N. (2013) 'Choices to Be Made and Prices to Be Paid: Potential Roles and Consequences in Roma Activism and Policy-Making' in Guy, W. (ed.) *From Victimhood to Citizenship: The Path of Romani Integration. A Debate.* Budapest: Kossuth Kiadó, pp. 40–97.

Goffman, E. (1963) *Stigma: Notes on the Management of Spoiled Identity.* Englewood Cliffs NJ: Prentice-Hall.

Goodwin, M. (2004) 'The Romani Claim to Non-Territorial Nation Status: Recognition from an International Legal Perspective', *Roma Rights*, 1: 54–64.

Gopnik, A. (2014) 'The People Who Pass: Pickpockets and Paranoia in France', *The New Yorker*, 13 January. http:// www.newyorker.com/magazine/2014/01/13/the-people-who-pass (accessed 29 April 2016).

Government of Slovakia (2012) *Strategy of the Slovak Republic for the Integration of Roma up to 2020.* Bratislava: Government of Slovakia.

Gustafson, P. (2009) 'Mobility and Territorial Belonging', *Environment and Behaviour*, 41(4): 490–508.

Guy, W. (1975) 'Ways of Looking at Roma: The Case of Czechoslovakia' in Rehfisch, F. (ed.) *Gypsies, Tinkers and Other Travellers.* London: Academic, pp. 201–29.

Hall, S. (1992) 'Cultural Identity in Question' in Hall, S., Held, D. and McGrew, T. (eds) *Modernity and its Futures.* Cambridge: Polity, pp. 273–316.

Hall, S. (1996) 'Introduction: Who Needs Identity?' in Hall, S. and Du Gay, P. (eds) *Questions of Cultural Identity.* London: Sage, pp. 1–17.

Hancock, I. (1994) *On the Origins and Current Situation of the Romani Population in Europe and the Responsibility of the American Media to Make that Situation Known.* Report Before the Congressional Human Rights Hearing on Abuses Against Gypsies in Eastern Europe, Washington, 14 April.

Harvey, D. (1996) *Justice, Nature and the Geography of Difference.* Oxford: Blackwell.

Hechter, M. (2000) *Containing Nationalism*. New York: Oxford University Press.

Horváth, K. (2012) 'Silencing and the Naming of Difference' in Stewart, M. (ed.) *The Gypsy 'Menace': Populism and the New Anti-Gypsy Politics*. London: Hurst, pp. 117–36.

Howarth, C. (2002) '"So, You're from Brixton?": The Struggle for Recognition and Esteem in a Multicultural Community', *Ethnicities* 2(2): 237–60.

Hušek, P. and Tvrdá, K. (2015) 'The Collective Singularity of Anti-Racist Actors: A Case Study of the Roma Minority in the Czech Republic', *Ethnic and Racial Studies*, 39(1): 49–67.

Hušová, M. (2010) 'Even After Demolition, Lunik IX Remains the Greatest Romani Ghetto in Europe', *Roma Transitions*, 16 December. http://www.romatransitions.org/even-after-demolition-lunik-ix-remains-the-greatest-romani-ghetto-in-europe/ (accessed 13 May 2016).

Ignatieff, M. (1994) *Blood and Belonging: Journeys into the New Nationalism*. London: Vintage.

Isin, E. (2008) 'Theorizing Acts of Citizenship' in Isin, E. and Nielsen, G. (eds) *Acts of Citizenship*. London: Zed Books, pp. 15–43.

Isin, E. (2009) 'Citizenship in Flux: The Figure of the Activist Citizen', *Subjectivity*, 29: 367–88.

Isin, E. (2012) *Citizens Without Frontiers*. London: Bloomsbury.

Isin, E. and Nielsen, G. (eds) (2008) *Acts of Citizenship*. London: Zed Books.

Ivancheva, M. (2015) 'From Informal to Illegal: Roma Housing in (Post-)Socialist Sofia', *Intersections: East European Journal of Society and Politics*, 1(4): 38–54.

Jacobson, D. (2002) *Place and Belonging in America*, Baltimore: Johns Hopkins University Press.

Jaspal, R. and Cinnirella, M. (2012) 'The Construction of Ethnic Identity: Insights from Identity Process Theory', *Ethnicities*, 2(5): 503–30.

Jasper, J. (2015) 'Introduction: Players and Arenas Formally Known as the State' in Jasper, J. and Duyvendak, J. V. (eds) *Breaking Down the State*. Amsterdam: Amsterdam University Press, pp. 9–24.

Jasper, J. and McGarry, A. (2015) 'Introduction: The Identity Dilemma, Social Movements and Contested Identity' in McGarry, A. and Jasper, J. (eds) *The Identity Dilemma: Social Movements and Collective Identity*. Philadelphia PA: Temple University Press, pp. 1–17.

Jenkins, R. (2008) *Social Identities*. London: Routledge.

Jones, P. R. and Krzyzanowski, M. (2011) 'Identity, Belonging and Migration: Beyond Describing "Others"' in Delanty, G., Wodak, R. and Jones, P. R. (eds) *Identity, Belonging and Migration*. Liverpool: Liverpool University Press, pp. 38–53.

Jovanovic, Z. (2016) 'On International Roma Day, A Call for Courage and Clarity', *Open Society Foundations: Voices*, 7 April. https://www.opensocietyfoundations.org/voices/international-roma-day-call-courage-and-clarity (accessed 5 May 2016).

Kabachnik, P. (2010a) 'England or Uruguay?: The Persistence of Place and the Myth of the Placeless Gypsy', *Area*, 42(2): 198–207.

Kabachnik, P. (2010b) 'Place Invaders: Constructing the Nomadic Threat in England', *Geographical Review*, 100(1): 90–108.

Kacarska, S. (2012) *Europeanisation Through Mobility: Visa Liberalisation and Citizenship Regimes in the Western Balkans*. CITSEE Working Paper 2012/21. Edinburgh: The

Europeanisation of Citizenship in the Successor States of the Former Yugoslavia (CITSEE), pp. 1–29.

Kapralski, S. (1997) 'Identity Building and the Holocaust: Roma Political Nationalism', *Nationalities Papers*, 25(2): 269–83.

Kapralski, S. (2012) 'Symbols and Rituals in the Mobilisation of the Romani National Ideal', *Studies in Ethnicity and Nationalism*, 12(11): 64–81.

Karaman, O. and Islam, T. (2012) 'On the Dual Nature of Intra-Urban Borders: The Case of a Romani Neighbourhood in Istanbul', *Cities*, 29: 234–43.

Kärrholm, M. (2007) 'A Conceptual Discussion of Territoriality, Materiality and the Everyday Life of Public Space', *Space and Culture*, 10(4): 437–53.

Klauser, F. (2012) 'Thinking Through Territoriality: Introducing Claude Raffestin to Anglophone Sociospatial Theory', *Environment and Planning D: Society and Space*, 30: 106–20.

Kóczé, A. (2009) *Missing Intersectionality: Race/Ethnicity, Gender and Class in Current Research and Policies on Romani Women in Europe*. Budapest: Central University Press.

Kóczé, A. (2015) 'Speaking from the Margins' in *Nothing About Us, Without Us: Roma Participation in Policy-Making and Knowledge Production. Roma Rights 2*. Budapest: European Roma Rights Centre, pp. 83–6.

Korkut, U., Bucken-Knapp, G., McGarry, A., Hinnfors, J. and Drake, H. (2013) *The Politics and Discourses of Migration in Europe*. New York: Palgrave.

Kovai, C. (2012) 'Hidden Potentials in "Naming the Gypsy": The Transformation of the Gypsy-Hungarian Distinction' in Stewart, M. (ed.) *The Gypsy 'Menace': Populism and the New Anti-Gypsy Politics*. London: Hurst, pp. 281–94.

Kristeva, J. (1991) *Strangers to Ourselves*. New York: Columbia University Press.

Kuus, M. and Agnew, J. (2008) 'Theorising the State Geographically: Sovereignty, Subjectivity, Territoriality' in Cox, K. R., Low, M. and Robinson, J. (eds) *The SAGE Handbook of Political Geography*. London: Sage, pp. 95–106.

Kymlicka, W. and Norman, W. (2000) *Citizenship in Divided Societies*. Oxford: Oxford University Press.

Lakhani, S., Sacks, A. and Heltberg, R. (2014) *'They Are Not Like Us': Understanding Social Exclusion*. Policy Research Working Paper 6784. Washington DC: World Bank.

Lamont, M. (2009) 'Responses to Racism, Health and Social Inclusion as a Dimension of Successful Societies' in Hall, P. and Lamont, M. (eds) *Successful Societies: How Institutions and Culture Affect Health*. New York: Cambridge University Press, pp. 151–68.

Lamont, M. and Fournier, M. (eds) (1992) *Cultivating Difference: Symbolic Boundaries and the Making of Inequality*. Chicago IL: University of Chicago Press.

Lamont, M. and Mizrachi, N. (2012) 'Ordinary People Doing Extraordinary Things: Responses to Stigmatization in Comparative Perspectives', *Ethnic and Racial Studies*, 25: 365–81.

Lemon, A. (2000) *Between Two Fires: Gypsy Performance and Romani Memory from Pushkin to Postsocialism*. Durham NC: Duke University Press.

Levine-Rasky, C., Beaudoin, J. and St Clair, P. (2013) 'The Exclusion of Roma Claimants in Canadian Refugee Policy', *Patterns of Prejudice*, 48(1): 67–93.

Liégeois, J. P. and Gheorghe, N. (1995) *Roma/Gypsies: A European Minority*. London: Minority Rights Group International.

Lípa, J. (1979) 'Cases of Coexistence of Two Varieties of Romani in the Same Territory in Slovakia', *International Research of the Sociology of Language*, 19: 51-7.

Lister, R. (1998) 'Citizenship and Differentiation: Towards a Differentiated Universalism', *European Journal of Social Theory*, 1(1): 71–90.

Loftland, L. (1998) *The Public Realm*. New York: Aldine de Gruyters.

Luccassen, L., Willems, W. and Cottaar, A. M. (1998) *Gypsies and Other Itinerant Groups*. Basingstoke: Macmillan.

Maddison, S. (2004) 'Young Women in the Australian Women's Movement: Collective Identity and Discursive Politics', *International Feminist Journal of Politics*, 6: 234–56.

Magdolenová, K. (2003) 'A So-Far Unfinished Story of Segregation – "Lunik Story"'. Unpublished manuscript. https://www.academia.edu/5950167/A_so_far_unfinished_story_of_segregation_-_Lunik_story_ (accessed 15 May 2016).

Marshall, T. H. (1992) 'Citizenship and Social Class: Part I' in Marshall, T. H. and Bottomore, T. (eds) *Citizenship and Social Class*. London: Pluto.

Marushiakova, E. and Popov, V. (2004) 'The Roma – A Nation Without a State? Historical Background and Contemporary Tendencies' in Burszta, W. et al. (eds) *Nationalisms Across the Globe: An Overview of Nationalisms in State-Endowed and Stateless Nations. Vol. 1: Europe*. Poznan: School of Humanities and Journalism, pp. 433–55.

Massey, D. (1991) 'A Global Sense of Place', *Marxism Today*, 38: 24-9.

Massey, D. (1998) 'The Spatial Construction of Youth Cultures' in Skelton, T. and Valentine, G. (eds) *Cool Places: Geographies of Youth Cultures*. London: Routledge, pp. 121–9.

Mayall, D. (2004) *Gypsy Identities 1500–2000. From Egipcyans and Moon-men to the Ethnic Romany*. London: Routledge.

Mayer, N., Michelat, G., Tiberj, V. and Vitale, T. (2016) 'Des Sentiments Plus Nuancés Envers les Roms' in Commission Nationale Consultative des Droits de l'homme (CNCDH) *La Lutte Contre le Racisme, l'Antisémitisme et la Xénophobie. Année 2016*. Paris: La Documentation Française, pp. 339–55.

McGarry, A. (2008) 'Ethnic Group Identity and the Roma Social Movement: Transnational Organizing Structures of Representation', *Nationalities Papers*, 36(3): 449–70.

McGarry, A. (2010) *Who Speaks for Roma? Political Representation of a Transnational Minority Community*. London: Continuum.

McGarry, A. (2011) 'The Roma Voice in the European Union: Between National Belonging and Transnational Identity', *Social Movement Studies*, 10(3): 283–97.

McGarry, A. (2014) 'Roma as a Political Identity: Exploring Representations of Roma in Europe', *Ethnicities*, 14(6): 756–74.

McGarry, A. and Agarin, T. (2014) 'Unpacking the Roma Participation Puzzle: Voice, Presence and Influence', *Ethnic and Migration Studies*, 40(12): 1972–90.

McGarry, A. and Drake, H. (2013) 'The Politicization of Roma as an Ethnic Other: Security Discourse in France and the Politics of Belonging' in Korkut, U., Bucken-Knapp, G., McGarry, A., Hinnfors, J. and Drake, H. (eds) *The Politics and Discourses of Migration in Europe*. New York: Palgrave Macmillan.

McGarry, A. and Jasper, J. (eds) (2015) *The Identity Dilemma: Social Movements and Collective Identity*. Philadelphia PA: Temple University Press.

Melucci, A. (1995) 'The Process of Collective Identity' in Johnston, H. and Klandermans, B. (eds) *Social Movements and Culture*. Minneapolis MN: University of Minnesota Press.

Mezzadra, S. (2003) 'The Right to Escape', *Ephemera* 4(3): 267–75.

Mezzadra, S. and Neilson, B. (2004) 'Né qui, né altrove: Migration, Detention, Desertion: A Dialogue', *borderlands* 2(1).

Mirga, A. and Gheorghe, N. (1997) *The Roma in the Twenty-First Century: A Policy Paper*. Princeton NJ: Project on Ethnic Relations.

Mishra, S. (2006) *Diaspora Criticism*. Edinburgh: Edinburgh University Press.

Mudde, C. (2005) 'Racist Extremism in Central and Eastern Europe', *East European Politics and Societies*, 19(2): 161–84.

Murphy, A. B. (2012) 'Entente Territorial: Sack and Raffestin on Territoriality', *Environmental Planning D*, 30(1): 159–72.

Nacu, A. (2011) 'The Politics of Roma Migration: Framing Identity Struggles among Romanian and Bulgarian Roma in the Paris Region', *Journal of Ethnic and Migration Studies*, 37(1): 135–50.

Newman, D. and Paasi, A. (1998) 'Fences and Neighbours in the Post-Modern World: Boundary Narratives in Political Geography', *Progress in Human Geography*, 22(2): 186–207.

Novak, P. (2011) 'The Flexible Territoriality of Borders', *Geopolitics*, 16(4): 741–67.

NPD (2015) *Submission to the Committee on the Elimination of Racial Discrimination*. 87th session in Geneva. Geneva: Network for Protection from Discrimination (NPD). http://tbinternet.ohchr.org/Treaties/CERD/Shared%20Documents/MKD/INT_CERD_NGO_MKD_21096_E.pdf (accessed 25 May 2016).

Okely, J. (1997) 'Non-Territorial Culture as the Rationale for the Assimilation of Gypsy Children', *Childhood: A Global Journal of Child Research*, 4: 63–80.

Olzak, S. (2003) 'Ethnic and Nationalist Social Movements' in Snow, D., Soule, S. and Kriesi, H. (eds) *The Blackwell Companion to Social Movements*. Oxford: Blackwell, pp. 666–93.

OSCE (2003) *Action Plan on Improving the Situation of Roma/ Sinti Within the OSCE Area*. PC.DEC/566. Maastricht: Organization for Security and Cooperation in Europe (OSCE).

OSCE and ODIHR (2008) *Implementation of the Action Plan on Improving the Situation of Roma and Sinti within OSCE Area. Status Report 2008*. Warsaw: Organization for Security and Cooperation in Europe (OSCE), Office for Democratic Institutions and Human Rights (ODIHR).

OSF (2015) 'Call for Concept Papers. Barvalipe Schools– Generation 2015'. New York: Open Society Foundations (OSF), Roma Initiatives Office. https://www. opensocietyfoundations.org/sites/default/files/ barvalipe-2015-guidelines-20150610_1.pdf (accessed 15 May 2016).

Painter, J. (2010) 'Rethinking Territory', *Antipode*, 42(5): 1090–118.

Parker, O. (2012) 'Roma and the Politics of EU Citizenship in France: Everyday Security and Resistance', *Journal of Common Market Studies*, 50(3): 475–491.

Penrose, J. (2002) 'Nations, States and Homelands: Territory and Territoriality in Nationalist Thought', *Nations and Nationalism* 8(3): 277–97.

Petrova, D. (2004) 'Between a Myth and the Future', *Roma Rights*, 1: 7–32.

Phillips, A. (1998) *The Politics of Presence*. Oxford: Oxford University Press.

Pickering, J., Kintrea, K. and Bannister, J. (2011) 'Invisible Walls and Visible Youth: Territoriality among Young People in British Cities', *Urban Studies*, 49(5): 945–60.

Powell, R. (2013) 'Loïc Wacquant's "Ghetto" and Ethnic Minority Segregation in the UK: The Neglected Case of Gypsy-Travellers', *International Journal of Urban and Regional Research* 37(1): 115–34

Prozorov, S. (2008) 'Belonging and Inclusion in European-Russian Relations: Alain Badiou and the Truth of Europe', *Journal of International Relations and Development*, 11: 181–207.

Raffestin, C. (1977) 'Paysage et territorialité', *Cahiers de Géographie du Québec*, 21(53/54): 123–34.

Rancière, J. (2004) *The Politics of Aesthetics*. New York: Continuum.

Robbins, J. (2010) 'A Nation Within? Indigenous Peoples, Representation and Sovereignty in Australia', *Ethnicities*, 10(2): 257–74.

Rokkan, S. and Urwin, D. (1983) *Economy, Territory, Identity: Politics of West European Peripheries*. London: Sage.

Roosens, E. (1989) *Creating Ethnicity*. London: Sage.

Ross, C. (2008) 'Visions of Visibility: LGBT Communities in Turin', *Modern Italy*, 13(3): 241–60.

Sack, R. (1986) *Human Territoriality*. Cambridge: Cambridge University Press.

Safran, W. (1991) 'Diasporas in Modern Society: Myths of Homeland and Return', *Diaspora: A Journal of Transnational Studies*, 1(1): 83–99.

Sardelic, J. (2015) 'Romani Minorities and Uneven Citizenship Access in the Post-Yugoslav Space', *Ethnopolitics*, 14(2): 159–79.

Sardu, M. and Kovats, M. (2015) 'Roma Identity as an Expert-Political Construction', *Social Inclusion*, 3(5): 5–18.

Sassen, S. (2008) *Territory, Authority, Rights: From Medieval to Global Assemblages*. Princeton NJ: Princeton University Press.

Savage, M., Bagnall, G. and Longhurst, B. (2005) *Globalization and Belonging*. London: Sage.

Scott, J. (1998) *Seeing Like a State: How Certain Schemes to Improve the Human Condition Have Failed*. Hartford CT: Yale University Press.

Scott, J. (2009) *The Art of Not Being Governed: An Anarchist History of Upland Southeast Asia*. Hartford CT: Yale University Press.

Sheffer, G. (1986) 'A New Field of Study: Modern Diasporas in International Politics' in Sheffer, G. (ed.) *Modern Diasporas in International Politics*. London: Croom Helm, pp. 1–15.

Sibley, D. (1981) *Outsiders in Urban Societies*. New York: St. Martin's Press.

Sibley, D. (1995) *Geographies of Exclusion: Society and Difference in the West*. London: Routledge.

Sigona, N. (2005) 'Locating "The Gypsy Problem". The Roma in Italy: Stereotyping, Labelling and "Nomad Camps"', *Journal of Ethnic and Migration Studies*, 31(4): 741–56.

Sigona, N. (2015) 'Campzenship: Reimagining the Camp as a Social and Political Space', *Citizenship Studies*, 19(1): 1–15.

Simhandl, K. (2009) 'Beyond Boundaries? Comparing the Construction of the Political Categories "Gypsy" and "Roma" Before and After EU Enlargement' in Sigona, N. and Trehan, N. (eds) *Romani Politics in Contemporary Europe: Poverty, Ethnic Mobilisation and the Neoliberal Order*. Basingstoke: Palgrave, pp. 72–93.

Skenderi, S. (2014) *Roma Housing and Social Integration in Republic of Macedonia*. Skopje: Roma Decade Focal Point Macedonia.

Smith, A. (1986) *The Ethnic Origins of Nations*. Oxford: Wiley.

Smith, M. P. (1994) 'Can You Imagine? Transnational Migration and the Globalization of Grassroots Politics', *Social Text* 39: 15–33.

Soja, E. (1971) *The Political Organization of Space*. Washington DC: Association of American Geographers.

Soros, G. (2011) 'George Soros message for the "Me sem rom, me sem romni"', YouTube, 10 October. http://www.youtube.com/watch?feature=player_embedded&v=dTHwKg7omwE#! (accessed 21 April 2016).

Soysal, Y. (1994) *The Limits of Citizenship: Migrants and Postnational Membership in Europe*. Chicago IL: University of Chicago Press.

Stewart, M. (1997) *The Time of the Gypsies*. London: Westview.

Stewart, M. (2012) 'Populism, Roma and the European Politics of Cultural Difference' in Stewart, M. (ed.) *The Gypsy Menace: Populism and the New Anti-Gypsy Politics*. London: Hurst, pp. 3–23.

Stewart, M. (2013) 'Roma and Gypsy "Ethnicity" as a Subject of Anthropological Inquiry', *Annual Review of Anthropology*, 42: 415–32.

Stråth, B. (2011) 'Belonging and European Identity' in Delanty, G., Wodak, R. and Jones, P. (eds) *Identity, Belonging and Migration*. Liverpool: Liverpool University Press.

Sudetic, C. (2013) 'Roma in Political Life: Macedonia – Pride and Prejudice', *Open Society Foundations: Voices*, 10 September. https://www.opensocietyfoundations.org/

voices/roma-political-life-macedonia-pride-and-prejudice (accessed 29 April 2016).

Szalai, J. (2014) 'Roma Marginalization and Exclusion in a Comparative Perspective' in Szalai, J. and Zentai, V. (eds) *Faces and Causes of Roma Marginalization in Local Contexts: Hungary, Romania, Serbia*. Budapest: Centre for Policy Studies, Central European University (CEU).

Taylor, P. J. (1994) 'The State as Container: Territoriality in the Modern World-System', *Progress in Human Geography*, 18: 151–62.

Taylor, R. (2014) *Another Darkness, Another Dawn: A History of Gypsies, Roma and Travellers*. London: Reaktion.

Theodosiou, A. (2011) 'Multiculturalism and the Catachresis of Otherness: Settling Gypsies Unsettling Gypsy Belongings', *Critique of Anthropology*, 31(2): 89–107.

Thobani, S. (2007) *Exalted Subjects: Studies in the Making of Race and Nation in Canada*. Toronto: University of Toronto Press.

Tilly, C. (1990) *Coercion, Capital, and European States, AD 990–1990*. Oxford: Blackwell.

Tremlett, A. (2009) 'Bringing Hybridity to Heterogeneity in Romani Studies', *Romani Studies*, 19(2): 147–68.

Tremlett, A. (2014) 'Making a Difference Without Creating a Difference: Super-Diversity as a New Direction for Research on Roma Minorities', *Ethnicities*, 4(6): 830–48.

Tremlett, A., McGarry, A. and Agarin, T. (2014) 'The Work of Sisyphus: Squaring the Circle of Romani Recognition', *Ethnicities*, 4(6): 727–36.

Turner, B. (1990) 'Outline of a Theory of Citizenship', *Sociology*, 24(2): 189–217.

Tyler, I. (2010) 'Designed to Fail: A Biopolitics of British Citizenship, *Citizenship Studies*, 14(1): 61–74.

Tyler, I. (2013) *Revolting Subjects: Social Abjection and Resistance in Neoliberal Britain*. London: Zed Books.

UNCERD (1995) *General Recommendation 19: The Prevention, Prohibition and Eradication of Racial Segregation and Apartheid*. 47th session, UN Doc. A/50/18 at 140. Geneva: United Nations Committee on the Elimination of Racial Discrimination (UNCERD).

UNCERD (2000) *General Recommendation XXVII on Discrimination Against Roma*. UN Doc. A/55/18, annex V. Geneva: United Nations Committee on the Elimination of Racial Discrimination (UNCERD).

Underwood, A. (2011) 'The Politics of Pride: The LGBT Movement and Post-Soviet Democracy', *Harvard International Review*, Spring: 42–6.

Vágvölgyi, A. (2014) 'On Roma Murders in Hungary', *OpenDemocracy*, 5 September. https://www.opendemocracy.net/can-europe-make-it/andr%C3%A1s-b-v%C3%A1gv%C3%B6lgyi/on-roma-murders-in-hungary (accessed 28 April 2016).

Van Baar, H. (2011a) 'Europe's Romaphobia: Problematization, Securitization, Nomadization', *Environment and Planning D: Society and Space*, 29(2): 203–12.

Van Baar, H. (2011b) 'The European Roma: Minority Representation, Memory and the Limits of Transnational Governmentality'. PhD thesis, University of Amsterdam.

Van Baar, H. (2014) 'The Emergence of a Reasonable Anti-Gypsyism in Europe' in Agarin, T. (ed.) *When Stereotype Meets Prejudice: Antiziganism in European Societies*. Stuttgart: Ibidem, pp. 27–44.

Van Baar, H. (2015a) 'The Perpetual Mobile Machine of Forced Mobility: Europe's "Roma" and the

Institutionalization of Rootlessness' in Jansen, Y., De Bloois, J. and Celikates, R. (eds) *The Irregularization of Migration in Contemporary Europe: Deportation, Detention, Drowning*. London: Rowman and Littlefield, pp. 71–86.

Van Baar, H. (2015b) 'Enacting Memory and the Hard Labour of Identity Formation: Rethinking the Romani Movement and its Historiography' in McGarry, A. and Jasper, J. (eds) *The Identity Dilemma: Social Movements and Collective Identity*. Philadelphia PA: Temple University Press, pp. 150–69.

Van den Hemel, E. (2008) 'Included but Not Belonging: Badiou and Rancière on Human Rights', *Krisis: Journal for Contemporary Philosophy*, 3: 16–60.

Vermeersch, P. (2006) *The Romani Movement: Minority Politics and Ethnic Mobilisation in Contemporary Central Europe*. Oxford: Berghahn Books.

Vidra, Z. (ed.) (2013) *Roma Migration to and from Canada: The Czech, Hungarian and Slovak Cases*. Budapest: CEU Press.

Vincze, E. (2013) 'Socio-Spatial Marginality of Roma as Form of Intersectional Injustice', *Studia UBB Sociologia*, 58(LVIII): 217–42.

Vincze, E. (2014) 'Faces and Causes of Roma Marginalization: The Case of Romania' in Szalai, J. and Zentai, V. (eds) *Faces and Causes of Roma Marginalization in Local Contexts: Hungary, Romania, Serbia*. Budapest: Centre for Policy Studies, Central European University (CEU).

Vincze, E. and Raţ, C. (2013) 'Guest Editors'. Foreword to the special issue on 'Spatialization and Racialization of Social Exclusion. The Social and Cultural Formation of "Gypsy Ghettos" in Romania in a European Context', *Studia UBB Sociologia* 58(LVIII): 5–22.

Vincze, E., Bartha, A. and Virág, T. (2015) 'Theoretical

Potential of Addressing Production of Marginality at the Crossroads of Spatial Exclusion and Development', *Intersections: East European Journal of Society and Politics*, 1(4): 4–13.

Vitale, T. (2015) 'Les Politiques Locales Face aux Roms: Entre Réification, Effets de Visibilité et Reconnaissance', *Métropolitiques*, 4 February. http://www.metropolitiques. eu/Les-politiques-locales-face-aux.html (accessed 5 May 2016).

Voiculescu, C. (2014) 'Voyagers of the Smooth Space. Navigating Emotional Landscapes: Roma Street Vendors in Scotland', *Emotion, Space, Society*, 30: 1–8.

Wacquant, L. (2007) 'Territorial Stigmatization in the Age of Advanced Marginality', *Thesis Eleven*, 91(1): 166–77.

Wacquant, L. (2008) *Urban Outcasts: A Comparative Sociology of Advanced Marginality*. Cambridge: Polity.

Wacquant, L. (2010) 'Crafting the Neoliberal State: Workfare, Prisonfare, and Social Insecurity', *Sociological Forum*, 25(2): 197–220.

Warf, B. and Arias, S. (2009) *The Spatial Turn: Interdisciplinary Perspectives*. London: Routledge.

Whittier, N. (1995) *Feminist Generations*. Philadelphia PA: Temple University Press.

Willems, W. (1997) *In Search of the True Gypsy: From Enlightenment to Final Solution*. Abingdon: Routledge.

Wilson, W. J. (1978) *The Declining Significance of Race*. Chicago IL: University of Chicago Press.

Wilson, W. J. (1987) *The Truly Disadvantaged: The Inner-City, the Underclass and Public Policy*. Chicago IL: University of Chicago Press.

Wimmer, A. (2008) 'Elementary Strategies of Ethnic Boundary Making', *Ethnic and Racial Studies*, 31(6): 1025–55.

Wimmer, A. (2013) *Ethnic Boundary Making: Institutions, Power, Networks*. Oxford: Oxford University Press.

Young, I. M. (1990) *Justice and the Politics of Difference*. Princeton NJ: Princeton University Press.

INDEX

gadje, use of term, 113
Gay Pride, 39, 184, 190, 200,
    253; reactions to, 216;
    results of, 205
gay rights, history of, 205
gender, 54
gens de voyage, use of term,
    60, 237
gerrymandering, 147
Gezi Park, 182
Gheorghe, Nicolae, 85
ghettoization, 39, 147, 167
ghettos, 79–81, 145–66;
    definition of, 145; use
    of term, 76, 164; in
    Macedonia, 145; in
    Slovakia, 145; in Hungary,
    134; in Romania, 79; in
    Slovakia, 134; in the Czech
    Republic, 134
Gitanos, use of term, 66,
    141
Goffman, Erving, 18–19
governance, 151–4
Grenoble, 238
Gypsies: in the UK, 57, 64;
    use of term, 1–2, 5, 99, 112,
    120; 'Gypsy ghetto', 80;
    history of term, 100–1
Gypsy Lore Society, 40

Habsburg Empire, 29

Hancock, Ian, 17, 106
health, 3
healthcare, access to, 138
heritage and culture,
    celebration of, 187
Holocaust, 11, 34, 118, 174,
    189; commemoration of,
    26, 198, 204; recognition of,
    123–4
home, meaning of, 43
homeland, 30–1, 43;
    protection of, 49
homogenization, 12
homophobia, 2
Horsdean Traveller Site, 63
horse-dealing, 70
housing, 3, 77, 127–70;
    amenities and services,
    159–60; destruction of,
    4, 238–9; impact of, 129;
    neglect of, 134; problems
    in, 129, 157–8
human rights, 223
Human Rights League, 143
Hungary, 17, 78, 233
'hybrid identities', 89

Ibraimovski, Samka, 148
identities, 89; group, 54;
    multiple, 240
identity, 44, 75, 85–126, 175,
    249; and authenticity, 86;

petitions, 198

Philip III of Spain, King, 66

'place', 44; understanding
of, 54

police, 158, 193; violence, 188

political authority,
organization of, 31

poverty, 77, 127, 147–8, 237;
and race, 83; cycles of, 159,
163–4, 250

power, cultural, 107

Prague, 188

prejudice, 95, 127, 191

pride marches, 171–209, 222

Prilep, 137–45

protests, 217, 239–40

public space: appropriation
of, 182, 205–7; use of,
181–2

punishment, policies of, 32

Puxon, Grattan, 117–18

queer communities, 37

racism, 16–18, 29, 81, 108,
247; acceptable forms of,
17; and power, 90; covert,
18; environmental, 167; in
Europe, 8; scientific, 40, 66;
state, 239; structural, 128

Raffestin, Claude, 56

Rancière, Jacques, 241–2

refugee camps, 234

religion, 8, 22, 106, 175

religious sectarianism, 66

relocation, 80

remittances, 46

Resande, use of term, 121

rhetoric, anti-Roma, 28

right to representation, in
Kosovo and Romania, 52

rights, 223; political, 34;
social, 34

right-wing: extremism, 233;
populism, 221–2

rituals, 34; of purity, 19

rob, use of term, 70

robi, use of term, 67

robia, use of term, 69

robie, use of term, 70

Rom politicians, 198

Roma: advocates for, 189;
agency of, 171, 194,
228, 237, 249; allies of,
195; and anachronism,
57; and criminality, 17;
art and culture of, 88;
as a perceived security
threat, 21, 28, 75, 99, 110,
186, 216, 229–31, 238,
243; as outsiders, 248; as
pilgrims, 65; as underclass,
14, 25; attacks on, 137;
celebrations of history and